NEW DIRECTIONS IN GERMAN STUDIES

Vol. 4

Series Editor:

Imke Meyer

New Directions in German Studies

Volumes in the series:

Improvisation as Art: Conceptual Challenges, Historical Perspectives
by Edgar Landgraf

The German Pícaro and Modernity: Between Underdog and Shape-Shifter
by Bernhard Malkmus

Citation and Precedent: Conjunctions and Disjunctions of German Law and Literature
by Thomas O. Beebee

From Kafka to Sebald: Modernism and Narrative Form
edited by Sabine Wilke (forthcoming)

Vienna's Dreams of Europe: Culture and Identity beyond the Nation-State
by Katherine Arens (forthcoming)

Image in Outline: Reading Lou Andreas-Salomé
by Gisela Brinker-Gabler (forthcoming)

Thomas Mann in English: A Study in Literary Translation
by David Horton (forthcoming)

Beyond Discontent

"Sublimation" from Goethe to Lacan

Eckart Goebel

Translated by James C. Wagner

continuum

Continuum International Publishing Group
80 Maiden Lane, Suite 704, New York, NY 10038
The Tower Building, 11 York Road, London SE1 7NX

www.continuumbooks.com

Library of Congress Cataloging-in-Publication Data
Goebel, Eckart.
[Jenseits des Unbehagens. English]
Beyond discontent : 'sublimation' from Goethe to Lacan / Eckart Goebel ; translated by James C. Wagner.
p. cm.
Includes bibliographical references and index.
ISBN 978-1-4411-7833-6 (pbk. : alk. paper) -- ISBN 978-1-4411-1391-7 (hardcover : alk. paper)
1. German literature--History and criticism. 2. Sublimation (Psychology) in literature. 3. Psychoanalysis and literature. 4. Germany--Intellectual life--History. I. Wagner, James C. II. Title.

BF175.5.S92G6313 2012
830.9›353--dc23
2012007350

ISBN: HB: 978–1–4411–1391–7
PB: 978–1–4411–7833–6

Typeset by Fakenham Prepress Solutions, Fakenham, Norfolk NR21 8NN
Printed and bound in the United States of America

Contents

Foreword and Acknowledgments

The idea for this book dates back to a graduate seminar I co-taught with Ulrich Baer at New York University in Fall 2005 on "Sublimation & Desire", and I would like to thank Uli and our graduate students for this wonderful semester, which was my first at NYU. While Uli's further research resulted in his seminal monograph on Rainer Maria Rilke (*Das Rilke-Alphabet*, Frankfurt am Main: Suhrkamp, 2006), it took me quite a while to come to terms with the problem of sublimation, although Rilke was, as it were, already taken care of.

In Spring 2008 I held a lecture series for undergraduate students at NYU, again under the title "Sublimation & Desire". There I presented a number of key texts of the European tradition from the scriptures and Greek antiquity through the twentieth century. Although Plato, Luther and Hobbes found their way into the present publication, I ultimately decided to focus primarily on Sigmund Freud, on some of his direct forerunners (Goethe, Schopenhauer and, most importantly, Nietzsche), and on some of his most compelling readers (Thomas Mann, Adorno, Lacan).

There remains a lot to be done with the concept of sublimation both within and far beyond literary studies. The term does not only imply the general and thus quite intimidating question of what "civilization" actually is. In Freud's case, "sublimation" can be deciphered as the name of "theoria" in the twentieth century; and from this follows that "sublimation" marks the abysmal interface of philosophy and psychoanalysis. I freely admit that I refrained from jumping into that abyss.

To my mind, further investigation into "sublimation" requires interdisciplinary research, co-operation with psychology, gender studies and advanced neural sciences, where the old problem returns as "affect-management". In addition, further research may seek cooperation with experts from art history and also from religious studies to discuss appropriately the overwhelming global heritage we have in the numerous traditions of contemplation and meditation. This became clear to me once more in Spring 2011 when I was meant to give a lecture at an interdisciplinary symposium on Buddhism in Göttingen. There again I decided to stick to my field of expertise and gave a talk on, *nota bene*, Hermann Hesse. The idea of *The Glass Bead Game* ushers towards these academic and spiritual challenges.

***

I would like to thank my friends and colleagues from the Department of German at NYU for lively discussions in the hallways, for their support at various levels, and for opening so many dossiers: Avital Ronell, Paul Fleming and Elke Siegel (now Cornell), Paul North (now Yale), John T. Hamilton (now Harvard), Friedrich Ulfers, Andrea Dortmann and Robert Cohen. I would also like to thank our distinguished visiting professors, especially Vivian Liska, Elisabeth Bronfen, Sigrid Weigel, Werner Hamacher and Laurence Rickels for their valuable advice and input.

Writing a book while chairing a pretty exciting department is not the easiest thing to do. So I want to give cordial thanks to the administrators of the department, Lindsay O'Connor and Harriet Asase, for all their help and for their patience. And I would like to thank Libby Garland and Christopher Leake for the time off in Manhattan.

Since parts of the book were written during my summers in Berlin, I also want to thank my friends over there: Mara Delius, Caroline Gille, Hella Tiedemann, Achim Geisenhanslüke, Gregor Gumpert, Hans-Christian v. Herrmann, Martin v. Koppenfels, and Martin Steffen.

The original German version of *Beyond Discontent* was published in 2009 by *transcript verlag* (Bielefeld) under the title *Jenseits des Unbehagens*. A short German version of the Goethe chapter appeared in the United States in 2008 in *Monatshefte* (Vol. 100, Nr. 4, pp. 461–88), and parts of the Adorno chapter were published in a different English version in *Cultural Critique* (Vol. 70, pp. 158–76). I want to thank the publishers for their permission to take advantage of this material for the present book.

After almost seven years in the United States, I am fully aware of the challenges German Studies is facing in this country. Against this backdrop it is admirable to see that the prestigious Continuum Press has decided to launch the book series *New Directions in German Studies* to help improve the situation, and I am grateful to the members of the editorial board and to editor Haaris Naqvi for accepting my book.

Finally I want to thank in a separate paragraph my translator James C. Wagner, currently a PhD student in our department, for the stunning job he did. Working with Jim was a wonderful and lasting intellectual experience. I highly benefited from our numerous discussions of linguistic details, especially when comparing different translations of the authors I deal with in my book. In our debates, Jim strongly reminded me of the reasons why I have left the German-speaking world again and again since I was a student. Learning in detail about international perspectives on the German tradition is crucial for Germans and for German Studies. In Germany, one can be inclined to forget that the reading of texts in one's native tongue is always the translation of an alleged "original text", which, since the text requires reading to become what it is, is already a difference from itself, and thus on the move.

Several of Jim Wagner's intellectual subtleties inscribed in his translations made me laugh, and in order to honor his work, I would like in closing to give a tiny example for those who read German. In German, the word *unerschwinglich* covers both things one cannot afford financially as well as a world of ideas in outer space far beyond the reach of our quite limited intellectual powers, since we lost, according to Plato, our metaphysical wings (*Schwingen*). By using this term, I tried somehow to bring together Schiller, cash, Thomas Mann and the Grand Hotel. The elegant, ironic English equivalent Jim found for *unerschwinglich* provides me now with the adjective to characterize the work he did: *exorbitant*.

Preface

Who's to say that passion
for the literal can be controlled,
that gaping and scarring
will not break through
to the real at any given moment?
Who can patrol symbolic territories and
assure secure frontiers among levels
and systems of transfer?

Avital Ronell, *The Test Drive*, p. 280.

"Sublimation of instinct is an especially conspicuous feature of cultural development; it is what makes it possible for higher psychical activities, scientific, artistic or ideological, to play such an important part in civilized life. If one were to yield to a first impression, one would say that sublimation is a vicissitude which has been forced upon the instincts entirely by civilization. But it would be wiser to reflect upon this a little longer."[1]

The following book takes up Freud's suggestion and offers in seven chapters the fruits of an effort to "reflect a little longer" upon the vicissitudes of sublimation. It is structured on the one hand according to the perspective of my chosen field, i.e. from the point of view of theoretical literary criticism, or more precisely: from the point of view of German philology. An art historian would perhaps be more likely to follow a path to Freud that proceeds from the figures of Leonardo da Vinci and Michelangelo. For a Germanist, however, it is an obvious choice to start with Goethe. Nor is it difficult to justify beginning with Goethe, as Freud's early engagement with the author influenced him and his writing – not just stylistically but also in terms of content – in ways that

1 Sigmund Freud: *Civilization and Its Discontents*, in: *The Standard Edition of the Complete Psychological Works of Sigmund Freud* (Ed. James Strachey and Anna Freud, London: Hogarth Press, 1956–74), Vol. 21, p. 97.

can scarcely be overestimated. Along with Plato, in whose *Symposium* the idea of sublimation was, as far as I can tell, first exemplarily articulated—with a singular effect, even today, Goethe is for Freud one of those figures who always held Eros in high esteem, as he noted in his speech upon receiving the Goethe Prize in 1930. Furthermore, Goethe himself, most notably in *Poetry and Truth*, characterized his own work as the sublimational processing of experiences, especially those which are overwhelming or erotic, describing poetry as a hot-air balloon that lifts us above the murky world of frustrations. As Goethe's late cycle of poems *Trilogy of Passion* not only "processes" the poet's love for Ulrike von Levetzow but also serves as a summary of the entire Goethean Passion, this study of sublimation begins with a reading of these great poems. Goethe chose as the motto for his *Elegy* two lines from the drama *Torquato Tasso* that formulate a theory of sublimation *in nuce*, while at the same time illuminating why Goethe's work delivers not only a paradigm but a provocation. Poetry does not allow suffering to disappear; rather, it exhibits it, as suffering:

> When in their anguish other men fall silent
> A god gave me the power to tell my pain.
>
> [Und wenn der Mensch in seiner Qual verstummt,
> Gab mir ein Gott zu sagen, wie ich leide.]

The passage from Freud's *Civilization and Its Discontents* cited at the beginning of this preface names the fundamental problem that even today continues to haunt both sublimation and its theory. Freud calls sublimation of the drives a vicissitude that has been *forced* upon the drives. Consequently, the entirety of civilization rests primarily upon compulsion, for which reason it is consistently met with hostility as a formation of life that is accepted only reluctantly. This assessment exemplifies an oft-noted pessimism on the part of Freud, who himself notes in *Beyond the Pleasure Principle* that by the time of the discovery of the death drive, the psychoanalytical theory of civilization had unwittingly steered its course into the harbor of Arthur Schopenhauer's philosophy. The influence of Schopenhauer's pessimistic metaphysics of the will on Freud has been well researched, yet there remain open questions regarding the theory of sublimation that will be discussed in the second chapter of this book. According to Schopenhauer's conception of dualism, sublimation of the drives cannot exist in the sense that, say, the sexual drive is directed towards non-sexual objects. Sublimation for Schopenhauer means the renunciation of the drives with an aim towards their ultimate mortification. As we will see, Freud's conception alternates between the sublimation of the drives and their renunciation; establishing a relationship between Freud and Schopenhauer's doctrine of asceticism would allow the pendulum to swing decisively in the direction of mortification. Yet this would stand in stark contrast to other elements of Freud's theory of sublimation, in which everything comes down to demonstrating the continued existence of erotic impulses beyond sexuality. A potential solution to the problem that Freud's reception of Schopenhauer implies can, I suggest, be found in relation to the metaphysics of music. For Schopenhauer, that which the will desires can never be understood but only experienced in the language-beyond-language of music. Freud turns away from the language of music, in turn demonstrating that what the will desires resounds in the language of man as well. Freud applies the practice of the trained musical ear to human language; musical improvisation is replaced by the art of free association, which first makes sublimation possible.

Friedrich Nietzsche, whose influence on Freud likewise has been brilliantly researched, introduces the concept of sublimation to psychology and, after turning away from Schopenhauer, outlines a history of European civilization that revolves around the poles of "false" sublimation understood as the weakening of the drives on the one hand, and on the other hand a "good" sublimation that, as "great self-control", utilizes the drives in the sense of an intensification of life. The third chapter of this book argues that, although it is historically antecedent, Nietzsche's concept of sublimation represents an enduring challenge to Freud's often self-contradictory theory. It is the pleasure principle, according to Freud, that defines our concept of happiness. By pointedly emphasizing that the dominion of the pleasure principle itself implies its own form of servitude, Nietzsche calls this idea of happiness into question and introduces the possibility of a conception of sublimation that exists in a space beyond discontent. A reading of the first book of *Morgenröthe* has greatly informed my elaboration of this hypothesis, in particular because here the will to power is still conceived as the expunction of the primary experience of powerlessness, the *Übermensch* as the person who knows how to integrate spirit and drive.

Sigmund Freud's fragmentary and desultory approach to the theory of sublimation, all the more astounding given that he so often concedes its central importance, has often been criticized. The fourth chapter of this book attempts to reconstruct the Freudian concept of sublimation as much as is possible given the limited and moreover frequently contradictory nature of the available material. Freud never really succeeded in satisfactorily describing the human capacity for sublimation; furthermore, he found it impossible to outline a concept of sublimation that would be free of the bitter taste of having renounced the "actual" object of desire (*das Eigentliche*). Few ever attain the realm beyond discontent, according to Freud, and even exceptional individuals are constantly exposed to the temptation of regressing, of undoing sublimation. Freud ultimately stresses the renunciation of drives, updating the theory of the strong state first articulated in Thomas Hobbes' *Leviathan* from the perspective of modern psychological expertise. Freud was long unable to decide whether or not he should subsume the idea of the individual's reconciliation with himself as well as with society and nature under the concept of sublimation. In the end, his remarks gravitate towards an emphasis on the moment of compulsion, toward defining sublimation as a destiny.

A book on sublimation obviously must deal with Thomas Mann, much of whose work can be understood as the sublimation of frustrated instinctual impulses. His celebrated novella *Death in Venice*, for example, appears not only to undertake the sublimational processing of an unsettling vacation, but also to illustrate exemplarily the process of sublimation itself. The scene in which Gustav Aschenbach writes his "sublime prose" the beautiful youth Tadzio standing before his eyes, can in fact be read as the epic emblem of the theory of sublimation. However, doubts about this perspective may arise upon longer reflection. One would first have to recognize that by making sublimation the unheard-of object of a novella, Thomas Mann stands on an equal footing with the psychoanalysis of his time. If one would even want to claim that Thomas Mann sublimates through the process of writing, one would then have to ask what it means to sublimate by portraying sublimation. Furthermore, the fact that Aschenbach's schematically delineated sublimation fails spectacularly would also have to be explained. Again and again, Thomas Mann surveys the abyss that according to Freud exists between narcissistically motivated ideal formation and sublimation. Thomas Mann offers an apologia of a process of writing that—and here the author anticipates Herbert Marcuse's reformulation of the doctrine of sublimation—postulates a "self-sublimation of Eros". In his underrated study of *A Man and His Dog*, an interpretation of which is offered in the fifth chapter of this book, Mann outlines a doctrine of sublimation that leaves renunciation behind. A sublimation that defines freedom only as compulsive emancipation from nature can only invoke fate; it will never progress beyond the idea of sublimation as a "fate" under constant threat. As a subtle, previously unrecognized rewriting of elements of Goethe's *Elective Affinities*, *A Man and His Dog* confirms the critique of the novel offered by Walter Benjamin. Through the idea of the "landscape"(*Landschaft*), itself already sublimated nature, Mann evokes an alternative understanding of sublimation that embraces man and creature in equal measure and describes their movement towards each other as a critical revision of an enlightenment dominated by "compulsion".

My reading of Thomas Mann's story about man and beast in the landscape sets up the following chapter on Theodor W. Adorno, which likewise takes a landscape as its starting point. Adorno's notes *Aus Sils Maria* are interpreted as an elaborate allegory that, mediated by the concept of natural beauty, prepare the idea of sublimation as shakenness (*Erschütterung*) as elaborated in his *Aesthetic Theory*. Adorno's posthumously published *Aesthetic Theory* includes a micrological analysis of Freud's theories, which are starkly contrasted with Kant's doctrine of disinterested delight. Adorno formulates his own position as the synthesis of the antitheses represented by the positions of Kant and Freud. Only a person who surrenders himself to *Erschütterung* through art becomes aware of the price that civilization exacts from human beings, and it becomes possible to conceive of an idea of happiness that lies both beyond the return to raw nature and beyond a civilization overshadowed by discontent. Adorno's description of the Upper Engadin landscape casts doubt on the widespread claim that his notion of "the remembrance of nature within the subject" represents a reformulation of the Rousseauian return to nature. Moreover, Adorno emphasizes the dialectical structure of experience, manifested as the history of object-choices, found in Freud's later works. Melancholia proves to be an exceptional case, in which the experience of consciousness is suspended. Sublimation, on the other hand, is conceived of as a change in interest itself resulting from experience. As interest becomes differentiated, the subject abandons raw desire and moves onto the path of spiritualization. At spiritualization's highest point, in the work of art, the entire process of experience itself becomes a shocking experience, and the possibility of a life beyond the discontent fatefully dictated by compulsion first becomes conceivable.

Jacques Lacan's research may be summarily characterized as an elaboration of the mechanisms explained by Freud in his essay *On Narcissism*. In his text on the mirror stage, Lacan places the experience of discontent at the beginning of the individual life. With both his analysis of narcissism and his development of Freudian cultural theory, Lacan unquestionably intensifies his skeptical view of human beings and their feeble chances for sublimation. More than almost any other author, Lacan, whose seminar on *The Ethics of Psychoanalysis* is discussed in this book's final chapter, confirms Nietzsche's aphorism that the realm of goodness begins where our psychological acuity no longer suffices. With Freud as his starting point, Lacan relentlessly deconstructs traditional ethics' concept of the highest good with the goal of paving the way for an ethics derived from psychoanalysis. Lacan augments Freud's studies of monotheism through a penetrating analysis of the figure of the "great reformer" Martin Luther. His illumination of the religious scenario does not offer illusion a new future but leads to a clear exposition of the split within the human psyche, which on the one hand abandons its ideals in the course of maturing, yet on the other hand always remains "creationist". The startling integration of these poles becomes possible when the soul exposes itself to the experience of utter helplessness. At the moment in which the subject experiences intensely the horror of helplessness, there arises the possibility that it will be able to assume the position of the father and cast off its enslavement to the imaginary. In Lacan's view, Luther's ecstatic description of the three lights—the weak light of nature, the flickering light of grace and the gleaming light of glory—documents this spiritual process of a healing immolation of the narcissistic imaginary, at the end of which sublimation may be recognized as the *via regia* to the disclosure of the real world.

1. Trilogy of Passion: Goethe as Paradigm and Provocation

The Secular Gospel

Lovers of classical German literature and philosophy who peruse the writings of Sigmund Freud will quickly note that his concept of sublimation is inherited from the anthropology of his literary fathers: "Hunger and love: that, after all, is the true philosophy, as our Schiller has said."[1]

Most relevant for Freud within the oeuvres of Goethe and Schiller, "whom he could recite at length",[2] are not their theories of the sublime but rather their prominent essays on aesthetic theory written at the turn of the nineteenth century, which attempt to define art as that medium which strikes a balance between duty and inclination, between the principle of reality and that of pleasure. Schiller's treatise *On Grace and Dignity* and series of letters *On the Aesthetic Education of Man* strive not only to reconcile the individual's reason with his drive to pursue particular interests, but also to reconcile the individual with society.[3]

Freud's concept of sublimation likewise covers both dimensions. It encompasses the individual balance between self-preservation and the demands of the drives, encountered in technical literature as

1 Sigmund Freud to his bride in 1884, cited in: Peter Gay: *Freud: A Life For Our Time* (New York: Norton, 1988), p. 46.

2 Peter Gay: *Freud* (Note 1), p. 166.

3 Freud's latent reference to Schiller is addressed by Herbert Marcuse. Cf. *Eros and Civilization: A Philosophical Inquiry into Freud* (New York: Vintage, 1962), pp. 157–79. Regarding Marcuse, cf. Stefan Matuschek: "'Was du hier siehest, edler Geist, bist du selbst.' Narziß-Mythos und ästhetische Theorie bei Friedrich Schlegel und Herbert Marcuse", in: *Narcissus. Ein Mythos von der Antike bis zum Cyber-Space* (Hg. Almut-Barbara Renger, Stuttgart: J. B. Metzler Verlag, 2002), pp. 79–97. Regarding Schiller's theory of grace as a theory of equilibrium, cf. Eckart Goebel: *Charis und Charisma. Grazie und Gewalt von Winckelmann bis Heidegger* (Berlin: Kulturverlag Kadmos, 2006), pp. 35–56.

"neutralization",[4] and also posits the necessary renunciation of the drives for the benefit of the society in which the individual lives, later given the term "adaptation".[5] Freud himself refers once to sublimation as an "art".[6] Whoever masters this art is capable either of directing uneconomical instinctual impulses towards a higher purpose with greater social value or of neutralizing them; ultimately, he is able to adapt himself completely. The analyzed soul becomes a beautiful one:

> "One refers to a beautiful soul when the ethical sense has at last so taken control of all a person's feelings that it can leave affect to guide the will without hesitation and is never in danger of standing in contradiction of its decisions".[7]

Freud's perspective on this, however, grows darker upon self-reflection, especially after the First World War. The possibility of a beautiful balance—even in clinical Freud research, sublimation is sometimes linked to the concept of "reconciliation"[8]—gives way to the concept of self-assertion through renunciation, asceticism and dignity. The serious idea of "control[ling] impulses through moral strength", the stoic habitus of "peace in suffering",[9] come increasingly to dominate Freud's writings. Only a distant echo of the Schillerian concept of *dignity* in the face of adverse destiny may be heard after 1930, when Freud offers the following formulation in *Civilization and its Discontents*:

> "Another technique for fending off suffering is the employment of the displacements of libido which our mental apparatus permits of and through which its function gains so much in flexibility. The task here is that of shifting the instinctual aims in such a way that

---

4 Cf. Heinz Hartmann: "Sublimierung und Neutralisierung" (1955), in: *Die Motivation menschlichen Handelns* (Hg. Hans Thomae, Köln/Berlin: Kiepenheuer & Witsch, 1966), pp. 339–48: "Furthermore, we can speak of sublimation only in cases involving the neutralization of the libido, for this was Freud's understanding of it which still dominates the structure of analysis" (p. 339). Translation JCW.

5 Cf. the chapter on Freud below.

6 Sigmund Freud: "Recommendations to Physicians Practising Psychoanalysis", in: *The Standard Edition of the Complete Psychological Works of Sigmund Freud* ((eds) James Strachey and Anna Freud, London: Hogarth Press, 1956–74), Vol. 12, p. 119.

7 Friedrich Schiller: "On Grace and Dignity" (trans. Jane V. Curran), in: *Schiller's "On Grace and Dignity" in Its Cultural Context* ((eds) Jane V. Curran and Christophe Fricker, Rochester, NY: Camden House, 2005), p. 152.

8 Cf. Hans W. Loewald: *Sublimation: Inquiries into Theoretical Psychoanalysis* (New Haven: Yale University Press, 1988), p. 33; see the chapter on Freud below.

9 Friedrich Schiller: "On Grace and Dignity" (note 7), pp. 158 and 160.

> they cannot come up against frustration from the external world. In this, sublimation of the instincts lends its assistance. One gains the most if one can sufficiently heighten the yield of pleasure from the sources of psychical and intellectual work. When that is so, fate can do little against one."[10]

The path of Freud's thought leads decidedly downwards, from Schiller's ideal of balance and the Hegelian concept of reconciliation to the dyspeptic philosophy of Schopenhauer, into whose gloomy harbor psychoanalysis entered, as Freud notes, in the wake of his depressing discovery of what lies *Beyond the Pleasure Principle*.[11] The concept of sublimation as the ideal of perfectly austere dignity is reserved in Freud for the exceptional individual. For the masses, represented by the common man ("that manufactured article of nature", according to Schopenhauer),[12] sublimation turns out to be a vicissitude of the drives enforced by institutions:

> "It is just as impossible to do without control of the mass by a minority as it is to dispense with coercion in the work of civilization. For masses are lazy and unintelligent; they have no love for instinctual renunciation, and they are not to be convinced by argument of its inevitability; and the individuals composing them support one another in giving free rein to their indiscipline. It is only through the influence of individuals who can set an example and whom masses recognize as their leaders that they can be induced to perform the work and undergo the renunciations on which the existence of civilization depends. All is well if these leaders are persons who possess superior insight into the necessities of life and who have risen to the height of mastering their own instinctual wishes."[13]

Such exemplary individuals of superior insight are the subject of several studies published by Freud. His enthusiastic treatise on Leonardo da Vinci, written before the First World War, may rightfully be read as an articulation of his ego ideal, woven into a portrait of the admired

---

10 Sigmund Freud: *Civilization and its Discontents*, in: *The Standard Edition* (London: Hogarth, 1956–74), vol. 21, p. 79.

11 Sigmund Freud: *Beyond the Pleasure Principle*, in: *The Standard Edition* (London: Hogarth, 1956–74), vol. 18, p. 50. Cf. the chapter on Arthur Schopenhauer below.

12 Arthur Schopenhauer: *The World as Will and Representation*, vol. 1 (trans. E. F. J. Payne, New York: Dover, 1969), p. 187.

13 Sigmund Freud: *The Future of an Illusion*, in: *The Standard Edition* (London: Hogarth, 1956–74), vol. 21, p. 7f.

artist-scientist. The author himself described the Leonardo essay as a "psychoanalytic novel", albeit defensively.[14] In it can be found the highest calling of sublimation, in the sense of a privilege of fate, ever offered by Freud. The highest sublimation may be achieved only by one who disdains all second-hand knowledge and whose view of reality, as it truly is, is thus no longer obscured. Knowledge again becomes an absolute in the sense of its disentanglement from all authority. Through the force of insight, it gains a new immediacy insofar as it is no longer clouded by the force of the drives:

> "[Leonardo] dared to utter the bold assertion which contains within itself the justification for all independent research: '*He who appeals to authority when there is a difference of opinion works with his memory rather than with his reason.*' Thus he became the first modern natural scientist, and an abundance of discoveries and suggestive ideas rewarded his courage for being the first man since the time of the Greeks to probe the secrets of nature while relying solely on observation and his own judgment. But in teaching that authority should be looked down on, and that imitation of the 'ancients' should be repudiated, and in constantly urging that the study of nature was the source of all truth, he was merely repeating—in the highest sublimation attainable by man—the one-sided point of view which had already forced itself on the little boy as he gazed in wonder on the world. If we translate scientific abstraction back again into concrete individual experience, we see that the 'ancients' and authority simply correspond to his father, and nature once more becomes the tender and kindly mother who had nourished him."[15]

This perspective, which thinks of sublimation as "renunciation" while at the same time conceptualizing it as a continual liberation from authority and a devotion to nature as the source of all truth, can in fact be traced back to Goethe, who between 1805 and 1819—the year his *West-Eastern Divan* appeared—had fully emancipated himself, even from his own imitation of the ancient Greeks. As with his assessment of Leonardo, an examination of Freud's well-documented "devotion to Goethe"[16] may shed further light not only on the ideal of the artist-scientist, but also on the concept of sublimation itself, which in Freud

---

14 Sigmund Freud: *Leonardo da Vinci and a Memory of His Childhood*, in: *The Standard Edition* (London: Hogarth, 1956–74), vol. 11, p. 134.

15 Ibid., p. 122.

16 David Rapaport: *The Structure of Psychoanalytic Theory: A Systematizing Attempt* (New York: International Universities, 1960), p. 11.

provides the name of this ideal. By his own admission, it was the fragment *On Nature*, allegedly written by Goethe, that led the teenage Freud to decide to study medicine.[17] Although he never directly invokes his "beloved Goethe"[18] in any of his various remarks on the subject, one can assume that Freud's conception of sublimation was inspired not only by the aesthetics of graceful play and the idea of reconciliation, but also by Goethe's works, particularly his autobiography, about which Freud published a short essay.[19] The reason for beginning a book on the concept of sublimation with a study of Goethe lies in the fact that the author's life, so often described as paradigmatic, offers a number of exemplary models for sublimation, at least at first glance.

In a speech delivered in 1930 on the occasion of his receiving the Goethe Prize, Freud directly compares the two Renaissance men Leonardo and Goethe, actually privileging the latter as the more harmonious spirit. Whereas in Leonardo's case the scientist disturbed the artist and in the end perhaps even "stifled" him, "Goethe's character was able to develop more freely." Unlike Leonardo, Goethe's versatility was not troubled by any "inhibition in his development."[20] Freud returns in the course of his remarks to the reason behind the uninhibited development of Goethe's character, citing him alongside Plato as the second great forerunner of the modern theory of the libido. A charmingly elegant allusion to the natural sciences leads to a chemical marriage between the author of *Elective Affinities* and the creator of psychoanalysis:

> "Goethe always rated Eros high, never tried to belittle its power, followed its primitive and even wanton expressions with no less attentiveness than its highly sublimated ones and has, as it seems to me, expounded its essential unity throughout all its manifestations no less decisively than Plato did in the remote past. Indeed, it is perhaps more than a chance coincidence when in *Elective Affinities* he applies to love an idea taken from the sphere of chemistry—a connection to which the name of psychoanalysis itself bears witness."[21]

Goethe himself, whose last novel bears "renunciation" in its title, had in *Poetry and Truth* programmatically described his poetry as the result

---

17 Gay: *Freud* (Note 1), p. 24

18 Ibid., p. 571.

19 Sigmund Freud: "A Childhood Recollection from *Dichtung und Wahrheit*," in: *The Standard Edition* (London: Hogarth, 1956–74), vol. 17, pp. 145–56.

20 Sigmund Freud: "The Goethe Prize", in: *The Standard Edition* (London: Hogarth, 1956–74), vol. 21, p. 208.

21 Ibid., p. 210.

of a sublimatory processing of experience. In one of the most well-known passages of his autobiography, he writes:

> "And so began that tendency which throughout my life I have never overcome, namely to transform whatever gladdened or tormented me, or otherwise occupied my mind, into an image, a poem, and to come to terms with myself by doing this, so that I could both refine my conceptions of external things and calm myself inwardly in regard to them. It is likely that no one needed this talent more than I, since my nature kept propelling me from one extreme to the other. Therefore all my published works are but fragments of one great confession."[22]

A further definition of true poetry appears in the third part of *Poetry and Truth* in the form of Goethe's lovely metaphor of the hot-air balloon, which not only accentuates the idea of writing as the working-through of experience, but also emphasizes writing's uplifting, literally sublimating aspect. Goethe's image succeeds on multiple levels; in chemistry, sublimation is a technical term designating the transition of a substance from a solid directly to a gaseous state. In the amusing, childlike image of the hot-air balloon, the bitter notion of sublimation as a sad substitution is gleefully sublated and sublimated in turn, a brilliant example of Goethe's care in selecting his metaphors. As in Freud, the question of what this description refers to—whether to the production of poetry, its reception or both—ultimately remains open. True poetry liberates the subject from the oppressive nature of existence, from depression, and lifts him up to a great height that rises even above the tight-lipped, deadly seriousness of the sublime:

> "True poetry makes itself known by the fact that it, as a secular gospel, can free us from our oppressive earthly burdens with its inner serenity and external delights. Like an air balloon it lifts us, with our ballast attached, into higher regions and lets the tangled maze of earth lie unrolled before us in bird's eye perspective. The sprightliest and the gravest works have an identical purpose, which is to moderate pleasure and pain by means of a felicitous, ingenious presentation."[23]

In his earlier play *Torquato Tasso*, Goethe had already articulated the

---

22 Johann Wolfgang Goethe: *From My Life: Poetry and Truth: Parts One to Three* (trans. Robert R. Heitner, New York: Suhrkamp, 1987), p. 214.

23 Ibid., p. 427.

idea of a moderating, neutralizing balance between the principles of reality and pleasure—those two extremes that threaten to tear the subject apart—compressing this concept into two lines that have become scarcely less famous than the above-cited passage from *Poetry and Truth*. Together they express *in nuce* what has become the popular conception of the Freudian theorem of sublimation:

> When in their anguish other men fall silent
> A god gave me the power to tell my pain.
>
> [Und wenn der Mensch in seiner Qual verstummt,
> Gab mir ein Gott zu sagen, wie ich leide.][24]

Goethe employs a slightly modified version of these lines from *Tasso* as an epigraph for the most significant poem of his later period, the so-called "Marienbad Elegy". The elegy first appeared in the definitive edition of Goethe's complete works, the *Ausgabe letzter Hand*, where it was presented in conjunction with two other poems to form the *Trilogy of Passion*, a kind of summing-up of the author's own life as well as of the era in which he lived. A reading of the elegy, its genesis and its context—the poems "To Werther" and "Reconciliation"—is illuminating for our attempt towards an exemplary understanding of sublimation as a culturally promoted processing of frustrated instinctual desires.

The *Trilogy of Passion* marks itself as an appropriate object of this study for another reason. If, on the one hand, it serves as a confirmation of Freud's theory both in its genesis and as a serious artifact, on the other hand, in terms of content, the trilogy already anticipates some of the crucial objections put forth by later metacritiques of Freud. Goethe's dark poems continue to cast a shadow over the promise of meaning of mainstream psychoanalysis. This observation applies as well to elements of *Poetry and Truth*: Goethe's conception of poetry as a Montgolfier balloon providing a cheerful view of the world below acts as a counterweight to his meager remarks on *Werther*, which succinctly articulate a theory of suicide—the catastrophic failure of sublimation, the plunge into utter senselessness. For Goethe, that "disgust with life" which culminates in suicide essentially arises when the subject, after an experience that destroys the balance of his life, finds himself cut off from the source of all contentment, the pleasure taken in "the regular recurrence of external things":[25]

---

24 Johann Wolfgang Goethe: *Torquato Tasso*, in: *Verse Plays and Epic* (trans. Michael Hamburger, New York: Suhrkamp, 1987), p. 138, lines 3423f.

25 Johann Wolfgang Goethe: *Poetry and Truth* (note 22), p. 425.

> "The more receptive we are to such pleasures, the happier we feel. If, however, these various phenomena surge and fall before us and we take no interest in them, if we are insensitive to these lovely offerings, then the greatest of evils sets in, the gravest illness, which is to view life as a repugnant burden."[26]

In an extraordinary twist that anticipates one of the main arguments put forth by Jacques Lacan, who understands sublimation as a necessary diffusion of desire,[27] Goethe teaches that it is above all the recurrence of love which may elicit this disgust:

> "But there is no more effective cause of this weariness than the recurrence of love. It is correctly said that the first love is the only one, for the supreme sense of love gets lost in the second and because of the second. The concept of eternity and affinity that really exalts and sustains love is destroyed, so that it seems as transitory as everything else that recurs. The separation of the physical from the moral part of it, which in the complex cultivated world divides the feelings of love from those of desire, also produces an exaggeration here that cannot bring good results."[28]

In his love for the nineteen-year-old Ulrike von Levetzow, Goethe once again suffers through this "division" between feelings of fatherly love and youthful desire. This love, too, much like that which had constituted the tragic theme of *Tasso* years earlier, led socially to an "exaggeration" which did not bring good results but might well, as Goethe remarked to Eckermann, produce a good poem. Goethe once described *Tasso* as "an intensified *Werther*". With the *Trilogy of Passion*, as an extreme expression of the destruction of man through the recurrence of love, there now emerges an intensified *Tasso* in the form of the poem "To Werther", composed by a 74-year-old poet who no longer simply narrates the destiny of an individual but speaks bluntly and unforgivingly about the *conditio humana*.

In the poem "To Werther", which opens the trilogy, Goethe lets his readers know that the experience which in the earlier novel had been depicted as a singular and tragic case now appears to him to be the rule when it comes to love; the doctrine of sublimation is revoked. As Marianne Wünsch aptly notes: "Rather than a meaningful development towards ever higher purposes, what occurs instead is a repetition of

26 Ibid.

27 Cf. the chapter on Jacques Lacan below.

28 Johann Wolfgang Goethe: *Poetry and Truth* (note 22), p. 425.

failure that negates meaning."[29] With this generalization of the tragic trajectory, Goethe's dreary doctrine of love has reached that state of existential disenchantment which would be confirmed in the twentieth century by Jean-Paul Sartre in his distraught study of passion, the argumentation of which Lacan deemed simply "irrefutable".[30] The "Elegy", the trilogy's center, mercilessly asserts the "breakdown of meaning"[31] that occurs via a series of failures. As a reading of the *Trilogy* demonstrates, Goethe's late work documents a "total catastrophe of meaning",[32] thus asserting the collapse of the era's idealist philosophy. As "Reconciliation", the trilogy's closing poem, shows, only music is capable of compensating for this conclusion, and even then only conditionally. The transition in aesthetic theory from Schiller to Schopenhauer is here already complete.

In but a small space, Goethe's *Trilogy of Passion* brings together the essential elements of the system of literature and thought that dominated his lifetime—Marianne Wünsch offers the pithy formula: "*Liebesbesitz = Selbstbesitz = Weltbesitz*",[33] i.e. being in love = having a strong sense of self = understanding the world—while at the same time documenting this system's downfall. A reading of the *Trilogy* as an exemplary case study thus not only prepares my reconstruction of both Nietzsche's and Freud's theories of sublimation but also provides the matrix for my studies of Adorno and Lacan, who emerge from a confrontation with the social and psychic consequences of this systemic collapse. There arises as well the question of whether the irreconcilability at the heart of the "Marienbad Elegy" does not in the end also haunt psychoanalysis and its concept of sublimation. To the extent that Goethe's poems exist as artifacts of sublimation, they offer an exemplary confirmation of Freud's theory. It is in this sense that Jürgen Behrens, one of the editors of the superb edition of the elegy's original manuscript first discovered in 1980, concludes his remarks on the history of the text as follows:

> "And so the enthusiastic tone, all this intensity, is only a means of productively withstanding the 'ebb and flow'. If the elegy's motif is loss—'What we had, where has it gone?/And what is it that we have?'— then in terms of its formation—how the poet says

---

29 Marianne Wünsch: "Zeichen – Bedeutung – Sinn. Zu den Problemen der späten Lyrik Goethes am Beispiel der 'Trilogie der Leidenschaft:'", in: *Goethe Jahrbuch* (Hg. Werner Keller, Bd. 108, 1991), S. 179–90, hier: p. 181. Translation JCW.

30 Jacques Lacan: *Freud's Papers on Technique, 1953–1954* (Seminar I) (trans. John Forrester, ed. Jacques-Alain Miller, New York: Norton, 1988), p. 216.

31 Marianne Wünsch (Note 29), p. 187. Translation JCW.

32 Ibid.

33 Ibid.

> what he suffers, what he endures—it is a making-present: 'O vis superba formae!' "[34]

Inasmuch as Goethe's poems, as a kind of summing up of the idealist age, document the downfall of a system of meaning, they constitute a double provocation—to a reality principle that must confront the largely uninterrogated category of meaning itself, and thus also to psychoanalysis as a promise of meaning or (as Lacan later criticizes it) of salvation. Just how radical the *Trilogy*'s view of the end of meaning is intended to be becomes clear in the light of Goethe's unusually casual remark to Eckermann regarding the "Marienbad Elegy": "I staked upon the present moment as a man stakes a considerable sum upon a card, and sought to enhance its value as much as I could without exaggeration."[35]

The discourse of high stakes applies to the trilogy as a whole and underscores the extent to which Goethe exposes himself socially as an individual and reveals himself to his readers as a specific person in particular agony, in such a way that he demolishes the framework of poetic immanence. Thus in the nihilistic poem "To Werther", the poet violates convention by directly identifying the lyrical subject with the empirical author Johann Wolfgang Goethe and abuses the hero of his first novel as though he were a real person. Moreover, the trilogy repeatedly invokes *Torquato Tasso*, Goethe's great, similarly unforgiving drama of the life of the aggressive artist *par excellence* who is incapable of adaptation. "Trilogy of Passion"—the title a proud summing up of the "simultaneity of passion and artistry"[36]—in this context also encompasses the three traditional literary genres: novel, drama and poem. To the extent that these three works—*Werther*, *Tasso*, and the *Trilogy*—mark decisive turning points in the life of Goethe, the pre-eminent representative of his age, the title "Trilogy of Passion" also

---

34 Jürgen Behrens: "Biographischer Hintergrund. Marienbad 1821–1823," in: Goethe: *Elegie von Marienbad. Urschrift September 1823* (Hg. Jürgen Behrens u. Christoph Michel, Frankfurt am Main: Insel Verlag, 1991), p. 116. Translation JCW.

35 Johann Wolfgang Goethe: *Conversations of Goethe with Johann Peter Eckermann* (trans. John Oxenford, New York: Da Capo, 1998), p. 25.

36 Jürgen Behrens: "Biographisches Hintergrund" (Note 34), p. 105. For a long time, research on the *Trilogy of Passion*, and on the "Elegy" in particular, has been marked by justifiable astonishment that Goethe succeeded so well in fusing the moving expression of extreme emotions with consummate artistic virtuosity. It is purely a rhetorical question when Arthur Henkel asks: "Must it be repeated that this 'Elegy' is considered by all sensitive readers to be one of the greatest poems of German, if not world literature?" Ibid. Henkel: "Geleitwort", p. 10. Translation JCW.

suggests a reading of Goethe's life as a *via dolorosa*, a tragic trilogy of passions in its own right.

The cheerful image in *Poetry and Truth* of poetry as a hot-air balloon may overshadow the fact that in this same passage Goethe provocatively describes poetry as a "secular gospel", thereby illuminating a telling characteristic not just of his own work but of the theory of sublimation itself. Included in the Gospels is the Passion of Christ, which culminates in the miracle of the Resurrection, in *"Stirb' und werde!"* ["Die and become!"], the epitome of sublimation. What was once perishable flesh becomes immortal spirit.

The double meaning of the title "Trilogy of Passion" is more evident in English than in the original German (*Trilogie der Leidenschaft*). It has already been suggested that *Werther* became such a literary sensation at least in part because it constituted a potentially blasphemous retelling of the Passion in terms of secular love; Goethe had written Werther's story with recourse to elements of Christ's ordeal.[37] *Werther* is in fact a secular Passion, and the *Trilogy of Passion* elicits both fascination and continued consternation because it once again blends the experience of love with religious experience, the experience of absolute meaning, and it does so in such a way that it is impossible to tell here whether a transcendent experience is disclosed through secular love, whether love alone makes religious experience comprehensible, or whether the senselessness of the psychological experience of love reveals the illusionary character of religious experience. Goethe's poetry is a secular gospel, a staging of the Passion. The soul perishes in the tragic experience of love, and its resurrection is sublimely and subtly fulfilled in poetry, and only in poetry. Sublimation is in fact achieved, but only over an empty abyss of meaninglessness that rips apart the "Elegy" at its terrifying end:

> The world's all lost, myself as well I'm losing,
> I, once the favourite of the gods on high;
> They tested me, for me Pandora choosing,
> So rich in gifts, in her more dangers lie;
> They urged me to that generous mouth to fate me,
> They separate me and annihilate me.
>
> [Mir ist das All, ich bin mir selbst verloren,
> Der ich noch erst den Göttern Liebling war;
> Sie prüften mich verliehen mir Pandoren,

---

37 Cf. Hans Leisegang: "Die Marienbader Elegie", in: *Beiträge zur Einheit von Bildung und Sprache im geistigen Sein. Festschrift für Ernst Otto* (Hg. Gerhard Haselbach und Günter Hartmann, Berlin: De Gruyter, 1957), pp. 385–404.

So reich an Gütern, reicher an Gefahr;
Sie drängten mich zum gabeseligen Munde,
Sie trennen mich, sie richten mich zu Grunde.]

On the Origin of the Text

Though historical documents about Johann Wolfgang Goethe's last great love are scarce, its poetic results have become quite famous. During the poet's stay at the spa resort town of Marienbad in the years 1821 to 1823, he struck up an active social relationship with the family von Levetzow. In particular, the old man cherished spending time with the family's teenage daughter Ulrike. The dramatic and public culmination of his love for the girl came in the summer of 1823, when the Grand Duke of Saxe-Weimar-Eisenach himself asked Ulrike's mother for her daughter's hand on behalf of the 74-year-old poet; his efforts, however, were in vain. The family von Levetzow departed for Karlsbad on 17 August, and Goethe followed shortly thereafter. After several days—including his own birthday on 28 August—Goethe took his leave of the family on 5 September. He made the following note in his diary: "general, somewhat tumultuous departure."[38] After the poet returned from his trip on 17 September, all involved at first treated the matter delicately. Nonetheless, the atmosphere had grown sour as a result of the grotesque social embarrassment of the previous summer; there was, as Goethe's son discreetly noted, "a certain awkwardness".[39] If the wedding had taken place, the young Goethes "would have gained a nineteen-year-old stepmother who would have become mistress of the house at Frauenplan for the foreseeable future. Their children would have gained a grandmother who was younger than their own mother. Goethe got into intense arguments with his son in Weimar."[40]

Faced with these conflicts, the old man retreated to the impenetrable solitude of his study to spare his family's embarrassment. He spread out before him the notes he had written in his *Schreib-Calendar* for the year 1822, which contained the original manuscript of a poem he had composed while traveling in his carriage, along with a nearly-complete transcription that apparently had been copied down at various points on his return trip from Karlsbad to Weimar between 5 and 17 September 1823. He took a large sheet of strong, valuable vellum paper and began to fold it. He had spent his entire life with paper and had expertly mastered the bookbinder's subtle art of folding; no improper or

---

38 Cited in: Goethe: *Gedichte 1800–1832* (Hg. Karl Eibl, Frankfurt am Main: Suhrkamp, 1998), p. 1051. Translation JCW.

39 August von Goethe to Ottilie on 13 September 1823. Translation JCW.

40 Jürgen Behrens: "Bibliographischer Hintergrund" (note 34), p. 92. Translation JCW.

unnecessary crease slipped by him. From the large vellum sheet he fashioned a beautiful, unwrinkled booklet of sixteen pages. Then came the artistic challenge of the calligrapher: none of the sixteen pages could be removed from the book or replaced, as each was an inextricable part of the larger white sheet. The transcription had to be flawless or the entire booklet would be ruined. The old man chose black ink, which could be erased only by scratching the immaculate paper, and in large, regular, perfectly legible strokes began to write in Latin script. The results were immaculate: no stray blots of ink, no slips of the pen, nothing crossed out. The scribe separated each part of the text with the figure of a spiral, a beautiful, doubly mirrored, serpentine line. The first page was left blank, as were the last two. As Goethe's diary attests, the transcription took three days, from 17 to 19 September 1823.

The poet fetched a portfolio made of red morocco leather, placed the booklet inside and affixed the poem with a silk cord. This was later "placed in a specially made portfolio overlaid with blue paper, on the cover of which was written in golden letters: Elegy. September 1823." At first, Goethe hid away the blue and red book, showing it to no one. "This clean copy [...] is one of the most beautiful examples of how Goethe accorded honor to the literary work of art through the work of his hands."[41] Goethe's clean copies are not the excesses of poetic narcissism but an expression of reverence toward language and its crystallization in poetry.

The manuscripts, still legible even today, underscore the objectivity of the linguistic artifact, of its disentanglement from the contingent individuality of the author whom language exceeds, passing through him as through a catalyst, and through this passage taking on poetic form. However, the clean copy of the so-called "Marienbad Elegy", as Goethe's idiosyncratic treatment of the manuscript attests, is a unique case, going beyond his frequently documented expressions of reverence. This copy is a test that Goethe took upon himself in his solitude. He passed triumphantly, with no trembling of the hand, no slip of the pen, no black marks. The clean manuscript of the elegy documents the poet's coming to terms with an experience that has resolved into a clear black figure against a white ground. Here again, Goethe expertly mastered the three arts of composing, of folding and of writing.

Goethe's engagement with the Asiatic world is rarely more directly apparent than in the gesture of the "Elegy". The author of the "Chinese-German Book of Seasons and Hours" knew of the connection between

41 Erich Trunz: "Kommentar", in: Johann Wolfgang Goethe: *Werke* (Hamburger Ausgabe), Bd. 1 (Hg. Erich Trunz, München: C. H. Beck Verlag, 1982), p. 761. Translation JCW.

calligraphy and combat, of the close relationship between the art of writing and the martial arts, of the parallels between commanding the pen and commanding the sword. In the *West-Eastern Divan*, the poem "Ecstatic Longing" [*Selige Sehnsucht*], which elevates the death in flames of two lovers, the experience of death in life[42]—"*Stirb' und werde!*"—to the principle of a life fully lived, is immediately followed by a short poem on writing. The old poet is testing himself, to see whether he has truly mastered and moved beyond the terrible experience of rejection and separation set down in the "Marienbad Elegy". The elegy represents a great example of the complete and successful sublimation of an unrequited love. The emphasis on material dimensions is strong, expressed not only in the great care given to the clean manuscript, but also in the number of stanzas, of which the 1823 elegy comprises exactly 23.

The well-documented history of the poem's origins paradigmatically confirms the theorem established by Freud that sublimation is the feasible substitution of a beloved object by something else that may help the subject to overcome a frustration of desire which is painful to the point where suicide becomes desirable. Taking the place of the lost or unreachable object, as both surrogate and compensation, is work towards the process of civilization, whose fragile yet potentially socially viable pinnacle is the cultural artifact, perhaps a threnodic poem, an elegy. Goethe read from or gave a copy of his elegy to two very old friends: an old musician, Carl Friedrich Zelter, and an old politician, Wilhelm von Humboldt. For the time being, he did not think of publishing the poem. Several lines appeared in *Art and Antiquity* in 1825, and eventually the elegy formed the central part of the *Trilogy of Passion*, first published in 1827. On 27 October 1823, Eckermann was also given the honor of being allowed to read the poem, which had been guarded like a treasure:

> "Stadelmann brought in two wax lights, which he set on the table. Goethe desired me to sit down, and he would give me something to read. And what should this be but his newest, dearest poem, his *Elegy from Marienbad*!
>
> I must here go back a little for a circumstance connected with this poem. Immediately after Goethe's return from Marienbad, the report had been spread that he had there made the acquaintance of a young lady equally charming in mind and person, and had been inspired with a passion for her. When her voice was heard in the Brunnen-Allee, he had always seized his hat, and hastened

42 Cf. Igor A. Caruso: *Die Trennung der Liebenden. Eine Phänomenologie des Todes* (Neuausgabe, Wien: Verlag Turia & Kant, 2001).

> to join her. He had missed no opportunity of being in her society, and had passed happy days: the parting had been very painful, and he had, in this excited state, written a most beautiful poem; which, however, he looked upon as a consecrated thing, and kept hid from every eye. [...] When I had finished [reading it], Goethe came to me again. 'Well,' said he, 'there I have shown you something good. But you shall tell me what you think a few days hence.' "[43]

Despite philologists' indefatigable search for precursors to the "Elegy", all that has been found is a single sheet of paper from the summer of 1822.[44] On this sheet is written, in Goethe's sober handwriting: "*Das Maß ist voll*" ["Enough is enough"]. On its own, this sentence does not constitute verse. It is merely a prosaic conclusion, an over-and-done-with, the double bar at the end of the score. The writing of the end, however, is also the transgression of the end qua objectification. "*Das Maß ist voll*"—literally, "The measuring cup is full"—stands apart from the screaming, weeping subject. It faces him, on a sheet of paper, and is readable. Pain, that which is senseless and inscrutable, thus seems to become comprehensible. In understanding a sentence, what the sentence says becomes understandable: this is the seminal illusion of writing. If unbearable pain is written down in such a way that meaningfulness and interpretability are established, then sublimation is introduced, the gap between the subject and his sorrow. The measuring cup, filled to the brim, is transformed into poetic measure, into two iambs, so that the sheet now reads:

> Das Maß ist voll.
> Warum streb' ich immer dahin,
> Wohin ich nicht soll.

The original articulation of pain is again framed by the addition of a fourth line above it; what had been the first line is now preceded by the codified articulation of sorrow in its lyrically conventional expression. The result is a four-line poem with alternating rhyme, in which pain is lyrically subdued, distant, sublimated:

> Könnt' ich vor mir selber fliehn!
> Das Maß ist voll.

---

43 Johann Wolfgang Goethe: *Conversations of Goethe with Johann Peter Eckermann* (note 35), p. 15f.

44 Cf. Erich Trunz's commentary (note 41), which reproduces the precursors to the Elegy discussed here, pp. 753ff.

Ach! Warum streb' ich immer dahin,
Wohin ich nicht soll.

[If only I could flee from myself!
The measuring cup is full.
Why do I always strive toward
Where I should not go.][45]

On the same sheet of paper can also be found a second quatrain, at the heart of which there is likewise a cry of suffering objectified and made distant by the act of writing: *Welch unerträgliche Schmerzen!* The poem itself, again spun in alternating rhyme, weaves poetic conventions about this cry, the codified "Ach!" on one side, on the other the classic metaphor of the snake, also employed by Goethe in his fairytale story *Das Märchen*. The poem reads:

Ach! Wer doch wieder gesundete!
Welch unerträgliche Schmerzen!
Wie die Schlange, die verwundete,
Krümmt sich's im eigenen Herzen.

[Oh! Who could ever recover!
What unbearable pain!
Like a wounded snake,
My own heart cringes.][46]

Goethe was quite literally heartsick in 1823, so much so that one must concur with Karl Eibl's observation that the poet's exasperated and exasperating references to the heart, both in the "Elegy" itself and in its fragmentary precursors, rise above the level of cliché:

> "Perhaps not insignificant for a deeper understanding of both the situation in Marienbad and the Marienbad poems is the fact that Goethe had become seriously ill in February 1823. The diagnosis today is a heart attack or pericardial inflammation, with a relapse in November. When Goethe speaks so frequently of his 'heart', of his 'fearful indecision' and his 'anxious heartvoid', or when he writes, 'Already in the storm my heart is rending', these are likely more than mere metaphors."[47]

---

45 Johann Wolfgang Goethe: *Werke*, Bd. 1 (note 41), p. 378. Translation JCW.
46 Ibid.
47 Johann Wolfgang Goethe: *Gedichte 1800–1832* (Hg. Karl Eibl, Frankfurt am Main: Suhrkamp, 1998), p. 1055. Translation JCW.

Goethe's physical breakdown was imminent when he presented the "Elegy" to Eckermann in October. For the ailing man, the triumphant success of the clean copy was only a seeming victory. When Goethe collapsed in November, his friend Zelter rushed to his side and was tasked with reading the "Elegy" aloud to him over and over again. An incredible entry in Zelter's diary offers a grim take on the idea of sublimation as the cauterization of that fatal wound, love:

> "What do I find? One who looks as though his body were filled with love, the entirety of love with all the anguish of youth. Now, if this is the case: he must get rid of it! No! He should keep it, he should glow like an oyster shell, but he should suffer pain like Hercules on Mount Oeta! No remedy should cure him; he should be strengthened and healed by his agony alone. And so it happened, so it was done. The loving heart gave birth to a divine child, beautiful and fresh. It was rough going, but the divine fruit [the 'Elegy'] was there and now lives and will live on in the name of its spirit, carried forth through time and space, and will be called love, eternal, all-powerful love."[48]

The snake that had been contorted in pain returns relieved in the clean copy of the "Elegy", now in the form of a beautifully curved spiral, as the epitome of that graceful figure which so elegantly separates and joins. The convulsions of the wounded creature dissolve in the poem into a serpentine line, the line of beauty and grace, described by William Hogarth as the original element of aesthetic representation. The metaphor of the snake disappears in the flowing river of the poem; all that remains of it is the pure curved form. The animal howl of pain stands at the source of an unblemished sublimation, as at the great poem's beginning there stands the unbridled, cathartic cry of an elderly man. *Torquato Tasso*, which provides the "Elegy" with both its motto and its matrix, informs us as well of beauty's terrible origins:

> Nature endowed us with the gift of tears,
> The agonized outcry when at last a man
> Can bear no more—[49]

To Werther

The dash in Goethe marks the site of what is unbearable, what is unspeakable, the limit of linguistic articulation. It establishes a moment of breathlessness that is at the same time a turning point. An exemplary

48 Cited in: Goethe: *Gedichte 1800–1832* (note 47), pp. 1053f. Translation JCW.
49 Johann Wolfgang Goethe: *Torquato Tasso* (note 24), p. 138, lines 3419–21.

instance of Goethe's use of the dash as a tense or terrified holding of breath may be found in the first stanza of the "Elegy." Here the dash occupies that unbearable second in which it is decided whether the day will bring the horror of separation or the bliss of presence:

In Paradise received, to Hell rejected;
How changeable my thoughts, my heart unsteady! –
She stands at Heaven's gate! Away with qualms!
She lifts you up and takes you to her arms.

[Das Paradies, die Hölle steht dir offen,
Wie wankelsinnig regt sich's im Gemüte! –
Kein Zweifeln mehr! Sie tritt ans Himmelstor,
Zu ihren Armen hebt sie dich empor.][50]

Apart from this fearful moment in the opening stanza and a later parenthetical remark, the dash appears twice more in the elegy to mark a shift in thought; otherwise, it is aestheticized as the beautifully curving spiral described above. It remains a sharp break, however, in the poem "To Werther", written in 1824. The dash disappears from the "Elegy", migrating to another poem which ranks as perhaps the most acerbic ever written by Goethe, and which allows to be heard the unsublimatable, potentially poisonous remnant that evidently remained after the composition of the "Elegy".[51] The incisive dash in "To Werther" represents an apologia of suicide: "You went before—how little you were losing." It marks as well the tragic moment in which happiness is overlooked: "So near – the happiness we do not prize." Finally, the dash marks the experience of death inherent in the separation of lovers: "At last to parting – parting is to die!" It is not only his sloppily written quatrains that the poet leaves behind him with the clean copy of the "Elegy". One year later, Goethe, who "had still a remnant of that passion in [his] heart",[52] unloads that unbearable

50 All citations of the *Trilogie der Leidenschaft* are taken from Johann Wolfgang Goethe: *Selected Poems* (trans. John Whaley, Evanston, IL: Northwestern University, 1998), pp. 134–45.

51 Cf. the chapters on Freud and Lacan below, which deal with the psychoanalytic hypothesis of the potentially corruptive "remnant". Jörg Löffler reads the dashes of the "Elegy" from a Lacanian perspective, with a view towards the dash of differential linguistic theory, which divides the classic symbol into signifier and signified, and from this dash interprets the melancholia of Goethe's late works; Jörg Löffler: *Unlesbarkeit. Melancholie und Schrift bei Goethe* (Berlin: Erich Schmidt Verlag, 2005), p. 152f.

52 Johann Wolfgang Goethe: *Conversations of Goethe with Johann Peter Eckermann* (note 35), p. 416.

remainder by transferring it to another poem. He publicly reestablishes the lost connection between *Werther*, *Tasso* and the "Elegy", however, in his 1827 *Ausgabe letzter Hand*.

Goethe's process of both framing and distancing himself from his experience through poetry and bookbinding continues with the publication of his lament. In the *Ausgabe letzter Hand*, Goethe published this long poem, which up to that point had been seen only by a few friends, for the first time. Given the title "Elegy", it was framed by the poem "To Werther", which had first been published in 1825 when it was included in a special anniversary edition of Goethe's first novel, and the short piece "Reconciliation", which had been written as an occasional poem for the Polish pianist Maria Szymanowska. The three poems were united under the now-famous title *Trilogy of Passion*.

The ordering of the poems in the trilogy, it should be noted, does not correspond with the dates of their original composition: "Reconciliation" was written first, in Marienbad during the summer of 1823, and "To Werther" last, in 1824, on the occasion of the fiftieth anniversary of the publication of *The Sorrows of Young Werther*. Goethe's arrangement of the texts creates a placatory narrative: the eerie séance with a suicide victim is followed by the accomplished stanzas of the "Elegy", and the trilogy closes with an expression of gratitude for the soothing consolation provided by sonorous music. The process of sublimation, already well-documented in regard to the origins of the "Elegy", is reproduced once again in the sequence of the poems: from suicidal despair through deep and irreconcilable sorrow to cathartic weeping. As Goethe noted from a distance in 1831, the trilogy evolved "gradually, and to a certain extent incidentally". It nonetheless attains its essential unity through the "love-sick feeling" that pervades it, and thus it succeeds in satisfying the formal demand of the three related parts: "that in the first there is a sort of introduction, in a second a sort of catastrophe, and in the third a satisfying denouement."[53]

With the *Trilogy of Passion*, Goethe attempts a stirring summation of the entirety of his poetic life with the authority of one for whom death is imminent. As noted above, the title has a double meaning, inasmuch as it not only refers to the collocation of three poems but also describes Goethe's life itself as a *Trilogy of Passion*, the three major stations of which are denoted by the three major genres: the novel *The Sorrows of Young Werther*, the art-and-society drama of the life of *Torquato Tasso*, and the three poems of the trilogy. Goethe's life is shown to have been continuously haunted by that "queer illness, as natural as it is unnatural", by disgust with life, by the *taedium vitae*.[54] The

53 Ibid.

54 Goethe's letter to Zelter of 3 December, 1812; cited in: Erich Trunz: "Kommentar" (note 41), p. 757. Translation JCW.

following reading of Goethe's Passion-journey examines its stations in the sequence specified by the poet, in order to arrive at a more sophisticated understanding of what may be meant by sublimation.

To Werther

Lamented shade, once more with unsure greeting
You venture to the light of day,
Here on new-flowered meadows we are meeting;
This time you do not shrink away.
It is as if you lived when all was starting,
When dew upon One field our life can mend
And when the sun enraptures us in parting
With one last ray as day's drear labours end;
I stayed, you left, our fate and not our choosing,
You went before – how little you were losing.

The life of man seems such a splendid fate;
The day how fair, and night as well how great!
And we, in this sheer Paradise so favoured,
The sun's magnificence we've hardly savoured
When our own striving muddles and confounds us
Now with ourselves and now with all around us;
And neither complements the other quite,
It's dark without when all within gleams bright,
And outward bright goes dulled before my eyes,
So near – the happiness we do not prize.

And now we think we see! By force compelled
In love of women's image we are held:
The youth, as happy as when childhood blooms,
In spring the form of spring itself assumes,
Enrapt, amazed, who worked such spell as this?
He looks around, and all the world is his.
Unfettered haste impels his onward need,
No wall, no palace, nothing can impede;

As flocking birds round woodland summits fly
He hovers round his love and keeps close by,
And glad to leave the air, he seeks and finds
The faithful look, and this it is that binds.

But warned at first too soon and then too late
He feels his flight is checked, ensnared by fate,

To meet again is joy, to part is sore,
Again to meet again is joy still more,
One moment can replace long years that passed;
But farewell's patient malice wins at last.

You smile, my friend, with feeling, as is due:
A fearsome parting brought such fame for you;
Memorials to your piteous fate we show,
You left us here behind for weal or woe;
Then we once more were drawn into the maze
Of chartless passion's labyrinthine ways;
And we, enmeshed in pains that multiply,
At last to parting – parting is to die!
How moving always when the poet sings
To sidestep death which every parting brings!
In torments snared of his half-guilt's procuring
May some god help him say what he's enduring.

[An Werther

Noch einmal wagst du, vielbeweinter Schatten,
Hervor dich an das Tageslicht,
Begegnest mir auf neu beblümten Matten,
Und meinen Anblick scheust du nicht.
Es ist als ob du lebtest in der Frühe,
Wo uns der Tau auf Einem Feld erquickt
Und nach des Tages unwillkommner Mühe
Der Scheidesonne letzter Strahl entzückt;
Zum Bleiben ich, zum Scheiden du, erkoren,
Gingst du voran – und hast nicht viel verloren.

Des Menschen Leben scheint ein herrlich Los:
Der Tag wie lieblich, so die Nacht, wie groß!
Und wir gepflanzt in Paradieses Wonne,
Genießen kaum der hocherlauchten Sonne,
Da kämpft sogleich verworrene Bestrebung
Bald mit uns selbst und bald mit der Umgebung;
Keins wird vom andern wünschenswert ergänzt,
Von außen düstert's, wenn es innen glänzt,
Ein glänzend Äußres deckt mein trüber Blick,
Da steht es nah – und man verkennt das Glück.

Nun glauben wir's zu kennen! Mit Gewalt
Ergreift uns Liebreiz weiblicher Gestalt:

Der Jüngling, froh wie in der Kindheit Flor,
Im Frühling tritt als Frühling selbst hervor,
Entzückt, erstaunt, wer dies ihm angetan?
Er schaut umher, die Welt gehört ihm an.
In's Weite zieht ihn unbefangene Hast,
Nichts engt ihn ein, nicht Mauer, nicht Palast;
Wie Vögelschar an Wäldergipfeln streift,
So schwebt auch er, der um die Liebste schweift,
Er sucht vom Äther, den er gern verlässt,
Den treuen Blick und dieser hält ihn fest.

Doch erst zu früh und dann zu spät gewarnt,
Fühlt er den Flug gehemmt, fühlt sich umgarnt,
Das Wiedersehn ist froh, das Scheiden schwer,
Das Wieder-Wiedersehn beglückt noch mehr
Und Jahre sind im Augenblick ersetzt;
Doch tückisch harrt das Lebewohl zuletzt.

Du lächelst, Freund, gefühlvoll wie sich ziemt:
Ein grässlich Scheiden machte dich berühmt;
Wir feierten dein kläglich Missgeschick,
Du ließest uns zu Wohl und Weh zurück;
Dann zog uns wieder ungewisse Bahn
Der Leidenschaften labyrinthisch an;
Und wir verschlungen wiederholter Not,
Dem Scheiden endlich – Scheiden ist der Tod!
Wie klingt es rührend wenn der Dichter singt,
Den Tod zu meiden, den das Scheiden bringt!
Verstrickt in solche Qualen, halbverschuldet,
Geb' ihm ein Gott zu sagen, was er duldet.]

Erich Trunz rightly notes that this poem frequently employs an "incisive sarcasm" that gives it a "nihilistic, illusion-destroying character".[55] Personal bitterness and despair are subdued in the poem only with great effort; beyond this, "To Werther" constitutes a declaration of the bankruptcy of intellectual history. From 1774 to 1824, Goethe had witnessed the blossoming of the intellectual movements of Enlightenment and Idealism. He had contributed to its development through a manifold exchange of ideas and, as a central figure of intellectual life, even inspired its flourishing both in the German-speaking world and abroad. Yet here this movement is certified a failure. Expressions of similar severity may be found in Goethe's letters; in

55 Trunz: "Kommentar" (note 41), p. 757. Translation JCW.

his literary works, he delegates this devastating voice to other figures, Mephistopheles being a quintessential example. The provocation of the poem consists in the fact that here the lyrical subject is identified as the author of *Werther*. The usually diplomatic Goethe does not hide behind a literary figure but speaks up ostentatiously for himself.

At first glance, the poem "To Werther" appears highly irregular, despite its consistent use of iambic pentameter (lines 2 and 4 providing the only exceptions). The first two stanzas contain ten lines each, and the third and fifth each comprise twelve; the fourth includes only six, i.e. it is exactly half as long as the stanzas that frame it. A skillfully realized hardening of sounds produces an impression that the poem is erratic, almost choppy. While the first stanza establishes a rhyme scheme of *ababcdcdee*, the rest of the poem is comprised solely of rhyming couplets. The result is the monotonous, hammering sound of the marking off of a checklist of hypotheses that allow for no dissent or debate whatsoever. This tone is only intensified by the near-total disappearance of so-called feminine rhyme beginning in the second stanza (after line sixteen; the exception *Wonne/Sonne* is discussed below). The contrast to the first stanza is striking, as here Goethe alternates between masculine and feminine endings and employs feminine rhyme in the stanza's closing couplet (*erkoren/verloren*). The short, six-line fourth stanza turns out to be literally hemmed in by the harsh "masculine" cut of the poem's hypotheses about the human condition. While the opening stanza of "To Werther" acts as a prelude to the sonorous form of the subsequent "Elegy", the short fourth stanza succinctly articulates its central theme: the final "malicious" separation that inevitably occurs at the end of an ever-increasing love, the loss of presence that constitutes the elegy's sole subject matter.

"To Werther" also has an uncanny effect: Goethe addresses the protagonist of his first novel as though he were a real person. The aesthetic boundary is torn down at two points: the lyrical subject reveals itself directly as the author Goethe, who claims responsibility for the content of his novel, which thus transcends the bounds of fiction to become the earnest document of a real life. The accentuation of the novel's autobiographical dimension suggests that, along with Werther, a part of Goethe took its own life, too. Something died, and a wound remained that even fifty years later had not been closed, but rather was opened anew. The strangeness of bringing Werther to life in this manner is only increased by the fact that his story, unlike those of picaresque novels or adventure narratives, does not end in such a way as would suggest the possibility of further adventures, or even the prospect of life under any circumstances whatsoever, as in Candide's embrace of gardening. For Werther, there is no "ever after". As a poetic device, addressing a fictional hero whose life goes on is certainly conceivable. Ariel migrates from Shakespeare's *The*

Tempest to Goethe's second *Faust* in just this way. Werther's end, however, is well-known: "The bullet had entered the forehead over the right eye; his brains were protruding."[56]

In the poem, Goethe speaks fearlessly with Werther's shade, the disfigured ghost of a suicide victim, condemned to hell according to the religious perspective of the age. Goethe underscores the poem's relationship to séance, to necromancy, in noting that the ghost does not avoid his gaze. The eerie nature of the poem, with its allusion to Odysseus' descent into Hades, is only intensified by the fact that the specter is encountered not in the underworld but against the contrasting backdrop of a bright spring day, "on new-flowered meadows". The setting is reminiscent of the opening scene of *Faust II*, in which Faust, in *A Pleasant Landscape* and "couched on grass and flowers", enjoys a rejuvenating, absolving sleep.[57] These omens are inverted in "To Werther". If the poem depicted the reunion of two old friends after half a century, it would be a lovely scene with an element of nostalgia. But the situation is given an unsettling shimmer; nature in spring rejuvenates itself, while in this shining brightness an aged man encounters the ghost of a dead youth. An echo of the situation at Marienbad: an old man suffers again through the springtime of love, a "reprint" of the time of *Werther*, and there is a kind of dark humor in the fact that the poem "To Werther" was in fact included in a new edition of the sorrowful novel. Freud would later seize upon the metaphor of the "reprint" or "new edition" (*Neuauflage*) to characterize the repetition compulsion.[58]

Finally, the poem produces its frightening character through its tonally dismissive, almost reckless turn toward cynicism. Perhaps most shocking for its contemporary readers were the following lines, which devalue Goethe's life after 1774 and decode the uncanny [*das Unheimliche*] as that which is secretly known [*das heimlich Bekannte*]. Werther is still, or perhaps once again, very near to Goethe:

> I stayed, you left, our fate and not our choosing,
> You went before – how little you were losing.
>
> [Zum Bleiben ich, zum Scheiden du, erkoren,
> Gingst du voran – und hast nicht viel verloren.]

---

56 Johann Wolfgang Goethe: *The Sorrows of Young Werther*, in: *The Sorrows of Young Werther – Elective Affinities – Novella* (trans. Victor Lange, New York: Suhrkamp, 1988), p. 87.

57 Johann Wolfgang Goethe: *Faust: Part Two of the Tragedy*, in: *Faust I & II* (trans. Stuart Atkins, New York: Suhrkamp, 1984), p. 121.

58 Cf. Freud: *Fragment of an Analysis of a Case of Hysteria*, in: *The Standard Edition* (London: Hogarth, 1956–74), vol. 7, p. 116.

If "To Werther" is openly autobiographical, one can perhaps imagine the mortification that Goethe's still-living companions—his friends, relatives, lovers, colleagues—experienced when faced with this bleak proclamation. The past fifty years of a life that had so often been envied and admired as rich and fulfilling apparently did not amount to much and are hardly worth mentioning. The poet could just as well have killed himself.

The disappointing elementary structures of life, the poet reveals, were already known to him during his *Werther* period. Nothing truly remarkable or new occurred in the half-century that followed. From the uncompromising perspective of passion, all "activity" is but a sad surrogate that takes the place of "actual" desire. The sole difference between the experiences of young Werther and those of the old poet consists in the crippling, perpetual repetition of a pattern that is always the same and only serves to deepen the tedium of life. Childhood is wonderful, the life of man seems to be "in this sheer Paradise so favored", yet there soon arise disconcerting discrepancies between the interior and exterior worlds, and these discrepancies compose an insulting *cantus firmus* that henceforth accompanies life and embitters it:

> And neither complements the other quite,
> It's dark without when all within gleams bright,
> And outward bright goes dulled before my eyes,
> So near – the happiness we do not prize.
>
> [Keins wird vom andern wünschenswert ergänzt,
> Von außen düstert's, wenn es innen glänzt,
> Ein glänzend Äußres deckt mein trüber Blick,
> Da steht es nah – und man verfehlt das Glück.]

In just a few provocatively relaxed lines, Goethe describes the philosophical movement of the age as a failed endeavor. The intellectual project that stretches from Kant to Hegel may be summarily characterized as an attempt to close the gulf between interiority and exteriority, between subject and object. In the history of philosophy, this effort is encountered as a working out of the problems that remained after Descartes. The lack of coherence between interiority and exteriority, the rift between subject and world, the discrepancy between that which lives and that which thinks and loves—all this is rooted, according to the poem "To Werther," in the unnatural incongruity between human time and the time of the world. The fatal consequence of the absence of any potential reconciliation between these two times is the frustration of the possibility of happiness achieved through unity, even and precisely at the moment when it stands immediately before us. When Goethe speaks of his "opaque expression" [*trüber Blick*] and of the "confused striving" [*verworrene Bestrebung*] that is the inevitable destiny of man, he passes judgment on the project of the Enlightenment, the goal of which since Leibniz was to elucidate all opaque perceptions and convert all confused impressions into clear and distinct ones. No one sees clearly here; everything remains murky and confused. The hot-air balloon that would provide a cheerful view of the labyrinth of life, that proud product of enlightened science, is nowhere to be found in this poem.

Love alone, appearing as the advent of what is eternal and absolute in what is temporal, in what is agonizingly confused and opaque, appears to offer an escape from a human condition plagued by distressful discrepancies. The lover regresses, becoming as blissful "as when childhood blooms" and believing that "all the world is his". Yet as this dark poem counsels, disappointment, too, follows inevitably from love, which is all the more dreadful because the longed-for feeling of oceanic harmony, of "paradise", has been tasted, even if only as an illusion. If love does not fail simply for missing the moment of its possibility, if it does not fail merely for arriving "too soon" or "too late", then it fails in and of itself; it is its own destruction. From this bitter insight, Werther draws the harsh conclusion:

> But farewell's patient malice wins at last.
> [Doch tückisch harrt das Lebewohl zuletzt.]

Interiority and exteriority fail to coincide. Man stands as a stranger in the opaque world, abandoned by God in his "biological deficiencies".[59] The time of man is not the time of the world, with its eternal orders and rhythms. As Herder and Schiller occasionally had done previously, the poem "To Werther" anticipates a fundamental insight of modern philosophical anthropology with its proposition of the "eccentric position" (Plessner) of the undetermined animal: "To say that man is 'world-open' means that he foregoes an animal adaptation to a specific environment."[60] Love, which offers us our only opportunity to comprehend what is absolute, eternal and true in this world, proves to be fickle, deceptive and fleeting. The suicide victim with whom Goethe speaks, and whom he vindicates in his actions—an act of blasphemy according to both Christian churches of the time—grins at the poem's tendentious depiction of life, yet it is unclear whether he is sneering at the complainer or smiling in knowing agreement. The equation *Liebesbesitz* = *Selbstbesitz* = *Weltbesitz* doesn't add up.

---

59 Arnold Gehlen: *Man: His Nature and Place in the World* (trans. Clare McMillan and Karl Pillemer, New York: Columbia University Press, 1988), p. 26.

60 Ibid. p. 27. Cf. Gehlen's discussion of Herder and Schiller's anthropologies.

The poem's sarcastic streak continues unsettlingly. Goethe confesses to the smiling dead youth that he well understood how to capitalize on his suicide, both symbolically and financially: "We celebrated your piteous fate." The author had become rich and famous thanks to his literary depiction of the fate of a person who took his own life when faced with love's fatal deception. The shocking nature of the passage becomes clear if one also understands the poem, as Heinrich Düntzer did, as a speech to Karl Wilhelm Jerusalem, the model for Werther.[61] Goethe soberly informs the wretched hero of his youth that he left him behind after this success to rush once again into the ever-present maelstrom of "weal or woe", into the bewildering labyrinth of the passions that leads only from separation to separation, and finally to separation in death. The advice of the poet is to avoid along the path of life—already marked by "day's drear labors"—the great sorrow that is love. Goethe finds this counsel "moving", yet it remains ambiguous whether he is moved by the memory of his own struggle or whether he sees in this advice a moving, naïve helplessness. To future generations he is able to offer only the wish that, should they, too, become ensnared by such torments, they will receive the divine assistance that was unavailable to both his poem and the hero of his youth. This pious wish is woven into a variation, marked by its subtle use of internal rhyme (*klingt/singt; meiden/Scheiden*),[62] of those lines from *Tasso* that open the "Elegy", through which the transition to the next poem is established:

> How moving always when the poet sings
> To sidestep death which every parting brings!
> In torments snared of his half-guilt's procuring
> May some god help him say what he's enduring.
>
> [Wie klingt es rührend, wenn der Dichter singt,
> Den Tod zu meiden, den das Scheiden bringt!
> Verstrickt in solche Qualen, halbverschuldet,
> Geb' ihm ein Gott zu sagen, was er duldet.]

The bitter poem "To Werther" can only be the apologia of suicide that it is because it also represents an acknowledgment that human life is meaningless. This radical expression of depression neither holds out the prospect of access to philosophical insight, to a conceptual formulation of life's meaning, nor does it find the possibility of consolation through

61 Cf. the commentary in: Goethe: *Gedichte 1800–1832* (note 47), p. 1050.

62 Cf. Jörg Löffler's discussion of the "moving" sound of these internal rhymes, in: Löffler: *Unlesbarkeit* (note 51), pp. 139f.

belief even worth mentioning. Man is trapped between nature on the one hand, which he confronts as a stranger in his reflexive existence as a finite being, and the unnatural character of his passions on the other, which have been emancipated from the cycle of nature and find their most extreme expression in suicide, an act of which only human beings are capable. Any reference in this poem to the supernatural, to the divine, is precarious. It is directly and exclusively tied to the possibility of poetic speech and finds expression only in the subjunctive mood of a quick prayer. The god thus addressed can neither soothe the pain one suffers, nor give it meaning, nor even sublate it. He can only impart the ability to say *what* that pain is, allowing for the possibility of catharsis. It is only this verbalization as such that seems to provide an alternative to suicide: the secular gospel. It must be noted that the pantheistic, gloriously radiant natural world, which Goethe courted throughout so much of his life, never appears in this poem as a potential source of consolation, nor do other fellow human beings, such as family or friends, beyond the object of the poet's delusional love. Missing as well is Goethe's oft-repeated advice that one must give one's life a stable structure of sublimations through work and "activity" and thus shield the time that is so incommensurate to man from the depressing void of idleness. Instead, the poet offers three possibilities for life: to write in solitude, to embrace passion that is necessarily doomed to failure, and finally to commit suicide. The poem to Werther, the dabbler and dilettante of art, is in fact a new *Werther*, one which, as Goethe announced in an 1812 letter, would make the public's hair stand on end:

> "When a man is gripped by the *taedium vitae*, he is only to be to be pitied, and not to be rebuked. That all the symptoms of this queer illness, as natural as it is unnatural, at one time also raged through my very core, *Werther* likely leaves no doubt. I know quite well what it cost me in terms of resolution and exertion to escape the waves of death at that time, just as I undertook the effort of my own arduous rescue and recovery from various later shipwrecks. [...] I entrusted myself with writing a new *Werther*, one which will make people's hair stand on end even more than the first."[63]

Elegy

With the long, calm flow of the "Elegy", Goethe leaves the rigid harshness of "To Werther" behind him, at least on the level of form. In the latter poem, the unsettling, choppy arrangement of irregular stanza lengths and rhyme schemes recalls the coarse gestures of the poet's *Sturm und*

63 Johann Wolfgang Goethe's letter to Zelter on 3 December, 1812 (note 54). Translation JCW.

Drang period. By contrast, the "Elegy", in the spirit of that classical style which the elderly Goethe had refined to the point of slick artificiality, is comprised of perfect six-line stanzas written solely in iambic pentameter with a consistently applied rhyme scheme of *ababcc*. The poem, epic in its scope, is difficult to take in all at once, as it conceals its clear psychological content beneath a veil of beautiful sounds and woven-together metaphors. For this reason, before the poem may be interpreted, an attempt at a summary breakdown of the complex whole is necessary. An analytical approach to the well-proportioned poem, with its melodious charms, seems inappropriate to the material. Rather, much more so than in other cases, one may feel compelled with respect to the "Marienbad Elegy" to refer apologetically to Schiller's exemplary phenomenology of theoretical work, which necessarily slights "natural feeling":

> "For alas! Intellect must first destroy the object of inner sense if it would make it *its own*. Like the analytical chemist, the philosopher can only discover how things are combined by analyzing them, only lay bare the workings of spontaneous nature by subjecting them to the torment of his own techniques. In order to lay hold of the fleeting phenomenon, he must first bind it in the fetters of rule, tear its fair body to pieces by reducing it to concepts, and preserve its living spirit in a sorry skeleton of words. Is it any wonder that natural feeling cannot find itself again in such an image, or that in the account of the analytical thinker truth should appear as paradox?"[64]

The first stanza, set apart from the rest of the poem by a curved figure, establishes the simple yet strict opposition that organizes the entire poem and that, despite every effort, is neither overcome nor sublated nor sublimated: to be with one's beloved is heaven, to be apart from her is hell. The entire elegy, from beginning to end, is concerned with working out this unalterable erotic *factum brutum*, this unapologetic insistence on "presence":

> Now from our meeting what can be expected,
> From this new day whose flowering's not yet ready?
> In Paradise received, to Hell rejected;
> How changeable my thoughts, my heart unsteady! –
> She stands at Heaven's gate! Away with qualms!
> She lifts you up and takes you to her arms.

---

64 Friedrich Schiller: *Letters on the Aesthetic Education of Man*, in: *Essays* (trans. Elizabeth M. Wilkinson and L. A. Willoughby, New York: Continuum, 1993), p. 87f. (First Letter).

[Was soll ich nun vom Wiedersehen hoffen,
Von dieses Tages noch geschloss'ner Blüte?
Das Paradies, die Hölle steht dir offen;
Wie wankelsinnig regt sich's im Gemüte! –
Kein Zweifeln mehr! Sie tritt an's Himmelstor,
Zu ihren Armen hebt sie dich empor.]

The second and third stanzas narrate the joy of an encounter, the bliss of a day spent with the unnamed beloved, whose presence is a kind of fulfillment that brings with it an extinguishing of the three modes of desire: "No need to *wish*, to *hope*, no more *demanding*" (my emphasis, E. G.). The fourth and fifth stanzas depict the cruel pain of the couple's parting and the forlorn state of the solitary lover, who reacts to the separation by falling into a downward spiral of dark thoughts. The list is exhaustive: *Mißmut* ("bad mood," the lover's current emotional state), *Reue* ("remorse," the negative perspective on the past), *Vorwurf* ("reproach," against himself or his beloved for the separation, or jealousy), *Sorgenschwere* ("cares," fear of the future). In stanzas six and seven, the poem follows the exemplary path of sublimation, however temporarily, in describing the lyrical subject's attempts to take his mind off his devastating misery by turning his thoughts outward toward nature: "But is the world not left?" Yet in the light of the fleeting and unstable character of natural phenomena that in the end serve only as reminders of the lost beloved, thus inhibiting sublimation from occurring, the eighth stanza recommends turning inward to erect a stable image of the lost object: "*Ins Herz zurück, dort wirst du's besser finden*" ["Back into your heart, you'll find its presence stronger there"]. Stanzas nine to fourteen thus devote themselves to remembrance and reflect precisely in memory what was chronicled at the poem's beginning: the lovers' meeting at the threshold (nine), the bliss of being in each other's presence (eleven), the breathless angst of wondering if they will see each other again (twelve). Finally, the blissful intensity of being in the presence of one's beloved is compared to the love of God that bestows inner peace. Like God's love, the presence of the beloved opens up, delights and fulfills the cold, withdrawn self (thirteen, fourteen): "Just so I adore her/And it is ecstasy to stand before her." Inasmuch as the beloved's presence signifies the highest joy, the circle of desire has been closed; the path seemingly leads upward, from science to the cultivation of the soul to religion. Yet this highest point is also the beginning: religion is nothing other than the desire to be in the presence of the beloved object; otherwise, it is empty.

In the light of this "revolution," in stanzas sixteen and seventeen it falls to the beloved herself, the lover's highest authority, to preach the doctrine of living in the present, of living like a child, in the moment, without allowing this moment to be spoiled by the foul prospect of an impending, inevitable separation, and of gratefully commemorating those happy moments even in that separation's wake: "Be so, be always childlike, wheresoever,/So you'll be everything, defeated never." The eighteenth stanza, however, rejects these teachings with a stunning brusqueness: "Well you may talk, I thought." The disagreeable lover is beyond help, insisting on presence. Stanzas nineteen to twenty-three follow his destiny after the departure of the beloved. The initially salutary effect of his "endless tears" proves transitory and is insufficient to allay his sorrow. Remembrance of his lost love is likewise incapable of soothing his agony. To the contrary, this flickering between shadow and the harsh, blinding presence of images can be neither tempered into a beautiful figure of memory nor stabilized into a narrative. In its convulsive instability, the flickering of images corresponds precisely to the coming and going of the "waves of death" to which Goethe refers in his letter on the *taedium vitae*. Remembrance thus does not soothe one's suffering but only intensifies it. Set apart by another curving figure, the final stanza comprises a psychologically compelling description of how a life, after the flickering of images, after the ebb and flow of pain, comes to an end. The collapse can no longer be averted, not even by the natural sciences, so dear to Goethe and practiced by him in loving and loyal co-operation with others. A second King Lear, the poet remains alone in moor and heath and is brought to ruin.

This overview of the "Elegy" allows the clinical precision with which Goethe traces the course of a passionate love to stand out. The enamored lover desires to spend his time, all time, at any price and without compromise, in physical proximity to his beloved, who becomes a transcendental signifier, the "sun" under which alone the world reveals itself as meaningful: "The heart's at rest, nought mars the deep, deep feeling/That we belong to her for life and healing." As soon as the beloved is no longer present, the entire world falls into a senseless darkness. Any attempt to take his mind off the situation fails, as the lover either senses only his beloved's absence or perceives her in everything around him. Thus the view of a tender image in the changing clouds calls up only the memory of the dancing beloved. The attempt to cope with separation by integrating it through memory fails. With great psychological acumen, Goethe notes that as long as passion endures, memory can only increase the burning desire for the beloved's presence to be restored. The imagined dialogue with the beloved about living in the moment makes clear how much Goethe in the "Elegy" truly bets on presence, in multiple senses. The "Elegy" plays subtly with two meanings of presence/present (*Gegenwart*). On the one hand, everything in the poem turns on the physical presence of the beloved. In opposition to this pressing desire for an abiding presence, the poem deploys an argument for living in the present and thus forgetting or gratefully remembering accordingly. Yet this argument cannot be accepted; the desire for physical presence proves too powerful. That Goethe forgets himself stylistically in his reaction to the doctrine of living in the moment—Well you may talk, I thought—dramatically underscores the fact that the lover can neither renounce nor sublimate the actual object of his desire: "Among what is authentic in this poem, to the extent that it bears witness to emotions, is its use of *litotes*: namely that lower volumes are chosen to express great inner pathos."[65]

Amazingly, Goethe's "Elegy" anticipates all of the most important forms of sublimation inventoried by Freud—science, religion, identification ("sublation"), stupefaction—yet they are portrayed negatively: none of them works. An attempt at scientific activity only conjures up the image of the beloved. Religion as the experience of the soul is only comprehensible in the beloved's presence; it can neither replace her nor offer consolation in her absence. In Goethe, it is not possible for the lover-subject to internalize in any stable way a lost object, whether through identification ("rejuvenation") or even as a psychically neutralized object of remembrance. The image of the beloved flickers in the grip of the repetition compulsion. The difference between trauma, melancholia and the pain of lost love here becomes clear. Whereas in trauma the mechanisms of the barrier against stimuli mechanically repeat the situation in which this barrier was breached, and in melancholia the self is unaware that its disparaging accusations against itself are actually an accusation against the lost object, the cruelty of being lovelorn lies in the fact that nothing is secret; everything is exposed to the light of day. *Everything* revolves around the longed-for presence of the beloved, the lover-subject's sole desire. And the flickering images are nothing but an expression of this pain, the result of a forced separation. Man in his agony *knows what* he suffers, and this is what makes the separation so horrible:

A thousand times her image it's defining.
It hesitates, is dragged off to the distance,
Now indistinct and now the purest shining;
But what's the use, what profit is it showing,
This ebb and flow, the coming and the going?

[Er wiederholt ihr Bild zu tausendmalen,
Das zaudert bald, bald wird es weggerissen,

65 Max Kommerell: *Gedanken über Gedichte* (Frankfurt am Main: Vittorio Klostermann Verlag, 1985), p. 157. Translation JCW.

Undeutlich jetzt und jetzt im reinsten Strahlen;
Wie könnte dies geringstem Troste frommen,
Die Ebb' und Flut, das Gehen wie das Kommen?]

Even the lower form of sublimation-as-surrogate, encountered in Freud as intoxication, is at best capable of soothing one's physical pain. Yet the spirit refuses to take sanctuary in medication. The lyrical subject knows that the moment the narcotic effect subsides, the pain of the separation will return with equal intensity (here I read *vermissen* – "give up" – as "forget"):

With herbs the body's torments may be treated;
Without resolve and will the mind's defeated,
Without the thought; how give up her existence?

[Wohl Kräuter gäb's, des Körpers Qual zu stillen;
Allein dem Geiste fehlt's am Entschluß und Willen,
Fehlt's am Begriff: wie sollt' er sie vermissen?]

The "Elegy" openly describes a state of embitterment, pain and sorrow, the hellish abyss that always remains open beneath the experience of love, and wonders, in the light of its parallels with the poem "To Werther", what exactly the difference is.

Goethe mitigates his depiction of these dark feelings not only through the restored melodiousness of his language (the elegy's end-rhymes are almost all "feminine"). He also softens the blow of these emotions through a well-established practice, by embedding them in a metaphorics of nature organized around the semantic fields of winter, associated with the lover, and of the sun, associated with the beloved. Moreover, Goethe objectifies his articulation of despair by orchestrating it with reference to literary history, e.g. through allusions to images of nature found in *King Lear*. Such measures serve to temper the immediate force of these emotions, which now appear merely as natural phenomena and not, as in "To Werther", as the expression of the insulating, unnatural nature of human passion and the melancholy that inevitably accompanies it as a result of being alienated from the world. Nonetheless, through his ordering of the poems in the trilogy, Goethe insists upon the essential connection that exists between them. He makes clear that the elegy's melodiousness and formal purity are possible because its lyrical subject is capable of channeling his black bile into another vessel.

The constellation of the poems furthermore underscores the fact that the worldview of "To Werther" is the elegy's precondition; the elegy does not recant this nihilistic perspective but rather presupposes it.

Its sovereign use of a metaphorics of nature legitimized by tradition—such as its successful variation of the topos of old age as a cooling of the emotions and freezing of the soul, or its imagery distilled from specifically Goethean interests such as the discourse of atmospheres or love for clouds—should not lead the reader to the false conclusion that the "Elegy" restores that unity between the life of man and the life of the world, whose absence "To Werther" had marked as man's fate, as a flaw intrinsic in the world itself. The "Elegy" does not stand in contrast to "Werther" in the sense that it repudiates that poem's worldview, say, as regards the adoration of nature. Rather, it documents a different reaction to the same condition of the soul. In terms of content, the former poem's apologia of suicide is replaced by a humble retreat and lonely death as a result of unrequited love. Suicide is the cruelest act that a lover can commit against his beloved, insofar as he thereby takes revenge for being denied her presence, remaining forever in her mind as a terrible memory that generates constant rumination. Suicide, even its literary representation, *compels* that presence which did not manifest itself without violence, and there are good arguments for the view that suicide as a result of unrequited love may be recognized as a death wish directed against the self that had originally been directed against the beloved: a permanent revocation of presence. The aggressive dimension so prevalent in "To Werther" is missing from the elegy entirely. In the "Elegy", suicide is substituted by a gesture of gratitude that is foreign to both the novel and the poem "To Werther". The distant beloved is paid the deepest thanks for illuminating the world and allowing her lover to find himself again. According to the "Elegy", it is only gratitude that may convert a pathological idealization of the beloved into the respect of truly *seeing* the other person, and letting her go. Authentic gratitude is the speech act of successful sublimation in the Marienbad elegy; the heart beats only "to thank her for all being".

The world of the "Elegy" establishes itself as different from the aggressive world of *Werther* most notably by following the only possible path that remains after the gesture of annihilation, i.e. by gratefully celebrating love as a great and fruitful illusion. The *form* assumed by the poem is one of profoundest gratitude. In terms of *motifs*, the "Elegy" achieves its enchanting formal beauty through the rhetorically dazzling identification of the beloved woman with the all-illuminating sun. The poem is so well-known that in reading it, it is easy to overlook the fact that until the third stanza, it is unclear whether the lyrical subject is singing the praises of the sun or of his beloved—and it is this ambiguity which constitutes the original twist Goethe gives to this topos. Even the third stanza's evening kiss could well refer to the red flowing rays of sunset. Only with its depiction of the final goodbye kiss that, "sweet and anguished", severs the thread of life does the poem allow the lover's lament to be heard unambiguously. The night of parting is followed by a description of reunion in which the beloved is celebrated as a rising sun:

The threshold now with gleams of hope is clearing
As she in gentle sunshine is appearing.

[Nun dämmert Hoffnung von bekannter Schwelle,
Sie selbst erscheint in milder Sonnenhelle.]

The beloved's streaming gaze is masterfully compared to the springtime sun that warms and melts away the rigid ice of winter. Love, and *only* love, makes understanding possible. Through love's radiant light, the world becomes clear "in gentle sunshine". Only through love does nature's abundance become visible. Through the figure of the beloved, through the transcendent experience of loving her, the perpetual changing of the clouds, "that vastness rounding,/Now formlessness and now all forms abounding", becomes an object of fascination, and with the poem's turn towards the self, the imagination is revived:

How light and delicate, how clear and tender,
From solemn clouds, seraphic, soaring high,
In lucid haze there floats an image slender,
As if herself, in blue ethereal sky;
So once you used to see her supreme dancing,
Of most entrancing forms the most entrancing.

But only moments dare you risk the danger
To grasp not her but mere hallucinations;
Within your heart, that's where you'll feel no stranger,
That's where she moves in forms and transformations;
To many One evolves through changing stages,
Thus thousandfold, and more and more engages.

[Wie leicht, und zierlich, klar und zart gewoben
Schwebt, seraphgleich, aus ernster Wolken Chor,
Als glich' es ihr, am blauen Äther droben,
Ein schlank Gebild aus lichtem Duft empor;
So sahst du sie in frohem Tanze walten,
Die lieblichste der lieblichsten Gestalten.

Doch nur Momente darfst du dich unterwinden,
Ein Luftgebild statt ihrer festzuhalten;
Ins Herz zurück, dort wirst du's besser finden,

Dort regt sie sich in wechselnden Gestalten;
Zu vielen bildet Eine sich hinüber,
So tausendfach und immer, immer lieber.]

Even faith becomes comprehensible to the agnostic poet in love's all-revealing light; through the secular gospel of love, the word of Holy Scripture comes alive. Yet with the casually skeptical remark, "*wir lesen's*"—as though the Bible were no more than the daily newspaper—, a hint of Voltairean derision is carried over into the "Elegy", giving the otherwise uniformly earnest poem a note of irony:

The peace of God, more happiness bestowing
Than all our understanding – scripture tells us –
Can be compared with peace that comes from knowing
The loved one's presence that serenely quells us;
The heart's at rest, nought mars the deep, deep feeling
That we belong to her for life and healing.

Towards a Higher, Purer, Unknown driven
We sense our purity of heart inclining
In grateful self-surrender freely given,
The Evernameless-One thereby divining;
We call this: reverence! – Just so I adore her
And it is ecstasy to stand before her.

[Dem Frieden Gottes, welcher euch hienieden
Mehr als Vernunft beseliget – wir lesen's –,
Vergleich' ich wohl der Liebe heitern Frieden
In Gegenwart des allgeliebten Wesens;
Da ruht das Herz, und nichts vermag zu stören
Den tiefsten Sinn, den Sinn, ihr zu gehören.

In unsers Busen Reine wogt ein Streben,
Sich einem Höhern, Reinen, Unbekannten
Aus Dankbarkeit freiwillig hinzugeben,
Enträtselnd sich dem ewig Ungenannten;
Wir heiβen's fromm sein! – Solcher seligen Höhe
Fühl' ich mich teilhaft, wenn ich vor ihr stehe.]

In the end, love is the ideal path towards a renewal of the self, which rejuvenates itself and becomes both accessible to itself and open to others. The subject, mediated through love, regains consciousness. What remains of the conceptual efforts of the philosophy of reflection is what is emphasized in Hegel's early writings, namely the dialectic of love. The path to the self must pass over the "threshold" of relinquishing oneself to another. Only he who is able to give himself away may potentially find himself:

Her look, as with the sun's commanding vigour,
Her breath as when I sense the springtime breezes
Dissolves the icy egotistic rigour
Of self that in its wintered caverns freezes;
No self-will, no self-serving, all that's vanished,
All by her coming swept away and banished.

[Von ihrem Blick, wie vor der Sonne Walten,
Vor ihrem Atem, wie vor Frühlingslüften,
Zerschmilzt, so längst sich eisig starr gehalten,
Der Selbstsinn tief in winterlichen Grüften;
Kein Eigennutz, kein Eigenwille dauert,
Vor ihrem Kommen sind sie weggeschauert.]

Love, according to the "Elegy", is that great seminal illusion from which sprout affection towards nature, religion, art, self-knowledge and sociability. Sublimation in this poem is precisely not a substitute for lost love, a surrogate in the face of rejection; rather, in Goethe the reverse is true: it is only through love, whose beam is directed away from the beloved object, that the world is disclosed. Sublimation does not take the place of love but rather becomes possible through love that elevates the world. The gesture of the "Elegy" is thus infinitely friendlier than that of "To Werther".

On the other hand, this lament serves to intensify the depths of grief, inasmuch as the poem lacks any aggression, any will to life in its negativity. The elegy is consistently silent regarding the difference in age between the lovers, and yet the old age of the poet, who like the fool King Lear takes leave of his trusted companions in moor and heath, is apparent. This poem no longer recognizes the future. The world does not disclose itself to those companions, perhaps because they, unlike the old lover, are not blinded by love. The situation is again reversed. New love, that all-illuminating illusion, still stands before those younger companions. This is the source of the elegy's deadly seriousness, which reaches well beyond the bitterness of the Werther poem: that there exists a last love, after which no more will follow. The poet, as noted above, allows his beloved to expound upon the doctrine of the fulfilled moment, the paradoxical claim that one must be "always childlike" and forget both past and future. The old age of the poet stands out here more clearly than at other points in the poem. He has no more time: "Well you may talk, I thought." The lyrical subject's stunningly prosaic reaction underscores why the beloved talks so well. Unlike the poet, she is actually young, and far from death. He, however, "shudder[s] at the hint of separation", as every parting could well be his last: "How am I helped by wisdom's education!" By revoking the principle of living in the moment and dismissing himself with a casual remark, Goethe makes clear that this poem documents the end of a life.

The "Elegy" thus confirms the breakdown, aggressively posited in "To Werther", of Marianne Wünsch's equation: "*Liebesbesitz* = *Selbstbesitz* = *Weltbesitz*." In a second step, however, the poem corrects this diagnosis, inasmuch as it celebrates love as an illuminating illusion, for the experience of which the beloved is owed thanks. Indeed, the experience of love signifies a renewal of the self and a more intense experience of the world. The recurrence of this experience is thus not merely an instance of *taedium vitae*, but rather is desired as an experience of rejuvenation. The "Elegy" paradoxically confirms the dire insight of "To Werther" regarding the collapse of the idealistic unity of love, self and world by gratefully preserving this fruitful illusion and opening itself for its recurrence. Ultimately, however, the elegy plunges its readers into sorrow over the finitude of an individual life. One's last love is not only the experience of a productive illusion; it is also the unbearable experience of a final separation. For an old man close to death, every parting becomes a *memento mori*; over the course of a love affair marked by the rhythm of repeated separations, the poet is laid low. In the end, nothing stands between him and death, not even an illusion.

The opposition between presence and separation that establishes the Marienbad elegy's law of motion is already present in the poem's original manuscript, first discovered in 1980, yet the gesture of gratitude is missing, as is the comparison of the beloved with the all-illuminating sun, which had already formed the organizing principle of "To Werther" in its courtship of "*paradiesische Wonne*" and "*hocherlauchte Sonne*." Gratitude is clearly possible only with increasing (physical) distance. In one of his last poems, Goethe again brings together gratitude and the sun; this late poem retrospectively sheds new light on the "Elegy".

In its bound clean copy, Goethe's lament bears the title "Elegy, September 1823." Five years later, another poem emerges with the title "Dornburg, September 1828." As far as I can tell, this objective connection between the two poems has not yet been observed; indeed, in some editions of Goethe's poetry, such as the Insel edition, the title of the later poem, which discreetly signals this intertextual link, is omitted entirely. Goethe published the *Trilogy of Passion* in the *Ausgabe letzter Hand* in 1827. The printing of this edition presumably sparked a renewed confrontation with his elegy's world of sorrow, which was then reflected in the Dornburg poem. The poem, one of the last Goethe wrote in his life, involves a compression and further development of the "Marienbad Elegy", a refined and simultaneously harrowing sublimation of sublimation. The poem reads:

Dornburg, September 1828
When, in garden, valley, mountains,
Dawn through misty veils is spilling,
Colours fill the flowers as fountains,
Every utmost longing stilling,

When the ether clouding over
Clarity of day oppresses
And the East Wind, airy drover,
Clears the blue as sun progresses,

If you feast your eyes then, purely,
Thank the gracious great on truly,
Parting sun shall redden surely,
Gild the whole horizon newly.

[Früh wenn Tal, Gebirg und Garten
Nebelschleiern sich enthüllen,
Und dem sehnlichsten Erwarten
Blumenkelche bunt sich füllen;

Wenn der Äther, Wolken tragend,
Mit dem klaren Tage streitet,
Und ein Ostwind, sie verjagend,
Blaue Sonnenbahn bereitet;

Dankst du dann, am Blick dich weidend,
Reiner Brust der Groβen, Holden,
Wird die Sonne, rötlich scheidend,
Rings den Horizont vergolden.][66]

The poem here subtly establishes its connection to *Werther*, whose fictional letter of 10 May, with its artful use of the hypotactic when-then construction, became a model for novelists such as Jean Paul. The poem consists of a single sentence that formulates a conditional structure: When the day begins and you are able to see your utmost longing fulfilled through the coloring of the flowers, when you are able to

66 Johann Wolfgang Goethe: *Selected Poems* (note 50), p. 148f.

observe calmly the drama of the day's strife, and when finally you are capable of thanking the sun for illuminating and coloring the world, then you will experience a radiant golden sunset.

The connection to Goethe's love of Marienbad and the processing of that love in the "Elegy" is woven into the poem insofar as here the interplay between sun and beloved is precisely inverted, i.e. is actually mirrored. If one might conclude, at the beginning of the "Elegy", that the poet is extolling the sun, the situation is reversed for a brief moment in the Dornburg poem: the "gracious great one" might well refer to the poet's beloved. Grammatically, it is even possible that giving thanks to the gracious great beloved fulfills the condition that allows the golden sun to set; the wording of the text makes it difficult, if not impossible, to decide how the poem should be read.

The Dornburg poem thus confirms the perspective taken up by the "Elegy", namely that it is sincere thankfulness, free of resentment and bitterness, which constitutes true sublimation. Only when one is able to feel gratitude toward one's beloved, despite that love story's tragic end, only then can one experience the sunset that gilds the entire horizon. It is of course also possible to read the sun as a metaphor of divine authority, to consider the poem as a kind of thanksgiving prayer. Such a reading, however, must rely on the convention of the sun as the eye of God or as God himself, which is not present in the poem. Rather, the Dornburg poem restricts itself to the level of what Walther Killy aptly called "the true image" (*das wahre Bild*).[67] From beginning to end, it remains on the level of the precise description of nature. There is the text, and there is the natural world in which the sun rises and sets. The poem follows this routine process with the precision of a camera and comes very close to that state of "contentment" which Goethe believes is achieved through joyful meditation on the regularity of cyclical processes. Nonetheless, the rift between man and world torn open in the *Trilogy of Passion* is not entirely closed, even in this late poem; there remains a faint confusion, namely the ambiguity which makes it impossible to determine whether it is the sun or the beloved being thanked. There emerges with this ambiguity the possibility in language to depict the uncertainty of visual perception. The potential polysemy of these lines corresponds to the blurred gaze of a finite man upon a world whose processes are subject to a time other than his own.

Reconciliation

Goethe cultivated the genre of occasional poetry like almost no other writer, to the point where almost the entirety of his lyrical output has

67 Cf. Walther Killy: *Wandlungen des lyrischen Bildes*, 8. Aufl. (Göttingen: Verlag Vandenhoeck & Ruprecht, 1998), s. 13ff.

been placed under this title, and rightfully so, inasmuch as Goethe himself called occasional poetry "the oldest and most genuine of all genres".[68] Three aspects come together under the concept of occasional poetry that are contained within the semantic field of the term *Gelegenheit* ("occasion"). First—as documented by the poem "Reconciliation", written as an homage to the Polish pianist Maria Szymanowska, whose playing Goethe admired—the occasional poem may be seen as an element of cultivated social intercourse. It participates in the sphere of play. Its various manifestations include extemporaneous improvisations and jovial competitions in salons, friendly greetings and respectful dedications to individuals, even erotic and chivalrous *billet doux*.

At the same time, the concept of occasional poetry preserves an essential relationship to the world that is particular to Goethe's poetry, a devotion to the concrete world that extends beyond mere social occasions. The world as a whole, its manifestations in nature, in society and in solitude all provide an infinite abundance of occasions for poetry, which thus becomes the preferred medium for capturing and preserving situations in their singularity and unrepeatability, for expressing them in their true image.

Finally, the concept of *Gelegenheit* includes the realm of *kairos*, chance, that joyful moment denounced in the gloomy "To Werther" as a missed opportunity. There are two sides to this sense of *Gelegenheit*; it refers both to that happy moment when life goes well, as well as the situation and mood employed by the quick-thinking poet as the occasion for his poetry. The poet, too, can either rise up to meet the moment in which poetry is possible, or miss it entirely.

Submitting the poem "Reconciliation" to an interpretative vivisection would amount to an ungallant overworking of a gallant homage. The poem praises the magic of music as an infinitely flowing therapeutic which is able to soothe the pain of heartache by eliciting tears, and which makes it possible for one to experience the feeling of gratitude towards love that stands at the center of the "Elegy". A reading of "Reconciliation" makes clear the precision with which Goethe wrote his great lament, as the poem includes one word that is consistently withheld from the "Elegy". The theme here is desire, joy, bliss. Goethe's phenomenology of love is precise; he ascribes many attributes to the experience of love, but not one: happiness. The lover in love is thrown back and forth between paradise and hell. That love—both heaven and hell together—was a joy, is only recognizable after the fact. Love is understood only after its end:

> Relieved, the supple heart then senses surely
> Its beat, its eager beat, its life resurgent;

---

68 Johann Wolfgang Goethe: *Poetry and Truth* (note 22), p. 295.

In gratitude itself it offers purely,
To bounteous gift makes its response convergent.
And then was sensed – oh could it last for ever! –
The double bliss of tones and love together.

[Und so das Herz erleichtert merkt behende,
Daβ es noch lebt und schlägt und möchte schlagen,
Zum reinsten Dank der überreichen Spende
Sich selbst erwidernd willig darzutragen.
Da fühlte sich – o daβ es ewig bliebe! –
Das Doppel-Glück der Töne wie der Liebe.]

The happiness of the poet Goethe is enshrined in the arrangement of the three poems that make up the *Trilogy of Passion*. Though "Reconciliation" was written first, it seems to constitute a synthesis of the two antithetical poems that precede it, to offer a summation in the form of an aphorism that has become a German proverb: "All passion has its pain!" (*Die Leidenschaft bringt Leiden!*). Thanks to a happy coincidence, this occasional poem acts as a "reconciliation" between "To Werther" and the "Elegy". It takes up the former poem's tropes of confused striving and opaque expression; from the latter, it draws the heart that beats with gratitude. Ultimately, "Reconciliation" formulates the structure of sublimation that guides the process of writing. As an *überreiche Spende* ("overly generous gift"), the *Überfülle* ("overflow") of art reacts to the *Allzuviele* ("all too much") that was lost, to that which has *überschnell* ("overly quickly") disappeared. These concepts, despite their polarity, converge in the prefix *über-*, which signifies disproportion.

The *Trilogy* thus comes full circle. Goethe defines *taedium vitae*, that disgust with life that can lead to suicidal tendencies, as an illness both natural and unnatural. For him, it is passion which transforms this doubling of the natural and the unnatural into experience, into an excruciating, unbearable experience. Affection for another human being—here a man's passion for a woman—can be conceived as a purely natural phenomenon. Yet man is subject to the great cyclical processes of the world, while his passion is not. Passion is decoupled from biological rhythms; it can occur at the wrong time, direct itself towards the wrong object. Failure in the face of nature, in the face of time's power, the powerlessness of man: love and passion are truly human phenomena. Animals do not know them in this sense. Goethe searched his entire life for an antidote to the illness that arises from passion. His sole solution is to turn to nature. Only a person capable of becoming one with nature is able to escape that natural-unnatural illness. The entirety of Goethe's efforts to understand nature can now be understood, in the light of the *Trilogy*, as a monstrous effort to escape what is unnatural; this is the fate of mankind.

According to the *Trilogy of Passion*, the paradoxical achievement of art is that it allows man to experience as happiness that overabundance which overburdens him and which in proportion to the world systematically becomes an endless lack. The joy in passion can be experienced only through its sublimation *in* the work of art. This is Goethe's formula of successful sublimation, which he derives directly from the sublime—the overabundance of what is absolutely great.

Running through the three poems of the *Trilogy* is the invocation of a third possibility which stands in relation to both the natural and the unnatural, i.e. the supernatural, the divine, religion. Goethe prays that when man falls silent in his anguish, a god will come to his aid so that he will be able to say what he is suffering. The famous epigraph of the "Elegy" is taken directly from *Torquato Tasso*:

> When in their anguish other men fall silent
> A god gave me the power to tell my pain.
>
> [Und wenn der Mensch in seiner Qual verstummt,
> Gab mir ein Gott zu sagen, wie ich leide.]

These lines from *Tasso* have frequently been understood as a gnomic summation of the Freudian theory of sublimation. According to this reading, the artist differs from other human beings in that he is able to satisfy his desires for power, success and erotic fulfillment, frustrated though they may be in the real world, through fantasies and daydreams that, formulated into a work of art, yield a social profit, such that the artist is now able actually to achieve what he previously had only dreamed of. The successful author Goethe would himself be the greatest example of this process. The drama *Torquato Tasso*, however, draws a different picture. Here Goethe depicts the social downfall of an artist who destroys his reputation in a struggle over his work, wrested from him by the powers that be, and thus comes to financial ruin. The quoted lines, in accordance with this tragedy of the modern artist, formulate a conception of sublimation different from Freud's. The difference between the artist and other men consists not in the artist's ability potentially to discharge his frustrated instinctual desires, but *only* in his ability to articulate beautifully those desires; a god may help the artist to say *what* his pain is, but not to soothe that pain nor to make it disappear simply through its utterance. Tasso is miserable, he is brought to ruin, despite the fact that his writing is so inspiring; the play's end offers him no hope for a successful life. It is the experience of suffering, not in the mode of silence but in the mode of speech.

Tasso is no neurotic artist standing in disproportion to the real world; rather, he is the hero of modernity who attacks the reality principle itself. Freud believed that the artist afforded the consumer a certain gentle "fore-pleasure". The artist as Goethe portrays him shocks and unsettles the world. Tasso leaves both his friends and adversaries as changed persons, having confronted them with a monstrous experience that is, strictly speaking, "incomparable". It is Antonio, the pragmatic man of the world and aggressive representative of the reality principle who, aghast, sums up the shock remaining at the play's end. If there exists nothing with which the harrowing experience of art can be compared, then this experience punctures the given structures of perception and cognition. It possesses an ontological force, as it allows us to understand what love is, our unnatural nature:

> Unhappy man, I scarcely yet can speak.
> When something quite unheard-of has occurred,
> When our own eyes have glimpsed a monstrous act,
> Then for a while our very minds are halted:
> All measure fails then, all comparison.
>
> [Unglücklicher, noch kaum erhol' ich mich!
> Wenn ganz was Unerwartetes begegnet,
> Wenn unser Blick was Ungeheures sieht,
> Steht unser Geist auf eine Weile still,
> Wir haben nichts, womit wir das vergleichen.][69]

The unheard-of, the monstrous, the incomparable returns in the *Trilogy* as the discourse of the *Allzuvieles* and the *Überschnelles*, as the discourse of *Überfülle* and of the *Überreiches*. What emerges here is the idea that the concept of sublimation should be disburdened of its moment of resignation, inverted and reconceived as the appearance of the sublime, of what is absolutely great. The experience and existence of the artist, the production and reproduction of his works, create neither "fore-pleasure" nor relief. Rather, art provides a glimpse of what is monstrous, that which takes one's breath way, which seizes the spirit for a single moment through the appearance of that which is incomparable, which escapes the differential order of opposites: "All measure fails then, all comparison."

Art and the existence of the artist are a transgression towards that which is absolutely monstrous, what in aesthetic theory is deemed the sublime. The production and reception of art neither brush aside nor replace nor even merely conceal that which is unbearable because

---

69 Johann Wolfgang Goethe: *Torquato Tasso* (note 24), p. 135, lines 3281ff.

it is monstrous. Art instead exposes what is monstrous—insatiable passion, desire—and makes possible its experience. Only through sublimation, Goethe teaches, does the monstrous scale of what is to be sublimated become apparent. Only through sublimation can what is to be sublimated be experienced as shock. And sublimation is achieved in art by the very fact that it is made manifest, that it is *spoken*. Art does not cause the monstrous to disappear, rather the monstrous *appears* in art: *Überfülle, Überreiches, Allzuvieles, Allzuschnelles, Alles*. This is why Goethe writes a *Trilogy of Passion*—a trilogy that writes, that is dictated by passion itself—and not a trilogy beyond passion. Sublimation means that what is destructive in life can be experienced through art. And this is Goethe's concept of happiness.[70]

---

70 In a recently published essay, Ernst Osterkamp points emphatically to loneliness as the great problem of Goethe's late work and later years. Osterkamp reconstructs Goethe's coping strategies, the goal of which was "not to sublate his loneliness but to transform it from an adverse fate inflicted upon him into a self-chosen state of creative solitude, of voluntary isolation". As a kind of "transformation", Goethe's vigorous and frequently successful attempts to master his loneliness may be described as another variety of sublimation. Yet in the case of the sublimation of loneliness, as in the case of passion, there remains a painful, unsublimatable remnant, a remaining scrap of empiricism, painful to carry: "Though he did not want it to be aired in public, Goethe often discussed with his closest friends what he called the empiricism of loneliness that could not be dealt with through the concept of renunciation." Here again, as in the case of passion, the elderly Goethe reveals himself as a forefather of the twentieth century, the existentialism of which period time and again invoked an "existential loneliness" of difference, though its best texts mediated this experience of "existential loneliness" through the depiction of bleak empirical solitude in social isolation. Ernst Osterkamp: "Einsamkeit. Über ein Problem im Leben und Werk des späten Goethe," Akademie der Wissenschaften und der Literatur, Mainz. Abhandlungen der Geistes- und sozialwissenschaftlichen Klasse. Jahrgang 2008. Nr 1. (Stuttgart: Franz Steiner Verlag, 2008), pp. 8 and 4. Translation JCW.

2. The Sound of Psychoanalysis: Arthur Schopenhauer

Non multa

The World as "Brain and Genitals"

Arthur Schopenhauer considered *Torquato Tasso*—that play in which Goethe "brings before our eyes not only suffering, the essential martyrdom of genius as such, but also its constant transition into madness"—"particularly instructive."[1] As discussed in the previous chapter, *Tasso* features those famous lines that define the prerogative of talent in a world marked by suffering, and which in 1823 would serve as a motto for Goethe's own "Marienbad Elegy", a chronicle of the downfall of a dejected man:

> When in their anguish other men fall silent
> A god gave me the power to tell my pain.
>
> [Und wenn der Mensch in seiner Qual verstummt
> Gab mir ein Gott zu sagen, wie ich leide.][2]

In concluding his *Trilogy of Passion* with a poem about the therapeutic, salutary function of music, Goethe also fulfills the transition that Schopenhauer orchestrated within the aesthetic order of things in 1819.[3] Music articulates the monstrous, the idea that beyond a

---

1 Arthur Schopenhauer: *The World as Will and Representation*, Vol. 1 (trans. E. F. J. Payne, New York: Dover 1969), p. 191.

2 Johann Wolfgang Goethe: *Torquato Tasso*, in: *Verse Plays and Epic* (trans. Michael Hamburger, New York: Suhrkamp, 1987). Final scene.

3 Goethe had read Schopenhauer's magnum opus, first published in 1819. One can thus suppose that Schopenhauer's metaphysics of music may have

phenomenal world split in two there exists a single driving force. Music, Schopenhauer writes, is "quite independent of the phenomenal world, positively ignores it, and, to a certain extent, could still exist even if there were no world at all."[4] This lofty description of the metaphysics of music documents not the descent of the monstrous into madness or folly, but rather the strict division of the world into representation and the will, whose constant urging may be heard in music. Schopenhauer's philosophy, as Thomas Mann notes in recalling his earliest encounters with it, is

> "[t]he erotic of death, as a musical, logical system of thought, born of an enormous tension of mind and senses – a tension whose issue and leaping spark is precisely eroticism: such is the parallel experience of youth in its encounter with this philosophy, which it understands not morally but vitally, personally – not because of its doctrine, I mean its preachment, but because of its essence – and with which they are well agreed."[5]

Allowing oneself the liberty to play around a bit with the much-venerated title of *The World as Will and Representation* reveals Schopenhauer's philosophy as historically Janus-faced, as the distinctive formulation of a potentially irreversible transition. Reading the title, with a view to the work's epigraph[6] and appendix,[7] as *The World as Goethe and Kant* places the book in the context of the time of its first publication, the year 1819. Schopenhauer's magnum opus appears as an ambitious attempt to redefine the relationship between transcendental philosophy and Goethean intuition, to integrate the two most potent trends of the age. Schopenhauer radicalizes transcendental idealism in the first book of his masterwork; in the second book, frequently criticized as an intellectually deficient argument by analogy,[8] he attempts an answer to the question of Kant's unknowable "thing-in-itself." Proceeding from bodily experience, which he claims is immediate and discloses the essence of the world, Schopenhauer defines the thing-in-itself as the

---

influenced Goethe's appreciation of music in the years that followed. However, the available documents on the genesis of the *Trilogy of Passion* provide no information about such a connection.

4 Schopenhauer: *The World as Will and Representation*, Vol. 1 (note 1), p. 257.

5 Thomas Mann: "Schopenhauer" (1938), in: *Essays of Three Decades* (trans. H. T. Lowe-Porter, New York: Knopf, 1965), pp. 372–410, here p. 395.

6 "Ob nicht Natur zuletzt sich doch ergründe. Goethe".

7 "Critique of Kantian Philosophy".

8 Cf. Jochen Schmidt: *Die Geschichte des Geniegedankens in der deutschen Literatur, Philosophie und Politik 1750–1945*, Bd. 1, 2. Aufl. (Darmstadt: Wissenschaftliche Buchgesellschaft, 1988), p. 471.

will, that blind urge, an undifferentiated unity that is wholly without cause: "All representation, be it of whatever kind it may, all *object*, is *phenomenon*. But only the *will* is *thing-in-itself*."[9] What remains from Kant's critical philosophy is the deceptive veil of Maya, woven into the thread of causality; from Goethe's observations of gloriously radiant nature there remains a nightmarish world, the obsessive description of which reveals "how essentially *all life is suffering*".[10]

This fusion of Kant and Goethe likewise implies a transformation of aesthetics and ethics. The phenomenal world (with which music has nothing to do) is beautiful, in Schopenhauer's view, only as an object of disinterested, superficial observation, as still life, as *nature morte*. In his ethical consideration of man's immersion in the essence of the world Schopenhauer recognizes only compassion as a moral driving force. Through compassion, the transcendent affect, we experience the unity of will behind all individualized phenomena in time and space. Through compassion we are liberated from our "colossal egoism"[11] and become conscious of the unity of that inner nature which exists within every living thing, what in Sankskrit is described by the formula "*tat tvam asi* (this art thou)."[12]

The artist, whose highest form is found in the figure of the composer—for Schopenhauer, specifically Beethoven—is fulfilled within this system as a resigned ascetic and ultimately as a saint. In Hegel's *Phenomenology of Spirit*, first published in 1806, infinity still frothed forth triumphantly over the lip of the champagne glass that is the realm of the spirit; in 1819, to the truly enlightened, "to those in whom the will has turned and denied itself, this very real world of ours with all its suns and galaxies, is—nothing."[13] If one accepts Friedrich Nietzsche's hypothesis that one of the fundamental conflicts in the history of Western civilization centers around sublimation as a process of intensification with an aim towards greater self-control on the one hand, and, on the other, "false" sublimation as the debilitation and mortification of the drives—for Nietzsche, a conflict exemplified by the poles of ancient Greece and Christianity[14]—then Schopenhauer takes his place squarely on the side of the latter. Thus Nietzsche writes in *Twilight of the Idols*:

"[Schopenhauer] is a first-rate case for a psychologist. Specifically,

9 Schopenhauer: *The World as Will and Representation*, Vol. 1 (note 1), p. 110.
10 Ibid., p. 310.
11 Arthur Schopenhauer: *On the Basis of Morality* (trans. E. F. J. Payne, Indianapolis: Hackett, 1998), p. 132.
12 Ibid. p. 210.
13 Schopenhauer: *The World as Will and Representation*, Vol. 1 (note 1), p. 412.
14 Cf. the following chapter.

> he is a viciously ingenious attempt to use the great self-affirmation of the 'will to live,' the exuberant forms of life, in the service of their opposite, a nihilistic, total depreciation of the value of life. He interpreted art, heroism, genius, beauty, great sympathy, knowledge, the will to truth and tragedy one after the other as consequences of 'negation' or some need to negate on the part of the 'will'—the greatest psychological counterfeit in history, Christianity excluded. On closer inspection, this just means that he is heir to the Christian interpretation."[15]

Taking into account the enormous influence of Schopenhauer's philosophy on Sigmund Freud, one might suppose that Freud's own ambiguous concept of sublimation likewise tends ultimately toward debilitation and mortification. For this reason, taking a look at Schopenhauer is instructive in preparing a reading not only of Nietzsche but also of Freud. If one reads the title of his masterwork as *The World as Ego and Id*, or—as Thomas Mann does—as *The World as "Brain and Genitals"*,[16] Schopenhauer is thus aligned with the twentieth century.[17] The tome then appears to highlight a watershed discursive moment directed towards the future, marking the transformation of philosophy into science. Take away its philosophically inexplicable mysticism and one is left with what Arnold Gehlen listed as the consequences of Schopenhauer: philosophical anthropology[18] and psychoanalysis.

---

15 Friedrich Nietzsche: *Twilight of the Idols*, in: *The Anti-Christ, Ecce Homo, Twilight of the Idols, and Other Writings* (trans. Judith Norman, ed. Aaron Ridley and Judith Norman, Cambridge, UK: Cambridge University Press, 2005), p. 202.

16 Cf. Thomas Mann: "Schopenhauer" (note 5), p. 405.

17 As is well known, Schopenhauer experienced the true height of his popularity during the 1800s, the century in which both Freud and Thomas Mann were socialized. The Schopenhauer of the nineteenth century—which also left its mark on the philosopher's late work, particularly in the form of aggressive anti-Semitism—has been studied by Max Horkheimer, among others, who noted one reason for the popularity of this notorious pessimist in the age of high capitalism: "Pessimistic philosophy became the rationalization of disturbing conditions in reality. It helped to push the absence of facilitations expected by technological progress onto the being of the world, instead of deriving the upcoming disaster out of a state of society in which technology has grown over the head of man." Max Horkheimer: "Schopenhauer and Society" (1955), in: *Qui Parle* 15.1 (2004), pp. 85–96. Here: p. 89. Regarding Schopenhauer's reception in the nineteenth century, particularly as it overlaps with Marx's, cf. Alfred Schmidt: *Idee und Weltwille. Schopenhauer als Kritiker Hegels* (München: Hanser Verlag, 1988).

18 Arnold Gehlen: "Die Resultate Schopenhauers", in: *Gesamtausgabe*, Bd. 4 (Frankfurt am Main: Vittorio Klostermann Verlag, 1989), pp. 25-49. Cf. the chapter below on Friedrich Nietzsche.

After all, in his *Metaphysics of Sexual Love*, Schopenhauer was one of the first to recognize the central importance of the sexual drive, which he deemed the "focal point" of the will.[19] Schopenhauer's divided world, however, offers no prospect of forcefully sublimating this focal point. Freud nonetheless conceded that Schopenhauer should be counted among the discoverers of the unconscious, as his "unconscious 'Will' is equivalent to the mental instincts of psychoanalysis."[20] The title of one of the essays appended to Schopenhauer's masterwork thus consistently asserts the "Primacy of the Will in Self-Consciousness", a provocative inversion of Idealist philosophy. The following passage reads like the earliest draft of what would later become known as Freud's second topography, under the banner of an insight into the unconscious that is derived from sound:

> "Therefore in self-consciousness the known, consequently the will, must be the first and original thing; the knower, on the other hand, must be only the secondary thing, that which has been added, the mirror. They are related somewhat as the self-luminous is to the

---

19 Schopenhauer: *The World as Will and Representation*, Vol. 1 (note 1), p. 203.

20 Sigmund Freud: "A Difficulty in the Path of Psychoanalysis", in: *The Standard Edition of the Complete Psychological Works of Sigmund Freud* ((eds) James Strachey and Anna Freud, London: Hogarth, 1956–74), vol. 17, p. 143f. Regarding Freud's reception of Schopenhauer, cf. primarily: Aloys Becker: "Arthur Schopenhauer – Sigmund Freud. Historische und charakterologische Grundlagen ihrer gemeinsamen Denkstrukturen", in: *Schopenhauer-Jahrbuch 1971*, pp. 114–56. On p. 115, Becker summarizes those points where Schopenhauer lays the groundwork for Freud: "The components of the mind (will/intellect – id/ego); the functioning of the 'mental apparatus' according to associational-psychological, dynamic and economic laws; the apparently materialistic concept of mental processes; understanding the mind-body problem in terms of psychophysical unity; the postulation of a uniform determinism in the empirical mental realm; the assumption of unconscious mental processes (unconscious thought); the principles that determine mental life (division of the will – pleasure and reality principle); nirvana principle; emotional ambivalence (identification, secret death wishes); the theory of repression; reaction formations and sublimation; sexual psychology (bisexuality, sexual neuroses, perversions); dream psychology (the *via regia* to the unconscious); psychology of religion [...]; the fundamental positions of metaphysical anthropology' (translation JCW). Whereas Becker strives to prove that Freud is highly dependent on Schopenhauer, Günter Gödde – 'Schopenhauers Entdeckung der Psychologie des Unbewuβten', in: *Schopenhauer-Jahrbuch*, 86. Band 2005, pp. 5–36 – offers a more sober assessment that in my view is more appropriate: "The prominent parallels between the psychologies of Schopenhauer and Freud support the assumption that the basic structure of Freud's (meta-)psychology of the unconscious is predetermined in Schopenhauer's 'philosophical discoveries.'" p. 32. Translation JCW.

> reflecting body; or as the vibrating strings are to the sounding-board, where the resulting note would then be consciousness. We can also consider the plant as such a symbol of consciousness. As we know, it has two poles, root and corona; the former reaching down into darkness, moisture and cold, and the latter up into brightness, dryness and warmth; then as the point of indifference of the two poles where they part from each other close to the ground, the collum or root-stock (*rhizoma, le collet*). [...] The root represents the will, the corona the intellect, and the point of indifference of the two, namely the collum, would be the *I*, which, as their common extreme point, belongs to both."[21]

The proximity of Schopenhauer's philosophy to the psychology of the unconscious becomes obvious if one holds up this astounding characterization alongside the illustration that Freud included in his introduction to the second topography in *The Ego and the Id*. Like Schopenhauer's root-stock, the ego in Freud "is not sharply separated from the id; its lower portion merges into it."[22] At the same time, Freud's departure from Schopenhauer's classical world of ideas, with its beauteous and graceful figures, can scarcely be more drastically illustrated than through this hideous drawing that presents the psychic apparatus as an amorphous lump or some kind of bagpipe with a small opening at the top. The title of Freud's 1923 study can be read as a paraphrase of *The World as Will and Representation*, yet it also suggests an inversion. For Freud, what comes first is the ego, which according to the ethics of psychoanalysis is supposed to emerge in that space where once there was only id. This inversion of Schopenhauer is ultimately seconded by Freud's peculiar suggestion "that the ego wears a 'cap of hearing" [*Hörkappe*]—on one side only, as we learn from cerebral anatomy. It might be said to wear it awry."[23] With his drawing, Freud implicitly rejects the metaphysics of music. Schopenhauer's pessimism survives as an unsightly sketch of our own amorphous soul; disenchanted, his theory of music returns in the form of a cap worn awry. One can hardly read this passage without thinking of Richard Wagner's similarly skewed beret, perhaps not entirely wrongly. It is decisive for his strictly dualistic philosophy that, unlike Freud, who emphasizes the flowing unity of his shapeless soul, Schopenhauer does not understand how to make his botanical metaphor conceptually fruitful.

---

21 Arthur Schopenhauer: "On the Primacy of the Will in Self-Consciousness," in: *The World as Will and Representation*, Vol. 2 (note 1), pp. 202–3.

22 Sigmund Freud: *The Ego and the Id*, in: *The Standard Edition* (London: Hogarth, 1956–74), Vol. 19, p. 24.

23 Ibid., p. 25.

Otherwise he might have taken up the task he so brusquely rejected, of shedding some light on the *commercium* between root and corona, between *corpus* and *mens*, i.e. he might have been in a position to identify the hitherto undiscovered solution to the problems left behind by Descartes. Schopenhauer's radical separation of spheres, intended as a solution, leads to the above-cited passage being dominated by the metaphor of strings stretched across the sounding-board of the will, which paves the way for a metaphysics of music that will take the exact place of a sublimation that has become impossible.

Wortlaut

In 1920, having discovered what lies *Beyond the Pleasure Principle*, Freud writes that we can no longer remain blind to the fact that

> "[w]e have unwittingly steered our course into the harbor of Schopenhauer's philosophy. For him death is the 'true result and to that extent the purpose of life', while the sexual instinct is the embodiment of the will to live."[24]

The founder of psychoanalysis rarely traveled to the "forbidden land" of philosophy.[25] That here he distinguishes Schopenhauer's system of thought with the suggestive topos of being rescued from the stormy sea, from disorientation and mortal danger—this gives us all the more reason to pay attention. Yet the ambivalence of this passage must be noted as well. It is also possible that, like the captain in Peter Jackson's psychoanalytic take on *King Kong*, we will emerge from the fog and, unwittingly, find ourselves in a harbor that we hadn't planned on entering. The harbor of Schopenhauerian thanatology may offer us the opportunity of a brief reprieve, but we must leave Skull Island as quickly as possible. Given the importance of *Beyond the Pleasure Principle* to the further development of psychoanalysis, the dualistic theory of drives, and trauma theory; to the formation of a new topography comprised of id, ego and superego; and to a new formulation of the concept of sublimation, it seems advisable to consider Schopenhauer's doctrine more closely. For the project of psychoanalysis has entered into the gloomy harbor of this philosophy, if only for a moment.

In any attempt to understand better Schopenhauer's powerful influence on Freud, which otherwise has been well reconstructed, there arises a question that must now be answered: How musical is

24 Sigmund Freud: *Beyond the Pleasure Principle*, in: *The Standard Edition* (London: Hogarth, 1956–74), Vol. 18, p. 50.

25 Becker: "Arthur Schopenhauer – Sigmund Freud" (note 20), p. 146. Translation JCW.

psychoanalysis? Or rather: How musical may or must psychoanalysis become? This question asserts itself inasmuch as Schopenhauer's aesthetics, as mentioned above, effects a revaluation of the hierarchy of the arts. Poetry, culminating in tragedy, is deposed, and it is music that now assumes the throne:

> "[M]usic is as *immediate* an objectification and copy of the whole *will* as the world itself is, indeed as the [Platonic] Ideas are, the multiplied phenomenon of which constitutes the world of individual things. Therefore music is by no means like the other arts, namely a copy of the Ideas, but a *copy of the will itself* [...]. For this reason the effect of music is so very much more powerful and penetrating than is that of the other arts, for these others speak only of the shadow, but music of the essence. [Inasmuch as music is an immediate copy of the will, it] therefore expresses the metaphysical to everything physical in the world, the thing-in-itself to every phenomenon."[26]

Considering how influential this metaphysics of music has been,[27] one might assume that it also played a role in the development of a psychology that explicitly recognized Schopenhauer's concept of the will as a stunning anticipation of the theory of unconscious drives. Yet Freud resolutely resists music. In his essay on *The Moses of Michelangelo*, he writes:

> "[W]orks of art do exercise a powerful effect on me, especially those of literature and sculpture, less often of painting. This has occasioned me, when I have been contemplating such things, to spend a long time before them trying to apprehend them in my own way, i.e. to explain to myself what their effect is due to. Wherever I cannot do this, as for instance with music, I am almost incapable of obtaining any pleasure. Some rationalistic, or perhaps analytic, turn of mind in me rebels against being moved by a thing without knowing why I am thus affected and what it is that affects me."[28]

26 Schopenhauer: *The World as Will and Representation*, Vol. 1 (note 1), pp. 257 and 262.

27 Cf. Lydia Goehr: "Schopenhauer and the musicians: an inquiry into the sounds of silence and the limits of philosophizing about music", in: *Schopenhauer, Philosophy and the Arts* (ed. Dale J. Jacquette, Cambridge, UK: Cambridge University Press, 1993), pp. 200–28. See also Lawrence Ferrara's musicological essay in the same volume: "Schopenhauer on music as the embodiment of Will", pp. 183–99.

28 Sigmund Freud: *The Moses of Michelangelo*, in: *The Standard Edition* (London: Hogarth, 1956–74), Vol. 13, p. 211.

Substitute "music"—the sound of the will—with "the unconscious" in this passage, and the connection to be examined here becomes apparent. Freud affirms Schopenhauer's hypotheses about music, inasmuch as he describes its effects as "moving" [gripping, *ergreifend*]. He reacts to music in exactly the same way as he reacted to the effects of the unconscious: by resolving to determine, through reason and the development of his "analytic disposition", the reasons behind this feeling of being gripped, from which he thus again emancipates himself. Both Schopenhauer and Freud discover the unconscious. Schopenhauer, however, declares communication with the unconscious, in the interest of a potential sublimation that would not be a mortification, to be impossible. Schopenhauer's reaction is one of resignation. As compensation, in a bold argument by analogy, he defines music as "in the highest degree a universal language", [29] one to which we abandon ourselves, shaken, without ever being able to comprehend it, explain it or open it up to analytical penetration.

Traditionally defined, metaphysics is the formal attempt to reproduce the world in its entirety in terms of concepts, i.e. in language; it is the "mental iteration of all that is."[30] In terms of content, metaphysics can be defined, according to Schelling, as the project of sublating the absolute opposition between "the conviction that all thinking and knowing are completely objective" and the principle "that nature is utterly without reason and thought" through knowledge of "[nature's] identity with the spiritual."[31] Given these definitions, Schopenhauer's magnum opus is not a metaphysical treatise at all, but rather, as an uncompromising *codification* of the *opposition* between will and representation, denotes metaphysics' end. Schelling's philosophy having fallen apart, Schopenhauer's is essentially silent. It is effectively a sign pointing to music, which shocks the body and makes it sing, though it cannot explain its will. Body and spirit are torn asunder, become hostile to one another. The radicality of Schopenhauer's descriptions of our misery may disguise its desolate emptiness; his arsenal of transcendental philosophical terminology may obscure the fact that Schopenhauer has abandoned metaphysics, in the place of which music resounds. In this light, post-metaphysical thought since 1819 can be understood as an attempt to express the codified opposition between representation (language)

---

29 Schopenhauer: *The World as Will and Representation*, Vol. 1 (note 1), p. 262.

30 Odo Marquad: *Skeptische Methode mit Blick auf Kant*, 3. Aufl. (Freiburg/München: Verlag Karl Alber, 1982), p. 11. Translation JCW.

31 Friedrich Wilhelm Joseph Schelling: *Philosophical Investigations into the Essence of Human Freedom* (trans. Jeff Love and Johannes Schmidt, New York: State University of New York, 2006), p. 4.

and will (music) in a non-idealist way, by discovering the musical, i.e. the erotic dimension of language.

Thomas Mann's claim in *Death in Venice* that "Eros is in the word"[32] bridges the gap between literature and psychoanalysis as two prominent modes of working with language. In his 1938 essay on Schopenhauer, which—in the light of historical experience—decidedly characterizes the trajectory of his own work as the path from Schopenhauer to Freud, Mann logically postulates that will and representation are intertwined in a captivating passage that does not invoke sublimation as a process of mortification, but rather figures it as the integration of will and representation in the *Klangkörper* ("sounding body") of language:

> "But suppose [Schopenhauer] had learned to reconcile [the unity of world and representation, E. G.] in his genius, in his creative life. Suppose he had understood that genius does not at all consist in sensuality put out of action and will unhinged, that art is not mere objectivation of spirit, but the fruitful union and interpenetration of both spheres, immensely heightening to life and more fascinating than either can be by itself! [...] But in Schopenhauer genius intensified both spheres until they took refuge in the ascetic. To him, sex is of the Devil, a diabolic distraction from pure contemplation; knowledge is that denial of sex which says: 'If thine eye offend thee, pluck it out.'"[33]

A further, highly ambiguous remark from Mann's essay takes on an incisive meaning in the context of the search for a post-metaphysical expression of the opposition between blind nature and empty subjectivity:

> "[W]hen we are speaking about truth, it is a matter of acceptableness. Truth, it seems to me, is not bound to words, does not coincide with a definite wording [*Wortlaut*]; perhaps that may even be its chief criterion."[34]

The nuance of this statement consists in the fact that Mann does not forsake language in favor of the language-beyond-language of music, but rather emphasizes the *sound* of language itself, its *Wort-Laut*. The will remains what it is, namely the constant urging of the drives: "[W]e untiringly strive from desire to desire [...], till we come to a wish that

32 Thomas Mann: *Death in Venice* (Trans. Michael Henry Heim, New York: Ecco, 2004), p. 85.

33 Mann: "Schopenhauer" (note 5), p. 406.

34 Ibid., p. 393.

is not fulfilled, and yet cannot be given up."[35] With this righteous remark, Schopenhauer succinctly articulates the challenge facing all theories of sublimation. Hovering over this statement is Freud's oft-articulated insight that we are unable truly to renounce anything, wherefore the veil of sorrow and the shadow of aggression seem to hang over all sublimation. This "truth" of Schopenhauer's is never disputed by either Thomas Mann or Freud. Consciousness remains the string stretched across the sounding-board of the will. Yet what the will desires can indeed be heard *within* language. Freud follows Mann's Venetian insight that "Eros is in the word," not poetically but—naturally—analytically. He conceives—and as a therapist later realizes—the project of a possible translation of the sounds of dreams and conversations. He applies the art of trained, structured listening to the effects of the unconscious in human speech. Freud listens for overtones, for nuances of discourse. He is attentive to dissonances, to modulations of the voice. He seeks out leitmotivs, pregnant pauses, rhythms and their syncopations and interruptions, shrill and strident tones, discordances, new themes, etc. Amazingly, the process of free association turns out to be precisely the technique of free musical improvisation transferred onto language. Schopenhauer's metaphysics falls silent; philosophical discourse is abandoned in favor of pointing to music proper, the language of which yet remains incomprehensible. Freud reacts rationally. He resists actual music, concentrates instead on human speech and attempts to ensure that this speech is heard, so that the will of the analysand may become clear.

Neither Freud nor, obviously, Thomas Mann has anything against music per se. They simply resist elevating music to the emblem of resignation and regression. Both Mann and Freud maintain Schopenhauer's insight that the unconscious will never fully disclose itself in language, nor allow itself to be raised into the light of the concept. A well-known passage from *The Interpretation of Dreams* here provides an echo of Schopenhauer's above-cited reflections on the rhizome from his essay on the *Primacy of the Will*:

> "There is often a passage in even the most thoroughly interpreted dream which has to be left obscure; this is because we become aware during the work of interpretation that at that point there is a tangle of dream-thoughts which cannot be unraveled and which moreover adds nothing to our knowledge of the content of the dream. This is the dream's navel, the spot where it reaches down into the unknown. The dream-thoughts to which we are led by interpretation cannot, from the nature of things, have any

35 Schopenhauer: *The World as Will and Representation*, Vol. 1 (Note 1), pp. 318–19.

> definite endings; they are bound to branch out in every direction into the intricate network of our world of thought. It is at some point where this meshwork is particularly close that the dream-wish grows up, like a mushroom out of its mycelium."[36]

It is *in this sense* that truth is not bound to words. On the other hand, this does not mean that musical resignation and regression necessarily follows from the impossibility of a perfect articulation of the truth in language, from the end of metaphysics. Rather, from the observation that the truth of what we actually want—what the id actually wants—does not coincide with a particular *Wortlaut* [sequence of words], there follows for Freud and Mann the demand that we constantly produce new *Wortlaute* or listen for *Wort-Laute*. Truth, including the truth of the body, is heard in the sounds of words. In turning away from music, psychoanalysis itself becomes musical. Schopenhauer's metaphysics perishes in the melancholy gesture of pointing. Freud answered this act of resignation with a famous conceptual compromise that allows the moment of being moved *and* rationalistic reserve *and* analysis all to be heard. He gave these methodological reflections a title that retains the excess of metaphysical inquiry within the framework of post-metaphysical thought, the insight that truth does not coincide with a particular *Wort-Laut*. Metaphysics has passed over into metapsychology.[37]

Melancholia

Inasmuch as the brusque rejection of any mediation between the world of representation and the world of the will is constitutive of Schopenhauer's worldview, one might point out that the above-outlined efforts towards such mediation cannot be extrapolated from Schopenhauer's thought itself. It is precisely this theory that I wish to challenge by demonstrating that an error may be discerned in Schopenhauer's reasoning that transcends dualism even according to its own argument. Schopenhauer naturalizes both compassion and music, which in his system converge to establish the immediate experience of the will, the unity behind all representation. Everyday language registers this convergence in the concept of shock or "shakenness" (*Erschütterung*) later elaborated by Adorno.[38] We are shaken when we hear great music or feel great compassion. Thus we are not

36 Sigmund Freud: *The Interpretation of Dreams*, in: *The Standard Edition* (London: Hogarth, 1956–74), Vol. 4, p. 564.

37 Cf. Achim Geisenhanslüke: *Das Schibboleth der Psychoanalyse. Freuds Passagen der Schrift* (Bielefeld: Transcript, 2008), pp. 115–28.

38 Cf. the chapter on Theodor Adorno below.

concerned here with Walter Gebhard's exquisitely established proof of the inconsistencies in Schopenhauer's analogical thinking:

> "Schopenhauer resolves the difficulty of ascribing to music a specific mimetic relationship to reality by hyperbolizing it as a parable of the world in its entirety: if it does not have to represent anything, it will presumably represent the entire world. Abstraction resolves the contradiction."[39]

Rather, what must be noted here is that Schopenhauer overlooks the basic fact that both compassion and music are peculiarly human. Animals neither experience compassion nor do they make music. Schopenhauer stops precisely where he should have begun. He refuses to acknowledge that the two phenomena he distinguishes, compassion and music, equally denote emotions and cultural practices that are uniquely human. Yet the moment he had conceived of compassion as a *humanum*, Schopenhauer would have taken the abhorrent plunge into ethical thought. As Ernst Tugendhat notes:

> "The real difficulty [of Schopenhauer's approach, E. G.], however, lies in the fact that [...] compassion simply more or less exists as a natural sentiment. There may well be people who spontaneously react with compassion to every instance of suffering, but most do this only partially, and some experience more strongly than compassion the opposite feeling of *Schadenfreude* or pleasure in cruelty. So can such a sentiment that is naturally predetermined and exists in varying degrees ever be the basis for an obligation? Are we obliged to compassion? One can certainly say that we should cultivate it as a general feeling. But what would motivate us to do this if we didn't already presuppose a moral perspective?"[40]

Tugendhat observes that at the moment he assigns *value* to compassion—the more compassion, the better the person—Schopenhauer has effectively reverted to the level of *reflection*. And this transition constitutes a valid ethical argument only by virtue of the fact that compassion is a distinctly human and not a natural phenomenon in the sense of the purely animal world. Tugendhat's argument can be applied as

---

39 Walter Gebhard: *Der Zusammenhang der Dinge: Weltgleichnis und Naturverklärung im Totalitätsbewusstsein des 19. Jahrhunderts* (Tübingen: De Gruyter Verlag, 1984), p. 112. Translation JCW.

40 Ernst Tugendhat: *Vorlesungen über Ethik* (Frankfurt am Main: Suhrkamp Verlag, 1993), pp. 182f. Translation JCW.

well to music, which Schopenhauer elevates to the same level. If he had begun to consider the human quality of music, he would have at that moment transcended the dimension of pure, empty performativity. On the one hand he would have come up against the question of the potential referentiality of musical language and, in the second step, been confronted with the musical, expressive character of human speech. Schopenhauer remains at the threshold of reflection in his keen recognition of phenomena such as repression, rationalization, etc. Yet ultimately he cannot reconcile these insights with the demands of his system.

Freud's fragmentary theory of sublimation—and here, too, Nietzsche laid the groundwork for him with his genealogical thinking—constitutes a theory of transformation *par excellence* that brings to light these processes of translation from will to knowledge. Between 1920 and 1923, i.e. during the critical phase of his development of a concept of sublimation, Freud re-engages in the paradigmatic conflict between Schopenhauer's dualism and the possibility of mediation. As it turns out, in 1923's *The Ego and the Id*, which directly followed the publication of *Beyond the Pleasure Principle* three years earlier, Freud refines his theory of sublimation by taking recourse to a dialectical model, thus leaving Schopenhauer's dualisms behind.

Schopenhauer is particularly relevant to a historical reconstruction of the theory of sublimation, not only in view of his theory of death, but especially with regard to his theory of a "fixed contemplation"[41] that sees through the world's essential meaninglessness. The sublime conception of a wholly objective and thus occasionally beatific worldview liberated from the urging of the will is nearly identical to certain of Freud's descriptions of successful sublimation. What for Schopenhauer was philosophy has for Freud become science in the form of an occasionally ascetic ideal: "Science is, after all, the most complete renunciation of the pleasure principle of which our mental activity is capable."[42]

When Freud's scattered remarks on sublimation are subjected to scrutiny, it becomes apparent that the concept's notorious nebulosity is at least partially a result of the fact that Freud allows two definitions of the term—one esoteric, the other exoteric—to exist side by side. For Freud, it is only a "minority"[43] of great individuals, and primarily

41 Schopenhauer: *The World as Will and Representation*, Vol. 1 (note 1), p. 178.

42 Sigmund Freud: "A Special Type of Choice of Object Made by Men (Contributions to the Psychology of Love I)," in: *The Standard Edition* (London: Hogarth, 1956–74), Vol. 11, p. 165.

43 Id.: "Civilized" Sexual Morality and Modern Nervous Illness,' in: *The Standard Edition* (London: Hogarth, 1956–74), vol. 9, p. 193.

multitalents like Leonardo or Goethe, who are able to achieve a kind of successful sublimation that amounts to more than mere substitution. As mentioned above in connection with Goethe, the apotheosis of Freud's esoteric concept of sublimation is articulated in his essay on Leonardo, where it is defined as an exhilarating liberation from all authority. Exoteric sublimation, by contrast, coincides almost completely with a forced renunciation of the drives; as a surrogate that is accepted by the masses only with much weeping and gnashing of teeth, it is constantly in danger of falling victim to regression, to desublimation. According to Freud, even the mere consumption of alcohol is sufficient to induce regression: "We know that drink removes inhibitions and undoes the work of sublimation."[44]

Both forms of sublimation in Freud are evidently derived from Schopenhauer's elitist model. With his dualistic, hydraulic model of drives, with his elitist concept of sublimation, and with his pessimistic view of civilization, the accomplishments of which can be annulled at any moment, Freud is clearly under the spell of Schopenhauerian thought. This is also the case when it comes to both authors' shared rejection of the notion of history. Freud is directly paraphrasing Schopenhauer when, in *Beyond the Pleasure Principle*, he notes: "The present development of human beings requires, as it seems to me, no different explanation from that of animals."[45]

In a third conception of sublimation, however, Freud achieves on the level of metapsychology what he had in fact begun with his musicalization of psychoanalysis. The concept of history returns. In *The Ego and the Id*, Freud writes:

> "It may be that this identification is the sole condition under which the id can give up its objects. At any rate the process, especially in the early phases of development, is a very frequent one, and it makes it possible to suppose that the character of the ego is a precipitate of abandoned object-cathexes and that it contains the history of those object-choices. [...] From another point of view it may be said that this transformation of an erotic object-choice into an alteration of the ego is also a method by which the ego can obtain control over the id and deepen its relations with it. [...] The transformation of object-libido into narcissistic libido [...] obviously implies an abandonment of sexual aims, a desexualization—a

---

44 Id.: *Psychoanalytic Notes Upon an Autobiographical Account of a Case of Paranoia (Dementia Paranoides)*, in: *The Standard Edition* (London: Hogarth, 1956–74), vol. 12, p. 64.

45 Id.: *Beyond the Pleasure Principle* (note 24), p. 42.

> kind of sublimation, therefore. Indeed, the question arises, and deserves careful consideration, whether this is not the universal road to sublimation, whether all sublimation does not take place through the mediation of the ego, which begins by changing sexual object-libido into narcissistic libido and then, perhaps, goes on to give it another aim."[46]

Attention to Freud's use of language here reveals that his breakthrough in metapsychology, discussed in detail in the chapter on Freud below, occurs in the form of a turning away from Schopenhauer. For Schopenhauer, a person's character is "innate and ineradicable. The wicked man is born with his wickedness as much as the serpent is with its poisonous fangs and glands [...]. *Velle non discitur.*"[47] Freud, by contrast, once again thinks character historically; it arises from an individual's history of object-choices.

He also introduces another concept that Schopenhauer ruthlessly rejects, that of mediation. Experience occurs when the ego integrates elements of the object world and is thus changed. Through experience, the ego becomes different and can move on. At the same time, experience implies that the ego grows ever richer, working through and leaving behind it the dichotomy of impelled subjectivity and the nightmarish world. It is clear that Adorno's dialectical understanding of the concept of sublimation, which reconstructs the life of the ego as the historical acquisition of experience, constitutes the absolute antithesis of the numbness of melancholia. Through sublimation, as the integrating, mediating history of object-choices, the future breaks free of the past that has thus been processed. Sublimation succeeds where melancholia catastrophically fails, in sublating the lost object. In coming to a dialectical understanding of sublimation in 1923, Freud demonstrates, via the same line of thought, that Schopenhauer's book about a rigidly fixed world, abruptly and irreconcilably divided into will and representation, is in fact a document of clinical melancholia; Arnold Gehlen, too, remarked on the "lack of any development" in Schopenhauer.[48] The gloomy harbor of the philosophy of division, into which Freud entered for but a moment in 1920, is a harbor of death, and the music that lures one into it is the song of the sirens, a seductive invitation to a regression that remains ever possible. The discovery of the sounding body of language allows us to leave this world and inaugurates our emancipation from a false sublimation that demands we pluck out the eye that offends us. Before the complicated development of Freud's

---

46 Id.: *The Ego and the Id* (note 22), p. 29f.

47 Arthur Schopenhauer: *On the Basis of Morality* (note 11), p. 187.

48 Gehlen: "Die Resultate Schopenhauers" (note 18), p. 26.

concept of sublimation can be studied, however, we must first turn our attention to Friedrich Nietzsche, who converted thinking in eternal oppositions into the project of a systematic genealogy that points far into the future.

3. Transfigured *Physis*: Friedrich Nietzsche

Gehen wir ans Meer!
Daybreak

Three Dimensions of Sublimation

Walter Kaufmann may count among his many accomplishments being the first to point out the central role of the concept of "sublimation" in Friedrich Nietzsche's thought. In his seminal book on the philosopher, Kaufmann not only collected many relevant and for the most part previously overlooked citations on the subject, but also offered interpretations of those passages in Nietzsche's work that, though they do not name the concept of sublimation explicitly, arguably describe the process referred to by that term, or at least processes closely related to it.[1] As Kaufmann explains, to understand more precisely what Nietzsche means by sublimation, it is necessary to look as well at his writings on *agon* or on asceticism; also relevant are his manifold remarks, scattered throughout his works, on refinement, spiritualization, sublation, and finally discipline and breeding.

Nietzsche's *methodical* use of "sublimation" in developing his ideas on genealogy and metamorphosis is exemplified by his richly variegated proposition that a trace of cruelty—i.e. delight in the pain of others, or in self-torture—not only haunts civilization as a shocking "relapse into barbarism" but in fact pervades or even underpins it in a sublimated form. Thus he writes in *Beyond Good and Evil*:

"Almost everything we call 'higher culture' is based on the

1 Cf. Walter Kaufmann: *Nietzsche: Philosopher, Psychologist, Antichrist*, 4th ed. (Princeton: Princeton University, 1974).

> spiritualization of *cruelty*, on its becoming more profound: this is my proposition. That 'savage animal' has not really been 'mortified'; it lives and it flourishes, it has merely become—divine. What constitutes the painful voluptuousness of tragedy is cruelty; what seems agreeable in so-called tragic pity, and at bottom in everything sublime, up to the highest and most delicate shudders of metaphysics, receives its sweetness solely from the admixture of cruelty."[2]

Nietzsche modifies this thought in his three treatises on the *Genealogy of Morality*; his explicit use of the word "sublimation" here representatively confirms the philological soundness of Kaufmann's hypothesis that the above-mentioned terms are germane to any reconstruction of Nietzsche's understanding of the concept. In the second treatise, Nietzsche considers the possibility that civilization's delight in cruelty, once so blatantly apparent (e.g. as in the public festivals of Roman antiquity), has not actually died out, even in the bourgeois world of the late nineteenth century:

> "[P]erhaps, just as pain today hurts more, it [pleasure in cruelty] needed, in this connection, some kind of sublimation and subtilization, it had to be transformed into the imaginative and spiritual, and adorned with such inoffensive names that they do not arouse the suspicion of even the most delicate hypocritical conscience ('tragic pity' is one such name, another is '*les nostalgies de la croix*')."[3]

These complicated reflections on cruelty—which, spanning from the individual soul to the idea of God, themselves merit a monograph devoted to their explication[4]—demonstrate that the concept of sublimation in Nietzsche has multiple dimensions, at least three, yet which Kaufmann, in the excitement of his first disclosing them, did not clearly differentiate. The first of these dimensions is rooted in cultural theory, the second in individual psychology and the third in philosophy.

Culture

As a term used in the field of *cultural theory*, sublimation refers to the fundamental accomplishment of civilization, namely the taming,

---

2 Friedrich Nietzsche: *Beyond Good and Evil*, in: *Basic Writings of Nietzsche* (trans. and ed. Walter Kaufman, New York: Modern Library, 2000), p. 348f.

3 Nietzsche: *On the Genealogy of Morality* (trans. Carol Diethe, Cambridge, UK: Cambridge University Press, 2006), pp. 47–8.

4 With *Discipline and Punish*, Michel Foucault delivered on Nietzsche's propositions. Foucault's Nietzscheanism is discussed further below.

ordering and channeling of pre-cultural chaos. Culture itself is a form of sublimation that ranges from simple practices to spiritual modes of living; Nietzsche, again anticipating Freud, conceives of saintliness as "the highest spiritualization of [the] instinct" to "cleanliness" (*Reinlichkeit*).[5] Following Kaufmann's lead, Rüdiger Safranski recently reformulated the most well-known distinction in Nietzsche's early writings as a theory of sublimation. The Apollonian, according to Safranski, turns out to be the sublimation of the Dionysian:

> "The Dionysian, in Nietzsche's vision, is the colossal course of life itself. Cultures are the fragile and always precarious attempts to create a zone of inhabitability within it. Cultures sublimate Dionysian energies; cultural institutions, rituals and explanations are representations that live off the actual substance of life and yet hold it at a distance. The Dionysian lurks before and under civilization. It is the dimension of the colossal power that both threatens and allures."[6]

Like Kaufmann before him, Safranski also draws attention to Nietzsche's perspective, probably inspired by his exchanges with Jacob Burckhardt, on the ubiquity of the contest in ancient Greece,[7] on *agon*, which by the early 1870s he understood as a form of sublimation for the pre-Homeric, pre-cultural world. In his preface to one of five unwritten books, *Homer's Contest*, Nietzsche interprets *agon* as the crucial foundation of a structure of sublimations that stabilizes the polis and prevents a relapse into a pre-cultural state. It is from his studies of ancient Greece that Nietzsche derives his later, generalized concept of sublimation, which, as will be demonstrated below, rests upon the implementation of a rule in general:

> "[I]f we take away competition from Greek life, we gaze immediately into that pre-Homeric abyss of a gruesome savagery of hatred and pleasure in destruction."[8]

---

5 Nietzsche: *Beyond Good and Evil*, in: *Basic Writings of Nietzsche* (note 2), p. 411.

6 Rüdiger Safranski: *Nietzsche: A Philosophical Biography* (trans. Shelley Frisch, New York: W. W. Norton, 2003), p. 66f.

7 "And now the agonal. While on the one hand the polis violently cultivates and promotes the individual, the agonal constitutes a second, equally powerful force that is known to no other nation. Agon is the common element that brings every desire and ability to fermentation, as soon as the necessary freedom exists." Jacob Burckhardt: *Griechische Kulturgeschichte*, in: *Das Geschichtswerk*, Bd. 2 (Frankfurt am Main: Zweitausendeins Verlag, 2007), p. 743, Abschnitt neun, Kapitel 3: "Der koloniale und agonale Mensch." Translation JCW.

8 Nietzsche: "Homer on Competition", in: *On the Genealogy of Morality and Other Writings* (note 3), p. 193.

As Reinhard Gasser succinctly notes, Nietzsche (unlike Freud, who always maintained a high degree of generality) ultimately connects his phenomenology of sublimation to the concrete (cultural) history of Europe and comes to a well-known, unambiguous judgment. According to Gasser, Nietzsche leaves no doubt

> "that history's manifold attempts to tame and conquer the drives were ultimately condensed into a prototypical form, namely the opposition between Greek and Christian civilization, a dichotomy which may be considered parallel to that of active and reactive, life-affirming and life-denying, healthy and sick. In a word, Nietzsche's concept of sublimation fundamentally implies a concept of judgment."[9]

Kaufmann, too, had already pointed out the initially surprising yet ultimately revealing fact that, in Nietzsche's estimation, Christianity, as opposed to ancient Greece, never developed a culture of sublimation (more on this below):

> "[T]he people to whom the Church addressed itself simply lacked the power to control, sublimate, and spiritualize their passions; they were 'poor in spirit.' "[10]

Psychology

As a *psychological* term, sublimation refers to a methodological concept that renders possible the genealogy of moral sentiments. Here sublimation is an instrument of the oft-admired, oft-imitated Nietzschean technique of "unmasking" (*Entlarvung*). One prominent example is the notion that an ostentatiously displayed "morality of distinction is in its ultimate foundation pleasure in refined cruelty," that such ostentatious irreproachability is marked by an immoral ulterior motivation to do harm to others.[11] Like others of his small masterpieces inspired by the French Moralists, Nietzsche's insight into the sadistic ulterior motives of irreproachability is reminiscent of Freud's observations on the psychopathology of everyday life—e.g. his theory of "gain from illness," the idea that a sick person can potentially draw narcissistic satisfaction from his own suffering.

9 Reinhard Gasser: *Nietzsche und Freud. Monographien und Texte zur Nietzsche-Forschung*, Bd. 38 (Hg. Ernst Behler et al., Berlin/New York: De Gruyter, 1997), p. 351. Translation JCW.

10 Kaufmann: *Nietzsche* (note 1), p. 231.

11 Nietzsche: *Daybreak: Thoughts on the Prejudices of Morality* (trans. R. J. Hollingdale, Cambridge, UK: Cambridge University Press, 1997), p. 23.

According to *The Gay Science*, psychological acuity is no evil eye, but rather an eye for sublimated evil:

> "At the point where the poor power of the eye is no longer able to see the evil drive as such, owing to its increasing subtlety, man posits the realm of goodness; and the feeling of now having stepped into the land of goodness excites all those impulses that had been threatened and limited by the evil drive, such as the feeling of security, of comfort, of benevolence."[12]

It is often assumed that it was Freud who first introduced the term sublimation to psychology and, later, to the theory of civilization. Kaufmann, however, endeavored to prove that Nietzsche not only generally refined the psychology of ulterior motives but also specifically "anticipated" Freud's concept of sublimation.[13] In light of the fact that it was Nietzsche who established this concept as a psychological *terminus technicus*, one is spontaneously inclined to concur with Kaufmann's observation, the elaboration of which was significantly promoted by Reinhard Gasser in his monumental study *Nietzsche und Freud*.[14] According to Gasser, sublimation in Nietzsche may be called "the epitome of the refinement of the drives",[15] and Nietzsche's imperative can clearly be identified as "recognizing that any 'pure' will to knowledge is rooted in the drives."[16] This insight into "the force of impulses in knowledge" [*die Gewalt der Triebe im Erkennen*][17] widens into a spectacular transformation of transcendental philosophy; if one follows to its logical conclusion the claim that all thinking is bound to the drives, then there no longer exists anything beyond "reality" as disclosed through the drives. Of course, this poses the question of what authority would be allowed to define the concept of a "reality" constituted by the drives. For now, we can note that the concept of a "world" structured by the drives, as the legacy of the Kantian apparatus of knowledge, could only be formulated by a person who has experienced sublimation in its perfection and thus positioned himself outside of this "world", in absolute solitude. And with his eye-opening transformation of transcendental philosophy in terms of drive theory, Nietzsche at the same time bequeathed to the generations that followed

12 Nietzsche: *The Gay Science* (trans. Josefine Nauckhoff, Cambridge, UK: Cambridge University Press, 2001), p. 63.
13 Kaufmann: *Nietzsche* (note 1), p. 218.
14 Gasser: *Nietzsche und Freud* (note 9), pp. 313–65.
15 Ibid., p. 326. Translation JCW.
16 Ibid., p. 338. Translation JCW.
17 Nietzsche: *The Gay Science* (note 12), p. 111.

him a new and enigmatic object of future research, namely the concept of the "drive" itself:

> "Suppose that nothing else were 'given' as real except our world of desires and passions, and we could not get down, or up, to any other 'reality' besides the reality of our drives—for thinking is merely a relation of these drives to each other: is it not permitted to make the experiment and to ask the question whether this 'given' would not be *sufficient* for also understanding on the basis of this kind of thing the so-called mechanistic (or 'material') world?"[18]

Philosophy

This ontological explication of the drive structure of "reality", which leaves open the pressing question of what a "drive" actually is, pointedly emphasizes the nexus between the psychological and philosophical dimensions of the concept of sublimation. From a *philosophical* perspective, sublimation refers to the hinge on which Nietzsche's philosophy swings from an idolatry of eternal being to the affirmation and celebration of ineluctable becoming. Descartes' theory of two substances, offshoots of which—and the Schopenhauerian variety in particular—defined so much of the eighteenth and nineteenth centuries, is substituted by a monism under the banner of the will to power. In gaining an understanding of Nietzsche's concept of "sublimation" it is important to note that, from a philosophical perspective, this concept serves to overcome the apparent dualism between reason and the body, discovering floating bridges where abysses of substantial difference were thought to be. The doctrine of "refinement" makes it possible from now on to stop "talk[ing] of opposites where there are only degrees and many subtleties of gradation".[19] According to Nietzsche's analysis, the Cartesian theory of two unmediated substances, *res cogitans* and *res extensa*, the enduring consequences of which dominate not only academic philosophy but also the life-world and specifically morality, rests upon a metaphysics of being that Nietzsche himself, as a young man, had passionately courted in his remarks on Schopenhauer:

> "In becoming, everything is hollow, deceptive, shallow and worthy of our contempt; the enigma which man is to resolve he can resolve only in being, in being thus and not otherwise, in the imperishable."[20]

---

18 Nietzsche: *Beyond Good and Evil* (note 2), p. 237.

19 Ibid., p. 225.

20 Nietzsche: "Schopenhauer as educator", in: *Untimely Meditations* (trans. R. J.

Nietzsche's juvenile attacks on the idea of becoming reproduce Schopenhauer's description of the world as one eternally and fatefully divided into will and representation, from which arose the theory of the veil of Maya, the doctrine of contempt towards becoming and particularly towards history in favor of a new Platonism in aesthetics, revived during the age of Weimar Classicism, and the principle of overcoming and ultimately denying the will altogether.[21]

Nietzsche broke away completely from Schopenhauer's metaphysics in 1878 with his book *Human, All Too Human*, in which he takes up the idea of ineluctable becoming and subsequently attacks any and all concepts of absolute being. "Sublimation" is the central methodological concept of what Nietzsche announces here as the project of a "historical philosophy"[22] as well as of a "history of the genesis of thought".[23] In the collection's opening aphorism on the "chemistry of concepts and things", Nietzsche employs for the first time the concept, taken from the natural sciences and now applied to the history of thought and culture, of sublimation. His language is distilled from chemistry and makes perfectly clear why terms like "refinement" belong to the

Hollingdale, Cambridge, UK: Cambridge University Press, 1997), p. 155.

21 In his enlightening essay on the consequences of Schopenhauer, Arnold Gehlen suggests that, with his removal of a metaphysical and spiritual framework, Schopenhauer anticipated a number of the fundamental insights of modern anthropology. The idea of an individual soul, Gehlen claims, could only impose itself on the individual in contemplation, when the intellect has been "shut down". By emphatically underscoring the secondary status of the intellect in relation to the will, and by defining the intellect as the medium of the will's motives, Schopenhauer effectively abandons the traditional distinction between body and soul. The intellect appears as the "organ of orientation", while psychology becomes "the doctrine of affect and motivation. It must be considered in its immediate connection to man's necessities and actions. Psychology thus becomes the 'biology of man from within'." Arnold Gehlen: "Die Resultate Schopenhauers" (1938), in: *Gesamtausgabe*, Bd. 4 (Frankfurt am Main: Vittorio Klostermann Verlag, 1989), pp. 25–49, here: p. 36f. (translation JCW). This ingenious updating of Schopenhauer highlights the point in his philosophy where Nietzsche was able to establish a foothold in developing his concept of the soul, which for him is something connected to the body. At the same time, as Gehlen himself admits, this revision must pay the price of discarding the entire mystical dimension of Schopenhauer's thinking. If in Schopenhauer the intellect of the empirical subject also becomes the instrumental organ of the will, his dualism yet remains intact; the radically inconceivable transcendental subject survives triumphantly as the sublime consciousness of the *tat-tvam-asi* which discloses itself in contemplation, indeed a shutting down of the intellect.

22 Nietzsche: *Human, All Too Human: A Book for Free Spirits* (trans. R. J. Hollingdale, Cambridge, UK: Cambridge University Press, 1996), p. 12.

23 Ibid., p. 20.

semantic field of "sublimation." Reason that argues from ahistorical concepts and thus assumes the existence of eternal entities commits an error if reason and unreason, disinterested pleasure and yearning desire, are defined as strict opposites. According to Nietzsche's new historical philosophy:

> "there exists, strictly speaking, neither an unegoistic action nor completely disinterested contemplation; both are only sublimations, in which the basic element seems almost to have dispersed and reveals itself only under the most painstaking observation."[24]

From this point on, Nietzsche's theory of the chemistry of concepts and sensations becomes a central theme of his writings, later informing the thinking of Michel Foucault: "The genealogist needs history to dispel the chimeras of the origin."[25] Emblematic of this is Nietzsche's proposition at the beginning of *Daybreak* of the "origin in unreason" [*Abkunft aus der Unvernunft*], rendered nearly invisible as a result of sublimation, of that which out of habit is held to be reasonable.[26] *Beyond Good and Evil* once again bestows upon psychology the title of "queen of the sciences" for its role in helping to articulate a "doctrine of the derivation of all good impulses from wicked ones".[27] And *Twilight of the Idols* castigates the idiosyncrasy of a philosophy that in its blindness to history decrees that "the highest should *not* grow out of the lowest, it should *not* grow at all."[28] Again alluding to the chemical definition of sublimation as the evaporation of a solid, Nietzsche articulates the claim that a philosophy which ignores the historicity of its concepts and terms places the *end result* of its development, "the emptiest, most universal ideas, the last wisps of smoke from the evaporating end of reality [...] at the beginning, *as* the beginning":[29] "as cause in itself, as *ens realissimum*".[30] Nietzsche's theory of sublimation paves the way for a thoroughly historical philosophy that, with recourse to the above-cited and similar passages, demonstrates the "fallacy" that "what persists is truer than what perishes."[31] In the introduction to his metacritique

24 Ibid., p. 12.

25 Michel Foucault: "Nietzsche, Genealogy, History", in: *Language, Counter-Memory, Practice: Selected Essays and Interviews* (Ithaca, NY: Cornell University Press, 1977), pp. 139–64, here: p. 144.

26 Nietzsche: *Daybreak* (note 11), p. 9.

27 Nietzsche: *Beyond Good and Evil* (note 2), p. 222 and p. 221.

28 Nietzsche: *Twilight of the Idols*, in: *The Anti-Christ, Ecce Homo, Twilight of the Idols, and Other Writings* (trans. Judith Norman, Cambridge, UK: Cambridge University Press, 2005), p. 168.

29 Ibid.

30 Ibid., p. 169.

31 Theodor W. Adorno: *Against Epistemology. A Metacritique* (trans. Willis Domingo,

of epistemology, Theodor W. Adorno cites Nietzsche, in the context of a historicization of philosophical concepts, as a direct forerunner of Critical Theory following the demise of the philosophy of history. Half a century after Nietzsche's death, the doctrine of becoming is transformed into a philosophy of the past, of that which perishes:

> "Heraclitus, whom Hegel and Nietzsche both praised, had already compared essence and the past. Ever since the first authentic formulation of the theory of Ideas, the past has always been ascribed to appearance, the kingdom of *doxa* and illusion. Infinity was reserved for essence. Only Nietzsche protested."[32]

The conceit of the Apollonian as a sublimation of the Dionysian; the notion of the contest, from the ancient Olympic games to the Greek tragedies, as an omnipresent ritualization, channeling and sublimation of the *bellum omnium contra omnes*; and numerous further remarks on the social sublimation of other drives and affects such as envy, egoism, altruism, hate, cruelty and ultimately the "will to power"—all of this rich Nietzschean material in fact appears to be a stunningly accurate anticipation of the Freudian theory of *civilization*. One of the most famous aphorisms from *Beyond Good and Evil*, moreover, reads like an abbreviation of that aspect of Freud's theory of sublimation which outlines the instinctual life of the *individual*, according to which, for example, anality is sublimated in the form of frugality, or curiosity and the will to power are sublimated as a compulsion to perform scientific research:

> "The degree and kind of a man's sexuality reach up into the ultimate pinnacle of his spirit."[33]

Sublimation as Liberation

At the same time, to assume that Nietzsche is a direct predecessor of Critical Theory is to introduce the problem that this book as a whole is devoted to addressing. Kaufmann's remark suggests that the meaning of sublimation in Freud is clear, which is not the case. As will be discussed in the next chapter, classical psychoanalysis never actually explained the relationship between the renunciation or suppression of the drives on the one hand and sublimation on the other; one might come to the conclusion that Nietzsche's own definitions have flourished thanks to their comparative clarity. Kaufmann himself claims that a closer understanding of Nietzsche is possible only if one takes

Cambridge, MA: M.I.T. Press, 1983), p. 17.

32 Ibid., p. 18.

33 Nietzsche: *Beyond Good and Evil* (note 2), p. 271.

into account "this contrast of sublimation and emasculation"[34] or likewise makes the important distinction between sublimation and mortification of the drives,[35] a distinction not consistently recognized in Freud's writings. Gasser notes critically that Freudian psychoanalysis, with its focus on "purely quantitative moments", is incapable of clearly defining "the difference between a life-affirming refinement and a pathological starving of the drives."[36] It is precisely this difference that concerns Nietzsche. A look at his comparison between (Greek) antiquity and Christianity illustrates why the distinction between sublimation and the mortification of the drives is so crucial to understanding his thought. Sublimation in Nietzsche is not a form of mortification, nor a somber renunciation that continually generates discontent with culture and civilization, nor a negation of the will to life in terms of Schopenhauerian metaphysics. On the contrary, Nietzsche recognizes in Schopenhauer the legacy of Christianity—to his mind, the opposite of sublimation. To return to a quotation from *Twilight of the Idols* cited in the previous chapter of this book:

> "[Schopenhauer] interpreted *art*, heroism, genius, beauty, great sympathy, knowledge, the will to truth and tragedy one after the other as consequences of 'negation' or some need to negate on the part of the 'will'—the greatest psychological counterfeit in history, Christianity excluded. On closer inspection, this just means that he is heir to the Christian interpretation."[37]

Sublimation in Nietzsche is not a negation of the will but an augmentation of power, or "great self-control".[38] A person who sublimates becomes more powerful, lives better and more intensely, and the most powerful person is the one who best understands how to sublimate. The doctrine of the corporeality of reason and the doctrine of the will to power come together under the banner of sublimation to form a structural unity that effectively articulates a strict counterargument against Schopenhauer:

> "The man who can develop his faculty of reason only by extirpating his sensuality has a weak spirit; a strong spirit need not

34 Kaufmann: *Nietzsche* (note 1), p. 224.
35 Cf. ibid., p. 227.
36 Gasser: *Nietzsche und Freud* (note 9), p. 61. Translation JCW.
37 Nietzsche: *Twilight of the Idols* (note 28), p. 202.
38 Ibid., p. 199.

> make war on the impulses: it masters them fully and is—to Nietzsche's mind—the acme of human power."[39]

The monism of the will to power is the heir to Nietzsche's prior opposition between the Apollonian and the Dionysian, which had yet stood under Schopenhauer's spell. A person with a strong will to power is capable of sublimating his drives, not in the sense of their mortification but in terms of their being put into service and even augmented. In the end, there appears on the horizon of Nietzsche's philosophy a concept of sublimation that is the opposite of renunciation, i.e. the antithesis of co- or subordination. Inasmuch as Nietzsche understands the will to power as nothing other than the *"instinct for freedom"*,[40] sublimation in no way implies a relinquishing of freedom but rather its pinnacle, its consummation. A person who knows how to sublimate becomes powerful and, ultimately, free; sublimation is the ideal path to liberation. Nietzsche thus anticipates the critiques of Herbert Marcuse, Theodor W. Adorno and Norman O. Brown regarding the concept of a "repressive sublimation".[41]

In her unfinished memoir *Looking Back*, Lou Andreas-Salomé discusses sublimation in the context of "The Freud Experience". Andreas-Salomé, friend of Nietzsche, paramour of Rilke and student of Freud, makes the connections between Nietzsche and Freud clearly visible. She achieves this with great subtlety and sophistication in her remarks on sublimation, as she professes to outline Freud's understanding of the term while effectively elaborating Nietzsche's, the cogency of which she had become convinced of during an intense encounter with Rainer Maria Rilke. Sublimation, she explains, is the point at which we experience simultaneously both "that which is most intimate *and* that which transcends us most completely." The following quotation combines the poetic, philosophical and psychological dimensions of sublimation and testifies to this concept's importance to any interdisciplinary study of culture:

> "One cannot stress enough that the power of sublimation is directly dependent upon how deeply and securely it is embedded in this primal ground of the mechanism of our soul, and upon the degree to which this vital source affects what we do or don't do in our conscious lives. The more strongly inclined one is toward eroticism, the greater are the possibilities for its sublimation, the longer one is able to withstand the demands involved, without generating a

39 Kaufmann: *Nietzsche* (note 1), p. 233.

40 Nietzsche: *On the Genealogy of Morality* (note 3), p. 64.

41 Cf. Herbert Marcuse: *Eros and Civilization* (New York: Vintage, 1962), pp. 187ff.

> conflict between the satisfaction of instinctual desires and accommodation to reality. *Such a person is in no sense an ascetic* whose desires are *weak*, and who tries to make a virtue out of necessity, nor someone atrophied by illness who finds comfort in the word 'sublimation'. It's not a matter of self-denying ascetics, but on the contrary those who even in the most adverse circumstances still realize their secret connection with those things which lie furthest from them, wielders of divining rods who sense the origin of springs beneath the driest earth—those who fulfill, not those who abstain—and thus are *capable* of abstaining for even longer periods of time because they know how close they remain to their inner home, their inner fulfillment. The crucial point is that they have not split themselves conceptually into body and soul, but instead gather themselves as human beings into a *single* vital strength—just as the jet of water in a fountain falls back into the same basin from which it rose."[42]

Of course, uncovering the connection between sublimation and freedom means dealing with the potentially greater problem of now having to define the concept of freedom, which for its part suggests at least two basic meanings, even beyond the inscrutable problem of "free will:"[43] liberation *from something* and freedom *for something*. A reading

---

42 Lou Andreas-Salomé: *Looking Back: Memoirs* (trans. Breon Mitchell, New York: Paragon House, 1991), p. 98.

43 Cf. for example Peter Bieri: *Das Handwerk der Freiheit. Über die Entdeckung des eigenen Willens*, 8. Aufl. (Frankfurt am Main: S. Fischer Verlag, 2007). (Below translations JCW.) Nietzsche's theory, articulated in his essay on Schopenhauer, of the freedom to be oneself (see below) survives in Bieri's "idea of the appropriated will". The disturbingly circular definition of free will formulated by Harry G. Fankfurt—"the statement that a person enjoys freedom of the will means that he is free to want what he wants to want" (cited in: ibid., p. 445)—can, according to Bieri, be overcome up to a certain point, but only if one understands "that freedom of the will is in part defined by the fact that the will is one which suits one's own self-image" (ibid.). Identification with one's will is possible—and here Bieri refers to Freud in a positive light—only "if we expand our understanding of our own inner world with respect both to its inner logic and its genesis" (ibid.). Only an individual who, to use Nietzsche's term, investigates the "unicum" that he or she is (see below) is capable of ascertaining what he or she actually wants. Bieri's appeal to psychoanalysis, according to Freud a decidedly deterministic discipline, is dubious. This critique of selfhood will be discussed below in the chapter on Jacques Lacan, for whom sublimation would mean overcoming the narcissistic will to selfhood. It is conceivable that selfhood may be grasped only within the network of the social, in its being determined by the other, and beyond that being without substance. The self-image to which Bieri refers is perhaps an actual image, that of the other: "The *you* is older than the *I*", as Zarathustra teaches. Friedrich Nietzsche: *Thus Spoke Zarathustra: A Book for None and All* (trans. Walter Kaufmann, New York: Penguin, 1966), p. 60.

of the first book of *Daybreak*, which is concerned with exactly this issue, should, as the study of an ambitious, coherent and internally consistent work of theory, provide a more precise explanation of Nietzsche's answers to the questions that continue to haunt Zarathustra:

> "You call yourself free? Your dominant thought I want to hear, and not that you have escaped from a yoke. Are you one of those who had a *right* to escape from a yoke? There are some who threw away their last value when they threw away their servitude. Free *from* what? As if that mattered to Zarathustra! But your eyes should tell me brightly: free *for* what?"[44]

Regarding the concept of freedom in its two meanings, it should first be noted that Nietzsche's argumentation with respect to the idea of "liberation from something" is less ambiguous than Freud's. In *Civilization and Its Discontents*, Freud claims that human freedom was greatest before the development of any civilization or culture, as the restraints imposed by the reality principle were at that time minimal. By contrast, Nietzsche makes it abundantly clear that the *domination* of the pleasure principle and its numerous derivatives ought not to be equated with freedom, but rather amounts to a peculiar form of servitude: the subjugation of man by his own tyrannical drives. The relevant dictum here is found in *Twilight of the Idols*, a summation of Nietzsche's own work that he was able to pull together just months before his mental breakdown: pursuit of the pleasure principle is no noble enterprise. In addition to developing the concept of the *noble*, Nietzsche also establishes a connection between the sublime and sublimation. Great self-control, the pathos of distance is developed by training one's "sense of distance," by learning not to smell or to touch, but to see:

> "This is the *first* preliminary schooling for spirituality: *not* to react immediately to a stimulus, but instead to take control of the inhibiting, excluding instincts. Learning to *see*, as I understand it, is close to what an unphilosophical way of speaking calls a strong will: the essential thing here is precisely *not* 'to will', to be *able* to suspend the decision. Every characteristic absence of spirituality, every piece of common vulgarity, is due to an inability to resist a stimulus—you *have* to react, you follow every impulse."[45]

Nietzsche pointedly calls into question the notion of equating the pleasure principle with freedom and bolsters his argument by

---

44 Nietzsche: *Thus Spoke Zarathustra* (note 43), p. 63.
45 Nietzsche: *Twilight of the Idols* (note 28), p. 190.

suggesting that there exists not only a pre-cultural, but also a "post-cultural," "decadent" form of disinhibition which indicates not a potentially joyful return to unadulterated nature, but rather, in modern terms, a neurosis, phobia or compulsion:

> "In many cases this sort of compulsion is already a pathology, a decline, a symptom of exhaustion—almost everything that is crudely and unphilosophically designated a 'vice' is really just this physiological inability *not* to react."[46]

Sublimation in Nietzsche means liberation both from the necessities of life (*Lebensnot*)[47] that are inflicted by an overpowering natural world as well as from the instinctual nature that urges from within. In this context, it is perhaps relevant to point out that Nietzsche also outlines the idea of a "discontentment with civilization," though the reasons he offers for this greatly deviate from Freud's. In Freud, discontent results from the curtailment of pleasure. To the extent that every civilization restricts pleasure, it inevitably and continually generates discontent. Freud's argument is convincing only if one first identifies the pursuit of the pleasure principle with happiness and second, assumes that happiness is something desirable and third, has in hand a legitimate understanding of happiness. Nietzsche, by contrast, having expertly deconstructed the entire concept of happiness, asks why morality in particular is supposed to be the only path to a "happiness" that is otherwise unachievable. The following passage can only be misunderstood as an invitation to amorality if one ignores Nietzsche's prior deconstruction of a concept of intersubjective happiness whose very existence implies that morality is the only path by which such "happiness" can be attained:

> "Has morality not, broadly speaking, opened up such an abundance of sources of displeasure that one could say, rather, that with every refinement of morals mankind has hitherto become *more discontented* with himself, his neighbor and the lot of his existence? Did the hitherto most moral man not entertain the belief that the only justified condition of mankind in the face of morality was the *profoundest misery*?"[48]

---

46 Ibid., p. 190f.

47 This, too, is a concept first introduced not by Freud, but by Nietzsche. Cf. for example Nietzsche: "Schopenhauer as educator", in: *Untimely Meditations* (note 20), p. 182.

48 Nietzsche: *Daybreak* (note 11), p. 62.

Nietzsche asks whether historically successful moral systems may have rested upon a concept of happiness that in fact engendered unhappiness (noting in particular that the idea of the inevitability of unhappiness logically implies an idea of happiness), and further inquires whether "happiness", as an untested formula, actually provides a genuine individual or collective compass. In proposing that sublimation, liberation from the tyranny of the drives, augments and enriches life, Nietzsche leaves "happiness" behind and outlines a concept of freedom beyond the pleasure principle that does not automatically give succor to the death drive. Only one who simply equates happiness with the pleasure principle must necessarily look into the darkness.

With respect to the question of "freedom for something," we can refer preliminarily to Nietzsche's remarks in his essay from *Untimely Meditations* titled "Schopenhauer as Educator", one of the founding texts of modern existential philosophy. Here sublimation means liberation from the "generation of public opinion,"[49] with the goal of enabling the possibility of selfhood. According to this early essay, the subject is a "unicum", a "strangely variegated [...] assortment" that chance has gathered together into a unity.[50] Liberation from the world of convention allows the *unicum* to fathom its own specificity. In the terms of the text's existentialist concept of freedom, the liberated subject comes to understand that its contingent facticity and radical openness are intertwined and, moreover, that it must accept responsibility for this existence that hangs in the empty space of contingency. "Schopenhauer as Educator" stands as an impassioned chapter in the history of "the true liberation of life"[51] hanging over the abyss:

> "But even if the future gave us no cause for hope—the fact of our existing at all in this here-and-now must be the strongest incentive to us to live according to our own laws and standards: the inexplicable fact that we live precisely today, when we had all infinite time in which to come into existence, that we possess only a short-lived today in which to demonstrate why and to what end we came into existence now and at no other time. We are responsible to ourselves for our own existence; consequently we want to be the true helmsman of this existence and refuse to allow our existence to resemble a mindless act of chance."[52]

---

49 Nietzsche: "Schopenhauer as educator," in: *Untimely Meditations* (note 20), p. 128.

50 Ibid., p. 127.

51 Ibid., p. 128.

52 Ibid.

Nietzsche seems to define his concept of sublimation less ambiguously than Freud defines his, including in regard to the value sublimation is assigned. In light of this fact, I will leave further comparison with Freud aside in favor of reconstructing the theoretical foundation of Nietzsche's concept of sublimation, in order to set up my reading of Freud in the next chapter. Nietzsche, I argue, conceives of a sublimation beyond discontent.

I will avoid direct comparison between the concepts of sublimation found in Nietzsche and Freud for another reason which has already been hinted at. Nietzsche and Freud begin their arguments from opposite poles. For Nietzsche, sublimation is an idea that belongs first to philosophy and only secondarily to Cultural Theory. As Kaufmann recognizes, to understand Nietzsche's concept of sublimation inevitably requires a consideration of its "cosmology",[53] the central insight of which Zarathustra had announced in his speech *On Self-Overcoming*. The always and everywhere perceptible motor of self-mastery—that process of overcoming life's necessities and one's own instinctual nature, and of maintaining a sublime distance in the name of selfhood—is the will to power:

> "Where I found the living, there I found will to power; and even in the will of those who serve I found the will to be master."[54]

In order to make Nietzsche's sweeping philosophical aspirations clear, Kaufmann, in a bold move, ultimately ties Nietzsche's concept of sublimation to the prominent Hegelian notion of "sublation" (*Aufhebung*),[55] a connection that in fact suggests itself: the German definition of the Latin verb *sublimare* is *"hoch erheben"*, "to raise up". Nietzsche's doctrine of sublime self-mastery is *his* tragic variation of a science of the experience of consciousness: "[E]xperience always seems to mean bad experience."[56]

Doctor Freud introduces his concept of sublimation in his *Three Essays on Sexual Theory* from 1905; unlike Nietzsche, his starting point is the physiological nature of the demands the drives place on the individual, and the possibility of their management. Freud's writings document the path from a "scientific" analysis of the individual and his instinctual life "upward" towards a theory of civilization. Sublimation becomes a conceptual linchpin that mediates between individual psychology and Cultural Theory. As will be detailed in the

53 Cf. Kaufmann: *Nietzsche* (note 1), p. 235.

54 Nietzsche: *Thus Spoke Zarathustra* (note 43), p. 114.

55 Cf. Kaufmann: *Nietzsche* (note 1), p. 274ff.

56 Nietzsche: *Beyond Good and Evil* (note 2), p. 311.

next chapter, however, it is precisely at this point of transition from a theory of the individual to a genealogy and theory of community that Freud's concept of sublimation tends unambiguously in the direction of renunciation and compulsion, including in his book on *Moses and Monotheism*: "But ethics is a limitation of instinct" [*Ethik ist aber Triebeinschränkung*].[57]

Nietzsche's philosophy, on the other hand, in thinking through the dualism of body and soul, leads downward, in the direction of psychology and physiology, and here too sublimation proves to be the connection between psychology and cosmology in the name of the will to power. The question of whether or not sublimation ultimately means "the same thing" to both men will be left open here, tempting though it may be to suggest that the doctor and the philosopher, having begun

---

57 Sigmund Freud: *Moses and Monotheism*, in: *The Standard Edition* (London: Hogarth, 1956–74), Vol. 23, p. 118. Freud's survey of the life of Moses, the testamentary character of which has often been noted, ultimately introduces a new perspective on sublimation theory and stands as a reminder that Freud's interests in cultural history biographically precede his education in neurology. *Moses* boldly casts the history of monotheism as a cultural history of spiritualization. The Egyptian Moses, a descendant of the court of Ikhnaton, imposes monotheism on the exiled Jews, the tragic result of which is his murder, for "[t]he Jewish people under Moses were just as little able to tolerate such a highly spiritualized religion [...] as had been the Egyptians of the Eighteenth Dynasty." (p. 47). As Freud explains in a continuation of the hypotheses developed in *Totem and Taboo*, the murder of the primeval father leads, after a period of latency, to "the return of a single father-god of unlimited dominion" (p. 84). Abstract monotheism, Freud writes, formed the character of the Jewish people "through its rejection of magic and mysticism, its invitation to advances in intellectuality and its encouragement of sublimations" (p. 86). Despite this digression, our primary concern here and below is the reconstruction of a Freudian theory of sublimation from the perspective of individual psychology, as even in this speculative study of Moses, the mechanisms that will be described in the next chapter remain in effect. Even as Freud distinguishes the Jewish people both culturally and historically as the people of sublimation, the question remains open as to the precise structural location of sublimation between the poles of successful spiritualization and "renunciation of instinct" [*Triebverzicht*], which here, too, makes possible "the first form of a social organization" (p. 82). Ethics in *Moses and Monostheism* remains a restriction of the drives whose notorious consequence is discontent. In this context, the groundbreaking insight that Freud's historico-cultural speculation introduces into the drama of sublimation is his theory of anti-Semitism. According to Freud, the delusion of anti-Semitism lies in its ability to assert that a single party, namely the people of sublimation, is guilty of producing the general discontent that is inevitable in any civilization (cf. footnotes 68, 78 and 100 below). Regarding *Moses and Monotheism*, cf. Achim Geisenhanslüke's clear depiction of the complex hermeneutic challenge in: *Das Schibboleth der Psychoanalyse. Freuds Passagen der Schrift* (Bielefeld: Transcript, 2008), pp. 139–50.

their excavations from opposite poles, in the end arrived at the same core that would provide the material, sought after since Descartes, to resolve finally the mystery of the *commercium mentis et corporis;* to quote Foucault's essay on Nietzsche: "Historical sense has more in common with medicine than philosophy."[58] What is beyond doubt is the fact that the philosopher and the doctor do in fact move towards each other. This is documented in the famous note at the end of the first essay in *On the Genealogy of Morality,* in which a lonely Nietzsche wishes for and anticipates an interdisciplinary collaboration to promote the study of the history of morality, thus gazing far into the future, well beyond his own time, to the research of Foucault and his disciples. In the note, which also hopes for the cooperation of philologists and linguists, Nietzsche writes:

> "[I]t is just as essential to win the support of physiologists and doctors for these problems (on the *value* of all previous valuations): we can leave it to the professional philosophers to act as advocates and mediators in this, once they have completely succeeded in transforming the originally so reserved and suspicious relationship between philosophy, physiology and medicine into the most cordial and fruitful exchange."[59]

"False Sublimation" (Weakening)

An overview of the semantics of sublimation would be incomplete without once again mentioning the special case that from Nietzsche's perspective can be called "false sublimation", and which he criticizes with increasing aggressiveness both in *Beyond Good and Evil* and especially in *On the Genealogy of Morality*. Nietzsche's critique is in fact directed against Paul's condemnation of the flesh in the Letter to the Romans. Whereas the Decalogue of the Old Covenant does not summarily condemn the flesh, but rather codifies the specific conditions under which an acted-out desire *becomes sinful,* the political theologian Paul does away with all these conditions and radically reformulates Exodus 20:17 as "Thou shalt not covet",[60] with major consequences for the history of civilization. If, in the Old Testament, it was against the law to covet your neighbor's wife or anything that

58 Foucault: "Nietzsche, Genealogy, History" (note 25), p. 156.

59 Nietzsche: On the Genealogy of Morality (note 3), p. 37. Regarding the exceedingly stimulating effect Nietzsche had on Foucault, cf. again Foucault's great essay on "Nietzsche, Genealogy, History" (note 25): "If genealogy in its own right gives rise to questions concerning our native land, native language, or the laws that govern us, its intention is to reveal the heterogeneous systems which, masked by the self, inhibit the formation of any form of identity." (p. 162).

60 King James Bible, Romans 7:7.

belonged to him, after Paul nothing good resides in the flesh at all: to desire is to sin. Spirit and flesh are torn apart, sublimation replaced with the mortification of the drives:

> "For to be carnally minded is death; but to be spiritually minded is life and peace. Because the carnal mind is enmity against God: for it is not subject to the law of God, neither indeed can be. So then they that are in the flesh cannot please God."[61]

Because man is created in the flesh, however, he is, according to Paul, inevitably sinful. In one of the more groundbreaking and enduring insights of his critique of Christianity, Nietzsche recognizes in Paul's terrorization and condemnation of the flesh the socio-politically momentous imposition of ecclesiastical authority, from which we neurotic moderns have "inherited millennia of conscience-vivisection and animal torture inflicted on ourselves".[62] If the flesh is *a priori* guilty, then man no longer knows innocence; there is nothing for him beyond sin. To live as a Christian means to exist in a state of consummate wickedness:

> "Guilt towards *God*: this thought becomes an instrument of torture. In 'God' he seizes upon the ultimate antithesis he can find to his real and irredeemable animal instincts, he re-interprets these self-same animal instincts as guilt before God [...], he emits every 'no' which he says to himself, nature, naturalness and the reality of his being as a 'yes', as existing, living, real, as God [...], as torture without end, as hell, as immeasurable punishment and guilt. We have here a sort of madness of the will showing itself in mental cruelty which is absolutely unparalleled: [...] his *will* to infect and poison the fundamentals of things with the problem of punishment and guilt [...]. Alas for this crazy, pathetic beast man!"[63]

In the context of this critique of Christianity, precise distinctions must be drawn among three different meanings of sublimation. In order to be able to recognize the subtle poisoning of man by *ressentiment* (false sublimation, 1), including in its spiritualized manifestations, one must apply the method of elucidating psychologically the paths of sublimation (2), in order finally to pave the way for a correct sublimation (3) that is oriented toward the paradigm of ancient Greece:

---

61 Romans 8:6–8.

62 Nietzsche: *On the Genealogy of Morality* (note 3), p. 70.

63 Ibid., p. 68f.

> "It is crucial for the fate of individuals as well as peoples that culture begin in the *right* place – *not* in the 'soul' (which was the disastrous superstition of priests and half-priests): the right place is the body, gestures, diet, physiology, *everything else* follows from this … This is why the Greeks are the *first cultural event* in history – they knew, they *did*, what needed to be done; Christianity, which despised the body, has been the greatest disaster for humanity so far."[64]

The three essays *On the Genealogy of Morality* together mark an attempt to exorcize Christianity from society and make possible a new beginning under the auspices of Plato and *agon*. Nietzsche's proposition that the "slaves" revolt in morality' began with the revaluation of the distinction between "good" and "bad" as that between "good" and "evil" is well known.[65] The *ressentiment* of those who in the Roman Empire had been impotent became a creative force; the powerful, noble and strong was denounced as morally reprehensible and subsequently ever further "improved", or, in Nietzsche's view: "discouraged, refined, molly-coddled, emasculated (so, almost the same as *injured*)" [›entmuthigt‹, ›raffinirt‹, ›verzärtlicht‹, ›entmannt‹ (also beinahe so viel als *geschädigt*)].[66] Christianity's victory march ushered in a false understanding of sublimation, no longer defined as "great self-control" but rather denoting an ideology of continual weakening that according to Nietzsche has led to the "*decline* of mankind". The misconception lay in the belief "that it is the *meaning of all culture* to breed a tame and civilized animal, a *household pet*, out of the beast of prey 'man.'"[67] The most subtle instrument of false sublimation was the invention of the bad conscience, Nietzsche's phenomenology of which—leaving aside the question of whether or not it is historically or culturally sound—anticipates Freud's theory of the cruelty of the superego, which is

---

64 Nietzsche: *Twilight of the Idols* (note 28), p. 221.

65 Nietzsche: *On the Genealogy of Morality* (note 3), p. 20f.

66 Ibid., p. 112.

67 Ibid., p. 26. A later reflection on Nietzsche's critique of "false sublimation" may be found in Alexander Mitscherlich's attempt at a definition of aggression that is specifically directed towards particular characteristics of Christianity: "The total expulsion of every natural, sexual expression, e.g. into the realms of the worthless, the immoral, the 'base'—to this extent an exaggerated demand for sublimation and neutralization in, for example, Calvinism and Puritanism—has led not only to a life-destroying collective neuroticization with an effective moral double standard but also to a form of unbridled aggression (separated out and emancipated from its true libidinal connection)." Alexander Mitscherlich: "Wesensbestimmung der Aggression", in: Hans Thomae (Hg.): Die Motivation menschlichen Handelns, 3. Aufl. (Köln/Berlin: Kiepenheuer & Witsch, 1966), pp. 210–15, here: p. 213. Translation JCW.

internalized in the form of a bad conscience.[68] To some extent, a bad conscience is the instinct for freedom violently made latent, and which now, imprisoned in the psyche, turns against its bearer and sickens him.[69] For Michel Foucault, this insight became the methodological foundation of his version of historical philosophizing:

> "The body—and everything that touches it: diet, climate and soil—is the domain of the *Herkunft* [descent]. The body manifests the stigmata of past experience and also gives rise to desires, failings and errors. These elements may join in a body where they achieve a sudden expression, but just as often their encounter is an engagement in which they efface each other, where the body becomes the pretext of their insurmountable conflict. [...] Genealogy, as an analysis of descent, is thus situated within the articulation of the body and history. [...] [The ritual] establishes marks of its power and engraves memories on things and even within bodies. It makes itself accountable for debts."[70]

With his radical condemnation of the flesh, Paul, as Nietzsche knew, not only leaves behind the old law, which according to him actually creates sin in the first place.[71] He also turns away from another tradition that held great power in antiquity, namely Plato's doctrine of sublimation, the classic formulation of which is found in the *Symposium*. According to the Platonic model of sublimation, emphatically invoked by both Marcuse and Adorno as an alternative to the Christian model of the condemnation of the flesh, the path to understanding the idea of the good leads directly through sensual love. Plato is aware "that all beauty is a temptation to procreate,—that this is precisely the *proprium* of its effect, from the most sensual all the way up to the most spiritual."[72] Philosophy is procreation in the spirit, and it is possible only through the experience of sensual love. Thus, as Socrates learns from Diotima, "The correct way [...] for someone to approach this business is to

---

68 A discussion of the extent to which Freud's psychoanalytic reconstruction of the Pauline doctrine of original sin was conceived as an alternative to Nietzsche would be the subject of its own investigation. Freud writes: "Paul, a Roman Jew from Tarsus, seized upon this sense of guilt and traced it back correctly to its original source. He called this the 'original sin'; it was a crime against God and could only be atoned for by death. With the original sin death came into the world. In fact this crime deserving death had been the murder of the primal father who was later deified." *Moses and Monotheism* (note 57), p. 86.

69 Nietzsche: *On the Genealogy of Morality* (note 3), p. 61.

70 Foucault: "Nietzsche, Genealogy, History" (note 25), pp. 148 and 150.

71 Cf. the chapter on *das Ding* in Lacan below.

72 Nietzsche: *Twilight of the Idols* (note 28), p. 203.

begin when he's young by being drawn towards beautiful bodies."[73] A corresponding note from among Nietzsche's unpublished writings corrects a Christian understanding of Plato that in philological terms is strictly false: "Plato says that love of knowledge and philosophy are a sublimated sexual drive."[74]

In analyzing the history of European civilization, Nietzsche not only attempts to reconstruct the consequences of both Paul's condemnation of the flesh and the continued devaluation and weakening of the powerful and noble as a result of *ressentiment*; he also seeks out phenomena that testify to the validity of Plato's model of sublimation even under the conditions of Christianity. This is the source of his adoration for the troubadours of Provence as well as for classical France, whose "whole higher culture and literature [...] also grew on the ground of sexual interest. You can search through it for gallantry, sensuousness, sexual competition, 'woman,'—you will never look in vain."[75]

Christian priests preach perversion, false sublimation. Yet in the context of his critique of Christianity and ascetic ideals, Nietzsche is repeatedly confronted by a phenomenon of cultural history that must be dealt with here in order to avoid certain misunderstandings. Nietzsche had in *Daybreak* already painted a portrait of the representatives of successful Christianity, a "very *spirited* religion" that has "chiseled out perhaps the most refined figures in human society." Regarding the figures of the high Catholic priesthood, he writes:

> "Here the human face attains to that total spiritualization produced by the continual ebb and flow of the two species of happiness (the feeling of power and the feeling of surrender) after a well-considered mode of life has tamed the beast in man; [...] here there reigns that noble contempt for the fragility of the body and of fortune's favor which pertains to born soldiers; one takes *pride* in obeying, which is the distinguishing mark of all aristocrats; in the tremendous impossibility of one's task lies one's excuse and one's ideal."[76]

Like Nietzsche's numerous other depictions of the figure of the ascetic priest, such as the Brahman, this portrait is clearly born of a deep

73 Plato: *The Symposium* (trans. Christopher Gill, London: Penguin, 1999), p. 47f. (210a).

74 Nietzsche: "Nachlass Frühjahr – Herbst 1881", in: Kritische Studienausgabe, Bd. 9 (Hg. Giorgio Colli u. Mazzino Montinari, München: Deutscher Taschenbuch Verlag, 1988), p. 486. Translation JCW.

75 Nietzsche: *Twilight of the Idols* (note 28), p. 204.

76 Nietzsche: *Daybreak* (note 11), p. 36f.

fascination. As the epitome of sublimation and an exemplar of the pathos of distance, the repeatedly conjured image of the great priest, who possesses "an inborn grace of gesture, the eye of command, and beautiful hands and feet",[77] eclipses even the ideal figure of the historically distant Greek warrior-philosopher, to say nothing of Renaissance *Übermenschen* such as Cesare Borgia, or the notorious "blond beast". Nietzsche's poignancy in his efforts to deconstruct this priestly ideal, in which sublimation and the sublime come together seductively under the banner of grace, was perhaps also motivated by his struggle against his own deep-seated fascination with asceticism and prophethood.[78]

Power

"Where I found the living, there I found will to power" – how are we to understand this key utterance of Zarathustra's, which became the mantra of Nietzsche's later writings, the core statement of his philosophy, his most notable catchphrase? And to what extent does it articulate the basis for Nietzsche's theory of sublimation in its subtle yet expansive development? At first glance, the statement reads like a qualifier appended to the definition of "life:" a living thing wants to go on living, to continue to live for as long as possible, eternally. This will of living things to keep living is described in Freud as a drive, the drive for self-preservation or the human ego drive (*Ichtrieb*). Freud calls attention to the fact that he inherits the term "drive" from the nineteenth-century concept of the will as conceived by Schopenhauer. The will to power is the will to live, the drive for self-preservation; it is manifested in the "instinct for freedom", since what most concerns man is his ability to realize his true self.

---

77 Ibid., p. 36.

78 Here again, Freud's remarks on monotheism can be read as an implicit, critical reaction to Nietzsche. Freud claims that monotheism formed the character of the Jewish people "through its rejection of magic and mysticism, its invitation to advances in intellectuality and its encouragement of sublimations." Against this backdrop, he deems Christianity to be regressive, with debilitating consequences over two millennia: "In some respects the new religion meant a cultural regression as compared with the older, Jewish one, as regularly happens when a new mass of people, of a lower level, break their way in or are given admission. The Christian religion did not maintain the high level in things of the mind to which Judaism had soared. It was no longer strictly monotheist, it took over numerous symbolic rituals from surrounding peoples, it re-established the great mother-goddess and found room to introduce many of the divine figures of polytheism only lightly veiled, though in subordinate positions. Above all, it did not, like the Aten religion and the Mosaic one which followed it, exclude the entry of superstitious, magical and mystical elements, which were to prove a severe inhibition upon the intellectual development of the next two thousand years." *Moses and Monotheism* (note 57), pp. 86 and 88.

Yet this explanation is insufficient; the suggestive everyday definition of power—dominance over others—remains inscribed in Nietzsche's statement and must be addressed. It is perhaps not immediately apparent why the will to power, in the sense of dominance over others, is necessary for survival. According to the modern—i.e. non-religious—theory of the state that Hobbes develops in the *Leviathan*, in the case of human beings, the opposite claim can be made: in order to survive, to be able to live longer and better, human individuals must relinquish their power to the state through a founding act; the state thus acquires absolute power. Man would therefore constitute an exception, a living thing that ensures its self-preservation through the *renunciation* of power. In a further, sophistic step, one might claim that this relinquishing of power to a sovereign creates a dialectic: the collective transfer of power to a sovereign thus constituted makes survival possible, but it also opens the door to the possibility of power struggles *within* the newly established political system. Whoever seizes social power potentially rises to the position of sovereign, thus becoming more powerful than he or she ever could have become before the polity was founded. Nietzsche's theory of the omnipresence of the will to power might then be understood as an expression of disillusionment. The formation of the state does not put an end to the *bellum omnium contra omnes*, but merely defers and sublimates it in *agonal* terms. Social warfare is conducted according to rules determined by the state, that is, within a legal framework: this is what constitutes sublimation. War with tooth and claw gives way to litigation. It is in this sense that Cornelius Castoriadis pithily defines sublimation as socialization:

> "'Sublimation' is nothing other than the psychogenetic or idiogenetic aspect of socialization, or the socialization of the psyche considered as a psychical process. This process can only take place by means of essential conditions which are rigorously external to it; it is the taking up again by the psyche of forms, *eide*, which are socially instituted and of the significations which they convey, or, in other words, the appropriation of the social by the psyche through the constitution of an interface between the private world and the public or common world."[79]

The danger here lies in the possibility that a person or group of people with a radical will to power may attempt to seize power through legal means with the goal of abolishing the state, thus effectively reversing the process of sublimation. Tyranny, under which the members of a

79 Cornelius Castoriadis: *The Imaginary Institution of Society*. (trans. Kathleen Blamey, Cambridge, MA: The MIT Press, 1998), p. 311f.

polity live in constant mortal terror, amounts to a return to the natural state of general anxiety. Hobbes' *Leviathan* takes this possibility into account: once the state no longer recognizes that it is tasked with protecting the lives of its subjects, but in fact threatens them, those subjects are relieved of their contractual obligation to the state, which thus ceases to exist.[80]

This application of Nietzsche's hypothesis of the omnipresence of the will to power with regard to the theory of the emergence of the state is merely a special case, however, and one which in no way exhausts the content of Nietzsche's idea. Taken by itself, this assertion of the will to power's ubiquity might at first appear to be merely an opinion with which one may agree or disagree according to one's own individual experience and worldview. Nietzsche's statement would thus immediately lose its persuasive power the moment it could be demonstrated that a hidden will to power does *not* underlie a particular action or behavior. The proposition that all living things are driven by the will to power articulates an extreme pessimism with regard to society; the prospect of any dissolution of the force of domination itself dissolves. The implication is that power structures can be found at the basis of even those relationships—such as love for a child,[81] love between adults,[82] friendship[83] etc.—in which one hopes to experience a space beyond the realm of power. We should recall here the above-cited passage on the realm of goodness, which according to *The Gay Science* begins where our power of psychological insight no longer suffices and where the finer, sublimated forms of the exercise of power escape us. Accordingly, the assertion that the will to power is omnipresent may be understood as the installation of a source of bright, gleaming light, in which power-free relationships are at first glance manifested as such, yet by which these relationships are also haunted. Nietzsche's statement implies that nothing can exist "beyond power". Yet he does not stop at this insight. The following passage from *Beyond Good and Evil*

---

80 Cf. Thomas Hobbes: *Leviathan* (Oxford, UK: Oxford University, 1998), p. 147.

81 "What child would not have cause to weep over its parents?" Nietzsche: *Thus Spoke Zarathustra* (note 43), p. 70.

82 The following aphorism from *Daybreak* (note 11) can be considered representative of many of Nietzsche's aperçus about love: "This one is hollow and wants to be full, that one is overfull and wants to be emptied – both go in search of an individual who will serve their purpose. And this process, understood in its highest sense, is in both cases called by the same word: love – what? Is love supposed to be something unegoistic?" p. 91f.

83 Regarding Nietzsche's politics of friendship, particularly with respect to his complicated relationship with Richard Wagner, cf. the final chapter of Avital Ronell: *The Test Drive* (Champaign, IL: University of Illinois Press, 2005), pp. 279–324.

can be read as a direct attack on Hobbes' model of the commonwealth constituted through the renunciation of power. The exalted conception of "life" as the untamed will to power that Nietzsche outlines here is irreconcilable with the idea of socialization in the form of a contract:

> "Refraining mutually from injury, violence and exploitation and placing one's will on a par with that of someone else—this may become, in a certain rough sense, good manners among individuals if the appropriate conditions are present (namely, if these men are actually similar in strength and value standards and belong together in *one* body). But as soon as this principle is extended, and possibly even accepted as the *fundamental principle of society*, it immediately proves to be what it really is—a will to the *denial* of life, a principle of disintegration and decay. Here we must beware of superficiality and get to the bottom of the matter, resisting all sentimental weakness: life itself is *essentially* appropriation, injury, overpowering of what is alien and weaker; suppression, hardness, imposition of one's own forms, incorporation and at least, at its mildest, exploitation."[84]

Nietzsche shows himself to be a poor reader of Thomas Hobbes, who would have agreed with this diagnosis but also would have called attention to the problem that Nietzsche fails to see, or no longer wants to see. Anarchy, according to Hobbes, can never truly lead to stability, as the life of even the strongest, most brutal individual or the most violent group is never safe in such an environment.[85] As Herfried Münkler brilliantly illustrated,[86] Hobbes' modernity consists in the fact that he abandons the metaphysically and religiously contaminated opposition between justice and injustice that had dominated traditional political philosophy and replaces it with the strictly empirical

---

84 Nietzsche: *Beyond Good and Evil* (note 2), p. 393.

85 Cf. Hannah Arendt's major treatise *On Violence*, which conceives of these two concepts as opposites and offers a striking twist on Hobbes' argument. According to Arendt, while "power" is the continuation of the original consensus of a people through institutions and laws, "violence" implies a disposition of strength (first of the body, then of the police and of the army) that can potentially be turned against the institutions of the people. Violence, understood purely in instrumental terms, can destroy power, though "it is utterly incapable of creating it." From this, Arendt extrapolates her theory that violence turned against the power of the people can, in the long run, never be stabilized, but rather will ultimately devour itself. Hannah Arendt: *On Violence* (San Diego: Harcourt Brace & Co., 1970), here: p. 56.

86 Herfried Münkler: *Thomas Hobbes* (Frankfurt am Main: Campus Verlag, 2001), p. 56ff.

difference between the state of nature and the political state. Hobbesian nominalism, the radical new beginning it imposed upon political philosophy, anticipates Nietzsche's antimetaphysics. Strictly speaking, Hobbes already argues from beyond good and evil. And his theory extends even beyond the idea that, without language, "there had been amongst men, neither commonwealth, nor society, nor contract, nor peace, no more than amongst lions, bears, and wolves."[87] Three hundred years before Ludwig Wittgenstein's *Philosophical Investigations*, Hobbes insists on defining the meaning of a word solely through its use in language. This applies particularly to words that, like good and evil or just and unjust, have lost their metaphysical dignity. In his *Genealogy of Morality*, Nietzsche reconstructs a paradigmatic conflict from late antiquity about the meaning of "good" and "evil", the fundamental contingency of which Hobbes had already asserted in the *Leviathan*:

> "For these words of good, evil and contemptible, are ever used with relation to the person that useth them: there being nothing simply and absolutely so; nor any common rule of good and evil, to be taken from the nature of the objects themselves; but from the person of the man (where there is no commonwealth); or (in a commonwealth) from the person that representeth it; or from an arbitrator or judge, whom men disagreeing shall by consent set up, and make his sentence the rule thereof."[88]

And furthermore:

> "To this war of every man against every man, this also is consequent; that nothing can be unjust. The notions of right and wrong, justice and injustice have there no place. Where there is no common power, there is no law: where no law, no injustice. Force and fraud are in war the two cardinal virtues. Justice and injustice are none of the faculties neither of the body, nor mind."[89]

Hobbes is thus aware that certain groups determine how a moral system is specifically constituted by positing values that are, by definition, relative: *auctoritas non veritas facit legem*. He also demonstrates greater insight than Nietzsche in recognizing that human life before the state is subject to a "principle of decay", something which can be observed whenever order collapses and the state of nature returns, as during a civil war. Hobbes' model of the state anticipates twentieth-century

87 Hobbes: *Leviathan* (note 80), p. 20.
88 Ibid., p. 35.
89 Ibid., p. 85.

anthropology, including the contributions of Arnold Gehlen, according to whom the development of higher culture with stable practices is possible only as a result of the emergence and maintenance of spaces of relative security, since man is by his nature "lacking [...] organic means and instincts, [and] dependent upon himself to develop his potential".[90] Gehlen developed the hypothesis of man's dire instinctual poverty into a theory of institutional "relief" [*Entlastung*], thereby deconstructing the fetish that is Nietzsche's concept of life. For human beings, the sublimation of nature is always already underway; this is what makes it possible in the first place to conceive of the chimerical idea that *human life* existed before sublimation. The idea of a pre-cultural state of pure human life can only be comprehended in retrospect *qua* sublimation and is thus a product of culture. Nietzsche's failure to reflect upon the belatedness of his understanding of life reveals him to be a conservative thinker who cannot or does not want to understand that his ideas are modern, secondary and not primary. Gehlen notes that it simply is not possible for man to exist in nature without changing or "decontaminating" it:

> "There are no 'natural men' in a strict sense—that is, no human society without weapons, without fire, without prepared, artificial food, without shelter, and without systems of cooperation."[91]

Nietzsche's plea for his concept "life", which he claims to have conceived without any illusion, proves to be poorly thought out, despite its supposed profundity. Life prior to society is subject to constant denial, disintegration and decay. Human beings are poor in terms of instinct and lack all organic means of survival. Thus human life *must* be institutionally structured, or it will self-destruct and implode. Against the backdrop of Hobbes' model of the social contract and Gehlen's theory of institutions, itself highly problematic,[92] Nietzsche's aphorism on life reads like an ill-considered invitation to work towards the disintegration of a state that guarantees the rights of its subject. A movement whose goal is the return of a state of general fear can always rely on *this* Nietzsche. Proceeding from his definition of

---

90 Arnold Gehlen: *Man: His Nature and Place in the World* (trans. Clare McMillan and Karl Pillemer, New York: Columbia University Press, 1988), p. 27.

91 Ibid., p. 29.

92 Cf. Jürgen Habermas: *Philosophisch-politische Profile. Erweiterte Ausgabe* (Frankfurt am Main: Suhrkamp, 1987), pp. 101–26, as well as Christian Thies: *Die Krise des Individuums. Zur Kritik der Moderne bei Adorno und Gehlen* (Reinbek: Rohwohlt, 1997), and finally the dispute between Gehlen and Adorno published in: Friedemann Grenz: *Adornos Philosophie in Grundbegriffen* (Frankfurt am Main: Suhrkamp, 1974), pp. 225–54.

life as a process of exploiting and overpowering, the path of Nietzsche's thought consequently leads to the proposition that "nothing damages freedom more terribly or more thoroughly than liberal institutions" and, just as logically, to the assertion that "[a] free human being is a *warrior*."[93] Statements such as the following—which, despite attempts to reduce Nietzsche to the level of harmless metaphor in the sense of "he didn't mean it that way", pave the way for euthanasia even if they don't explicitly endorse it—thus become utterly repulsive:

> "Sick people are parasites on society. It is indecent to keep living in a certain state. There should be profound social contempt for the practice of vegetating in cowardly dependence on doctors and practitioners after the meaning of life, the *right* to life, is gone. Doctors, for their part, would be the agents of this contempt – not offering prescriptions, but instead a daily dose of *disgust* at their patients ..."[94]

In the light of recent history, that is, after the Shoah—after the world's confrontation with a German science of medicine that lacked any and all humanity—and in the shadow of the bomb, Thomas Mann rebuked the absurdity and "folly" of this and similar passages:

> "As if it were really necessary to defend life against mind! As if there were the slightest danger of too much intellectualism on earth! Elementary fairness should counsel us to cherish and protect the feeble little flame of reason, intellect and justice, not join sides with power and the instinctual life and riotously whoop it up for negatives, for every sort of criminality. In our contemporary world we have seen the folly of this. Nietzsche did a great deal of mischief by acting as if man's moral consciousness were a devil threatening life, like Mephistopheles, with a cold diabolic fist. [...] Far more pressing is the danger that life on this planet may abolish itself by means of the atom bomb."[95]

Mann's essay is revealing with respect to his generation's reception of Nietzsche. It documents a fascination with the psychologist and theorist of aesthetic experience, but also a sense of horror: in its hostility towards the state, the ideology of National Socialism was able to derive at least some of its slogans from passages in Nietzsche's

---

93 Nietzsche: *Twilight of the Idols* (note 28), p. 213.

94 Ibid., p. 209f.

95 Thomas Mann: "Nietzsche's Philosophy in the Light of Recent History" (1947), in: *Last Essays* (trans. Richard Winston, New York: Knopf, 1966), p. 162.

writings like the one cited above. Thomas Mann calls the dilemma of conservatism "folly".[96] What Nietzsche either does not see or does not want to see is that culture itself produces the phantasm of an "authentic life". Furthermore, it is highly doubtful that Nietzsche—who, through his acquaintance with his sister's husband, with Richard Wagner and with one of his publishers, had frequently come into direct contact with anti-Semitism—was unaware of the incendiary potential that lay in remarks such as the following, which put anti-Semitic paranoia into circulation:

> "It was the Jews who, rejecting the aristocratic value equation (good = noble = powerful = beautiful = happy = blessed) ventured, with awe-inspiring consistency, to bring about a reversal and held it in the teeth of their unfathomable hatred (the hatred of powerlessness)."[97]

This dead end emerges as the dire consequence of Nietzsche's notorious inability, documented even in his early essays, to conceive of the modern state as anything other than a "threat" to individualists and "geniuses",[98] a failure that finds its culmination in a famous phrase from *Zarathustra*:

> "Only where the state ends, there begins the human being who is not superfluous: there begins the song of necessity, the unique and inimitable tune."[99]

---

96 Cf. Martin Greiffenhagen: *Das Dilemma des Konservatismus in Deutschland* (München: Piper Verlag, 1984).

97 Nietzsche: *On the Genealogy of Morality* (note 3), p. 19.

98 According to Nietzsche's essay on Schopenhauer, the production of geniuses is the highest purpose of culture. It is this proposition that leads Nietzsche to an understanding of the state as an instrument that should use its power to protect interiority: "Every state in which anyone other than the statesman has to concern himself with politics is ill organized and deserves to perish by all these politicians." Nietzsche: "Schopenhauer as educator", in: *Untimely Meditations* (note 20), p. 181. Rapaport's note on the sociological deficiencies of classical psychoanalysis is also relevant to Nietzsche: "Society is not merely a prohibitor or provider; it is the necessary matrix of the development of all behavior. Indeed, the development and maintenance of the ego, of the superego, and perhaps of all structures are dependent on the social matrix; behavior is determined by it and is possible only within it." David Rapaport: *The Structure of Psychoanalytic Theory. A Systematizing Attempt* (New York: International Universities, 1960), p. 65.

99 Nietzsche: *Thus Spoke Zarathustra* (note 43), p. 51. A discussion of this concept of the state is unnecessary, as Nietzsche does not explain how the state is to be understood here. In its generality, Zarathustra's statement could well be the

Nietzsche's understanding of his own hypothesis about the ubiquity of the will to power, which becomes exceedingly murky in the wake of his various post-*Zarathustra* exaltations, may best be delineated by moving backwards chronologically through his writings. From this perspective, the repulsive passages in Nietzsche's later works give way to insights that he himself had previously gained, and which persist even alongside his regressive lapse into a hysteric vitalism.[100] In *Beyond Good and Evil*, Nietzsche defines man as the *"as yet undetermined animal"*.[101] It is *this* insight that, along with similar formulations found in Herder, represents one of the initial sparks that led to Gehlen's anthropology. The nexus that exists between constitutive "world-openness" and the will to power had already become visible by *Daybreak*.

Powerlessness

The first book of 1881's *Daybreak* articulates a proposition that may spare the principle of the will to power from the accusation that it is a mere opinion. This proposition is hinted at in the phrase "will *to* power" itself; whoever possesses such a will evidently lacks power. In fact, *Daybreak* locates the origin of the will to power in a *primary* experience of powerlessness, which explains why Nietzsche could

---

slogan of outsiders and fascists alike. More fruitful is Nietzsche's critique of Bismarck's Reich and, in connection with this, his critique of educational institutions and the role of philosophers employed by universities, such as may be found in the essay on Schopenhauer.

100 Sigmund Freud's famous commentary on anti-Semitism in *Moses and Monotheism* relates as well to Nietzsche's construction of the history of European culture. Alongside his theory of the "jealousy" directed toward the first-born children of God the Father, which, according to Freud's speculation, emerges "from the unconscious of the peoples", Freud claims that it is primarily the grudge held by "misbaptized" Christians which is articulated as anti-Semitism. Here Nietzsche's aggression would be exemplary, not something new, but something truly ancient: "[W]e must not forget that all those peoples who excel today in their hatred of Jews became Christians only in late historic times, often driven to it by bloody coercion. It might be said that they are all 'misbaptized'. They have been left, under a thin veneer of Christianity, what their ancestors were, who worshipped a barbarous polytheism. They have not got over a grudge against the new religion which was imposed on them; but they have displaced the grudge on to the source from which Christianity reached them. The fact that the Gospels tell a story which is set among Jews, and in fact deals only with Jews, has made this displacement easy for them. Their hatred of Jews is at bottom a hatred of Christians, and we need not be surprised that in the German National-Socialist revolution this intimate relation between the two monotheist religions finds such a clear expression in the hostile treatment of both of them." Freud: *Moses and Monotheism* (note 57), p. 91f.

101 Nietzsche: *Beyond Good and Evil* (note 2), p. 264.

later define "happiness" as "the liveliest feeling of power".[102] From this primary human experience of fear-inducing powerless, the idea unfolds that it is desirable to command power. However, because "the feeling of impotence and fear was in a state of almost continuous stimulation so strongly and for so long", and because it could, at any moment, reassert its dominance,

> "the *feeling of power* has evolved to such a degree of *subtlety* that in this respect man is now a match for the most delicate gold-balance. It has become his strongest propensity; the means discovered for creating this feeling almost constitute the history of culture."[103]

This precious aphorism is perhaps the most plausible explanation ever produced by Nietzsche of the doctrine of the will to power,[104] a brilliant example of his "history of the development of thinking" here applied to the concept of power. What is crucial about this argument is that it separates "power" from Nietzsche's vague conception of the drives. The will to power is not a drive, but rather an increasingly habitual *reaction* to the experience of being wholly at the mercy of an overpowering natural world, of the fragility and finitude of one's own body, of other people who are not always benevolent or sympathetic. The history of culture is to a large extent the history of the means employed to combat a sense of life-threatening powerlessness; in this respect, it is consistently and continuously shaped by the "will to power". From the perspective of this aphorism, one might be able to establish an approach to Nietzsche's philosophy that does not necessarily lead down the dead-end streets which mar his later work.

---

102 Nietzsche: *Daybreak* (note 11), p. 68.

103 Ibid., p. 19.

104 As late as 2007, Ernst Tugendhat offered the criticism "that Nietzsche never offered a precise explanation of how the word 'power' (*Macht*) should be understood. Two meanings blend together in the way he employs it. First, one has power over the will of others. Yet Nietzsche also understands the term in its more innocent meaning, according to which it stands for strength and potency generally." Tugendhat thus does not find it reasonable to conclude that "the aim of all egoism is domination over others", even if one assumes that egoism is the motivation of all action. By calling attention to Nietzsche's derivation of the will to power from an experience of powerlessness, one can respond to this objection and point out that man's addiction to domination does not follow, analytically speaking, from the will to power in this sense of a liberation from powerlessness. Ernst Tugendhat: "Nietzsche und die philosophische Anthropologie. Das Problem der immanenten Transzendenz", in: *Anthropologie statt Metaphysik* (München: Verlag C. H. Beck, 2007), pp. 13–33, here: p. 16. Translation JCW.

Daybreak does not stop with Nietzsche's insight into the primacy of powerlessness, which is easily compatible with Freud's theories on the origins of civilization as developed in his treatise on discontent. Nietzsche takes the next step, into the prehistory of subjectivity. The fundamental threat to interiority—and this is Nietzsche's real discovery—lies in the amorphous character of the pre-cultural human soul, which does not enjoy the relief of being embedded in a solid instinctual framework and which moreover is subjected to the uncontrolled, chaotic production of alogical representations. Nietzsche outlines his central proposition later in *Daybreak*, in his aphorism on *The Rule*, which could easily serve as a motto for the major works of Michel Foucault, the theorist of discourse and power whose writings can be seen as a working out of the Nietzschean project of genealogy:

> " 'I always find the rule more interesting than the exception'—he who feels like that is far advanced in the realm of knowledge and is among the initiated."[105]

Nietzsche recognizes that the discussion of individual elements within established moral systems does not touch upon the fundamental function of such systems, which consists in the establishment of a rule in general. Nietzsche takes this insight into the relativity of social and moral systems (inevitable in the wake of the proliferation of knowledge about history and the world since the Renaissance, and particularly since the discovery of the New World) to its logical conclusion. The specific *content* of a normative system is deemed irrelevant; what is crucial is that it provides human beings, unstable and amorphous, with a general *structure*: *the rule*. Yet Nietzsche neglects to link this insight with the concept of the state.

The dimension of experience that Nietzsche evokes here can still be experienced today in the form of dreams. Years later, Cornelius Castoriadis, reading Freud, recalled the archaic dimension into which Nietzsche gazes here with his critique of morality, describing it as a

---

105 Nietzsche: *Daybreak* (note 11), p. 187. In his essay on Nietzsche, cited above (note 25), Michel Foucault notes: "The isolation of different points of emergence does not conform to the successive configurations of an identical meaning; rather, they result from substitutions, displacements, disguised conquests and systematic reversals. If interpretation were the slow exposure of the meaning hidden in an origin, then only metaphysics could interpret the development of humanity. But if interpretation is the violent or surreptitious appropriation of a system of rules, which in itself has no essential meaning, in order to impose a direction, to bend it to a new will, to force its participation in a different game, and to subject it to secondary rules, then the development of humanity is a series of interpretations. The role of genealogy is to record its history." p. 151f.

sphere whose characteristics may be experienced in the chaos of dream-life: "'[Dream thoughts] branch out in every direction into the intricate network of our world of thought': they are magmas in a magma."[106] This archaic character is already lost as soon as the amorphous world of human dream-time is read, ordered and subjected to hermeneutics; the alogical, which rests on what Castoriadis calls "originary phantasmatization", the "radical imagination",[107] is already transformed "into a multiplicity of consciousnesses opposing one another".[108] According to Castoriadis, even Freud's concept of a "primal phantasm" constitutes a world of objects, a stability whose derivative character becomes clear even in the modern age, when the work of dream interpretation is confronted with the dream's navel, the incomprehensibility that precedes the "rule". The dimension of "magma" (which Nietzsche's investigations in *Daybreak* touch upon), the *apeiron*, is present even today in the profound experience of the dream, about which Freud notes, in a famous passage already cited in the previous chapter on Schopenhauer:

> "There is often a passage in even the most thoroughly interpreted dream which has to be left obscure; this is because we become aware during the work of interpretation that at that point there is a tangle of dream-thoughts which cannot be unraveled and which moreover adds nothing to our knowledge of the content of the dream. This is the dream's navel, the spot where it reaches down into the unknown. The dream-thoughts to which we are led by interpretation cannot, from the nature of things, have any definite endings; they are bound to branch out in every direction into the intricate network of our world of thought. It is at some point where this meshwork is particularly close that the dream-wish grows up, like a mushroom out of its mycelium."[109]

Freud's marvelous text on the unknown can here serve as a description of what Nietzsche considers to be pre-cultural "consciousness", which exists in harrowing powerlessness, and which further amplifies that powerlessness vis-à-vis the external necessities of life through the fact that it is internally confronted with "magma", the mycelium of dream-soaked thoughts which constantly escape in every direction and cloud one's perceptions. From this dream state, the impotent

---

106 Cornelius Castoriadis: *The Imaginary Institution of Society* (note 79), p. 280.
107 Ibid., p. 286.
108 Ibid., p. 280.
109 Sigmund Freud: *The Interpretation of Dreams*, in: *The Standard Edition* (London: Hogarth, 1956–74), Vol. 4, p. 564.

human being salvages the implementation of the rule. It is the rule, and not the exception that a previously established rule permits, that for Nietzsche constitutes a disturbing and unexplained object of fascination which illuminates why the most profound adoration of any culture is offered to the "great legislator", and why the legislator yet remains an uncanny figure treated with ambivalence.[110] Given the chaos of a "consciousness" that flickers between wakefulness and dreaming, thought and fantasy, reality and phantasm—a chaos which, according to the poetry of Goethe, is again endured in the experience of passion—any rule is better than no rule at all. The moment the rule is established, the subject casts up his eyes and constitutes world. With a view to archaic social orders, Nietzsche writes:

> "*First proposition of civilization*—Among barbarous peoples there exists a species of customs whose purpose appears to be custom in general: minute and fundamentally superfluous stipulations (as for example those among the Kamshadales forbidding the scraping of snow from the shoes with a knife, the impaling of coal on a knife, the placing of an iron in the fire—and he who contravenes them meets death!) which, however, keep continually in the consciousness the constant proximity of custom, the perpetual compulsion to practice customs: so as to strengthen the mighty proposition with which civilization begins: any custom is better than no custom."[111]

Nietzsche's critique of morality does not stop with its demonstration of the inconsistencies inherent in existing moral systems; it progresses rather from that which is constituted to that which is constituent. Nietzsche discovers what he calls the concept of a "morality of custom" [*Sittlichkeit der Sitte*], the implementation of a structure that, though it cannot end man's inner chaos, yet orders, channels, contains—in short, sublimates it. In a second step, this *original sublimation* allows for the mitigation of powerlessness, insofar as it opens one's eyes for something like world: generating the differentiation between interiority and exteriority, setting history in motion, allowing for the transformation

---

110 Inasmuch as the rule guarantees stability prior to any specific content, crime is a challenge to order itself. The criminal is reminiscent of the pre-cultural dimension, which is why the creator of a new morality, the installation of which must pass through a moment of chaos, is considered a criminal: "There is a continual moiling and toiling going on in morality – the effect of *successful crimes* (among which, for example, are included all innovations in moral thinking)." Nietzsche: *Daybreak* (note 11), p. 59.

111 Nietzsche: *Daybreak*, (note 11), p. 15.

of "psychical monads" into a social individual "for whom there exist other individuals, objects, a world, a society, institutions":[112]

> "*Concept of morality of custom*—In comparison with the mode of life of whole millennia of mankind we present-day men live in a very immoral age: the power of custom is astonishingly enfeebled and the moral sense so rarefied and lofty it may be described as having more or less evaporated. That is why the fundamental insights into the origin of morality are so difficult for us latecomers, and even when we have acquired them we find it impossible to enunciate them, because they sound so uncouth or because they seem to slander morality! This is, for example, already the case with the *chief proposition*: morality is nothing other (therefore *no more*!) than obedience to customs, of whatever kind they may be; customs, however, are the *traditional* way of behaving and evaluating."[113]

Even in his early work, Nietzsche is concerned with exposing the constitutive function of the rule. For him, Greek tragedy is "not agonal speech but a silent theater of movement"; in tragedy, the archaic dimension is evoked as a condition of culture. Hans-Christian von Herrmann emphasizes that *The Birth of Tragedy* draws its principal arguments from contemporary medical studies on widespread diseases, epidemics, dancing mania, etc.

> "Among the neurophysiological symptoms to which Nietzsche's theory of tragedy is subject, linguistically articulated communications are replaced by non-linguistic media, which are themselves the message. What actually constitutes 'the character of Dionysian music' is 'the shocking violence of sound,' the effects of which incite only 'dread and horror' in theoretical ears. It is a music whose power no longer 'borrows from the medium of language and its significances' 'but rather is pure media technique, purely a chain of command.'"[114]

Attic tragedy is thus not primarily the representation of a dramatic plot, but rather "a spatial-temporal movement with a contagious

---

112 Castoriadis: *The Imaginary Institution of Society* (note 79), p. 274.

113 Nietzsche: *Daybreak* (note 11), p. 10.

114 Hans-Christian von Herrmann: "'Induction psycho-motrice.' Zur technischen Wiederkehr der Kunst in Hysterie und Hypnose", in: *Electric Laokoon. Zeichen und Medien, von der Lochkarte zur Grammatologie* (Hg. Michael Franz et al., Berlin: Oldenbourg Akademieverlag, 2007), pp. 82–96, hier: p. 86. Translation JCW.

effect".[115] Art reveals a monstrous nature, the *apeiron*. To the extent that art accomplishes this within the framework of tragedy, however, it likewise serves—via catharsis—the project of sublimation, which achieves its stability when emotions are purged in the space of the theater.

By uncovering the original dimension of sublimation, which consists in nothing else but the introduction of a rule in general, Nietzsche possesses the key that allows him to disclose as derivative the phenomena of morality, as in his proposition that morality itself is nothing moral, but rather is the result of an act of subjection:

> "*To become moral is not in itself moral* – Subjection to morality can be slavish or vain or self-interested or resigned or gloomily enthusiastic or an act of despair, like subjection to a prince: in itself it is nothing moral."[116]

Both in *Daybreak* and in his subsequent writings, Nietzsche extensively pursues further epiphenomena of this "primal morality," such as the question of "utility". Regarding the individual dimension of sublimation, i.e. self-overcoming, Nietzsche offers a systematic derivation of his original insight:

> "Self-overcoming is demanded, *not* on account of the useful consequences it may have for the individual, but so that the hegemony of custom, tradition, shall be made evident in despite of the private desires and advantages of the individual: the individual is to sacrifice himself – that is the commandment of the morality of custom."[117]

This insight into the necessity of the "rule" that is able to give structure to pre-cultural chaos provides the manual for Nietzsche's observations about cruelty discussed at the beginning of this chapter. Nietzsche's view that every culture can be said to rest on cruelty makes sense if one recognizes the implementation of the "rule" as the original sublimation. In his *Genealogy of Morality*, Nietzsche analyzes the origins of memory; the relevant passages confirm why Freud's striking description of dream-life as the trace of the archaic in modernity is helpful here. In dream-time, amid the uncontrolled surging of alogical representations, the pre-cultural "human-animal" lacks a stable memory that would be able to order those shimmering representations into thoughts and

115 Ibid., p. 83. Translation JCW.
116 Nietzsche: *Daybreak* (note 11), p. 59.
117 Ibid., p. 11.

deduce logical plots from them.[118] Rather it is equipped with a "partly dull, partly idiotic, inattentive mind" that is incapable of consistently retaining anything. The step from human-animal to human being is taken in the shadow of violence; this is why Nietzsche—and after him Foucault—can assert that all religions, the oldest moral systems, are "at their most fundamental, systems of cruelty", systems of surveillance and punishment, which for their part do not allow for any inferences regarding a meaning that would be transcendentally guaranteed:

> "This age-old question was not resolved with gentle solutions and methods, as can be imagined; perhaps there is nothing more terrible and strange in man's pre-history than his *technique of mnemonics*. 'A thing must be burnt in so that it stays in the memory: only something which continues *to hurt* stays in the memory' – that is a proposition from the oldest (and unfortunately the longest-lived) psychology on earth."[119]

With his discovery of the "rule", the quintessence of the *Sittlichkeit der Sitte*, Nietzsche's excavations have reached bedrock—that point, to take up Wittgenstein's metaphor, on which the spade is turned. From this perspective, the great themes pertaining to Nietzsche's investigations demonstrate their connection to one other. The phrase "will to power" is given a comprehensible meaning in the context of primary powerlessness, just as Nietzsche's genealogy of morality can be traced back to the idea of the implementation of the rule in general. It becomes clear that, alongside "power" and "immoralism", a third popular slogan from *Daybreak*—namely, Nietzsche's discourse of the *Übermensch*—also possesses a clear meaning.

According to *Daybreak*, the establishment of any enduring institution is an arrow that points in the direction of the *Übermensch*. *Übermensch* here means something understandable. Man is and remains constantly at the mercy of the *apeiron*; it is always possible that he will sink back

---

118 With his phenomenology of *Befindlichkeit* ("state-of-mind"), Martin Heidegger in *Being and Time* confirms the secondary nature of an ordered view of things; the "flickering" imagery may derive from his reading of Nietzsche: "It is precisely when we see the 'world' unsteadily and fitfully [*flackernd*] in accordance with our moods, that the ready-to-hand shows itself in its specific worldhood, which is never the same from day to day. By looking at the world theoretically, we have already dimmed it down to the uniformity of what is purely present-at-hand, though admittedly this uniformity comprises a new abundance of things which can be discovered by simply characterizing them." Martin Heidegger: *Being and Time* (trans. John Macquarrie and Edward Robinson. Oxford, UK: Blackwell, 1962), p. 177.

119 Nietzsche: *On the Genealogy of Morality* (note 3), p. 41.

into a chaotic, pre-cultural state. Institutions establish as their *telos* an ideal concept of man as being no longer subject to this danger. Flickering, transitory emotions are institutionalized, and in this context a fourth concept is illuminated, namely that of "formation" [*Schaffen*] and "transformation" [*Umschaffen*]. Formation, transformation—this means the conversion of what is constantly slipping away into something enduring which, established as an institution, has a stabilizing and "elevating" effect, as Nietzsche notes, on the wheelhouse of human emotions.[120] Expressed at the limit of paradox: in *Daybreak*, the *Übermensch* is that human being who has left the "human-animal" behind:

> "All institutions which accord to a passion, *belief in its endurance* and responsibility for its endurance, contrary to the nature of passion, have raised it to a new rank: and thereafter he who is assailed by such a passion no longer believes himself debased or endangered by it, as he formerly did, but enhanced in his own eyes and those of his equals. Think of institutions and customs which have created out of the fiery abandonment of the moment perpetual fidelity, out of the enjoyment of anger perpetual vengeance, out of despair perpetual mourning, out of a single and unpremeditated word perpetual obligation. This transformation has each time introduced a very great deal of hypocrisy and lying into the world: but each time too, and at this cost, it has introduced a new *suprahuman* [*übermenschlich*] concept which elevates mankind."[121]

Nietzsche leads his consistent chain of arguments regarding the morality of custom to a brilliant conclusion, by connecting the violent implementation of the rule that becomes an intersubjectively shared "truth" to the actual animal world. "Truth", according to *Daybreak*, is in its origins that which serves life, which guarantees security. The original sublimation makes "self-control" possible in the sense of distancing oneself from and mastering one's internal chaos. This

---

120 The repercussion of the rule on feelings makes possible the following insight into the secondary character of emotions: "[F]eelings are nothing final or original; behind feelings there stand judgments and evaluations which we inherit in the form of feelings (inclinations, aversions). The inspiration born of a feeling is the grandchild of a judgment." Nietzsche: *Daybreak* (note 11), p. 25. Beyond this, Nietzsche strengthens his hypothesis on the origin of morality in the implementation of a rule through comparative studies of the relative valuations of phenomena such as envy or hope, which are "transformed by moral judgments". Ibid., p. 26.

121 Nietzsche: *Daybreak* (note 11), p. 21f.

is why it is so "true", like the life-preserving instincts of animals, of which the sense for security has remained in humans. The experience of brutal violence is offset by promises of security that soothe the animal within us:

> "[T]he sense for truth, which is really the sense for security, man has in common with the animals [...]. With it too self-control springs from the sense for what is real (from prudence). [...] The beginnings of justice, as of prudence, moderation, bravery – in short, of all we designate as the *Socratic virtues*, are *animal*: a consequence of that drive which teaches us to seek food and elude enemies. Now if we consider that even the highest human being has only become more elevated and subtle in the nature of his food and in his conception of what is inimical to him, it is not improper to describe the entire phenomenon of morality as animal."[122]

Training

Reading through Nietzsche's individual observations on sublimation and reconstructing his definition of sublimation's origins in the introduction of the rule, it becomes clear that there is an inherently consistent theory hidden behind his many maxims and aphorisms, which certainly are not exhausted here. Nietzsche's theory of sublimation is effectively a genealogy of culture that ultimately leaves open the murky, speculative question of how this culture came to exist in the first place. The "rule", thrust violently into the archaic soul of man, looms like the black monolith in Stanley Kubrick's Nietzschean film *2001: A Space Odyssey*, to which Bernhard Dotzler dedicated a compelling study. In Kubrick's film, the black monolith of extraterrestrial origin induces intelligence, "the sudden ability to use tools", in the ape-people; it is also, after its return in the era of space travel, "a *black box* in the strictest sense and to this extent represents non-knowledge, as does the odyssey that is prompted by it, an expedition into the unknown of space."[123]

Nietzsche discloses this original dimension, the moment at which the alogical dream-consciousness is subjected—with a brutal, memory-generating, monolithic violence—to an order, the *Sittlichkeit der Sitte*,

122 Ibid., p. 21.

123 Bernhard J. Dotzler: "Vom Vorteil des Nachteils, dass Medien geistlos sind. Wissen und Nichtwissen in *2001: A Space Odyssey*," in: *Ignoranz. Nichtwissen, Vergessen und Missverstehen in Prozessen kultureller Transformationen* (Hg. Achim Geisenhanslüke und Hans Rott, Bielefeld: Transcript, 2008), pp. 175–202, here: pp. 182 and 184. Translation JCW.

the rule. The order that substitutes for man's missing ensemble of drives may be based not only on violence but also on the primary experience of powerlessness, which corresponds to the elementary will to survive. The "truth value" of this order rests upon the feeling of security and stability it affords; to this extent, it is linked with the animality that yet remains in human beings. The origin of morality is not itself moral; order emerges and subjugates its subjects.[124] It is the critique of this primary, constitutive subjugation that Theodor W. Adorno undertakes in his work on the concept of sublimation. Adorno attempts to conceive of an alternative model of subjectivity that would not forever be at the mercy of the inescapable destiny described by Nietzsche's dire proposition that any rule is better than no rule at all.

In the beginning there is the rule that must be implemented through training. The history of culture is to some extent a history of cruelty and thus at the same time a history of attempts to mitigate this cruelty, to consign it to oblivion, perhaps to heal the wound that has been there since the beginning. Animism, myth, monotheism, other phantasmatic worlds beyond our own, the various forms of romanticism as the courting of an oceanic feeling, art, refinement, ennoblement, sublimation of morals and improvement of material life, but also the forced will to power (exemplified for Nietzsche by the German Empire under Bismarck)—Nietzsche investigates all of these cultural techniques with

124 Judith Butler calls attention to the fact that Nietzsche "offers us a political insight into the formation of the psyche and the problem of subjection, understood paradoxically not merely as the subordination of a subject to a norm, but as the constitution of a subject through precisely such a subordination." Thus emerges the circle in which "the subject who would oppose violence, even violence to itself, is itself the effect of a prior violence without which the subject could not have emerged." The reference to Nietzsche's insight into the amorphous structure of pre-cultural subjectivity can be viewed as a way out of Butler's clearly defined circle, inasmuch as subjectivity did not exist as a stable entity before subjection. There is subjection 1, the constitution of the subject, and subjection 2, the violence that constituted subjects commit against each other. What the subject remembers—in a dream, in love, occasionally in the experience of art—is a world without authority or rules; returning to this world, however, requires the psychotic loss of identity. The way back is a Fata Morgana, for in regressing, the entity that could relish this regression—consciousness—is extinguished. To live with and in this separation: this is the demand implicit in Nietzsche and made explicit by psychoanalysis, the path from id to ego. The remembrance of the supposedly lost paradise becomes the motor of hope for a better future; cf. the chapter on Adorno below. Judith Butler: "Circuits of Bad Conscience. Nietzsche and Freud", in: *The Psychic Life of Power: Theories in Subjection* (Stanford, CA: Stanford University Press, 1997), pp. 63–82. Citations: pp. 66 and 65.

respect to their increasingly forgotten yet still consequential origins in cruelty, which *is* the process of becoming a subject: "Nietzsche's thought [regarding immanent transcendence, E. G.] was in fact nothing other than philosophical anthropology."[125]

The Renaissance, the first age of globalization and thus the age of an irreversible relativization of culture, inaugurated the project of modern enlightenment and, along with modern skepticism (Montaigne) and atheism, generated the most historically successful *theological* attempt to consign to oblivion the memory of man's origin in a contingent rule and once again to reverse radically the nature of causal relationships in favor of the black monolith, God. Nietzsche re-establishes the atheistic perspective of anthropology in 1881 and systematically takes back the Reformation, oriented by Paul's Letter to the Romans, of Martin Luther:[126]

> "Works, first and foremost! That is to say, training, training, training! The 'faith' that goes with it will soon put in an appearance—you can be sure of that!"[127]

Daybreak

After living for ten years in the solitude of the mountains, Zarathustra rises "one morning [...] with the dawn [*mit der Morgenröte*]."[128] In light of the fact that the book of the same name represents the apex of Nietzsche's work, it is perhaps more than just fun to suppose that before beginning his descent, Zarathustra greets the sun, if not with a copy of Nietzsche in his hand, then with Nietzsche's thoughts in his head and heart. Zarathustra is free. The dawn illuminates the world, making visible the four points of the compass and thus simultaneously revealing the four directions in which Zarathustra can go. Zarathustra can walk the path of religion, the path of the worship of the black monolith. He can take the path that leads in the direction of the *apeiron* and choose to drown his soul in the flood of alogical representations; he can choose regression, psychosis; he can choose to be swallowed up.

---

125 Ernst Tugendhat: "Nietzsche und die philosophische Anthropologie" (note 104), p. 18. Translation JCW.

126 Alongside Martin Luther, it is the Catholic mathematician Blaise Pascal who famously merits Nietzsche's attention time and again. In Nietzsche's view, Pascal commits against himself the cruelty that stands at the origin of civilization, in the hope of finding in this way salvation in faith. Regarding Luther as a key figure, cf. the chapter on Jacques Lacan below.

127 Nietzsche: *Daybreak* (note 11), p. 19. Translation slightly altered, JCW.

128 Nietzsche: *Thus Spoke Zarathustra* (note 43), p. 9.

He can maintain the cold position taken up in *Daybreak*: the position of science, from which sublimation reaches its highest peak, as it has recognized and seen through itself. This will be the path of Sigmund Freud who, in his essay on Leonardo da Vinci, defines *liberation from all authority* as the highest sublimation achievable by man. The precondition for maintaining the scientific position—which is a consciousness of the *apeiron* that does not abandon itself to it, but dwells above the abyss—is "great self-control". Six different methods that make self-control possible through the mastery of the drives are outlined by Nietzsche in the 109th aphorism in *Daybreak*. He mentions:

> "avoiding opportunities, implanting regularity into the drive, engendering satiety and disgust with it and associating it with a painful idea (such as that of disgrace, evil consequences or offended pride), then dislocation of forces and finally a general weakening and exhaustion."[129]

The point of this little catechism of great self-control, however, lies in its ultimate revelation that self-mastery is never realized by a disembodied reason that declares war against a particular drive, but rather represents the achievement of another drive that battles against its rivals. We may complain about one of our drives, yet "at bottom it is one drive *which is complaining about another*." This perpetual tension among the drives heralds a conflict "in which our intellect is going to have to take sides."[130]

The knowledge that our drives define the horizon of our knowledge and of the world points to the fourth path that lies open to Zarathustra in his moment of freedom, indifferent to this conflict. He can re-conceptualize sublimation, not as mortification but as intensification. He can transform the enmity between body and spirit promoted by Christianity into the productive game that in the *Symposium* had been distinguished as the path towards the Idea and that now returns in Nietzsche as the *Übermensch*, who at bottom is more than a mere catchphrase: he is man in his entirety. As early as in his essay on Schopenhauer, Nietzsche had discovered a post-Christian understanding of sublimation that not only leaves behind the irreconcilable, melancholically paralyzed dualism of will and representation, but also defines an alternative to that fateful plunge into the *apeiron*. Within the frame of his portrait of Schopenhauer, Nietzsche had also hung a self-portrait, the image of

129 Nietzsche: *Daybreak* (note 11), p. 65.
130 Ibid.

a philosopher who may be counted "among the mightiest promoters of life, of the will to live", a philosopher who "from out of [his] own exhausted age [...] long[s] for a culture, for a transfigured *physis*."[131] Transfigured *physis*: this is the title that Nietzsche finds for successful sublimation.

131 Nietzsche: "Schopenhauer as educator", in: *Untimely Meditations* (note 20), p. 145.

4. Self-Control: Sigmund Freud

"Now things are becoming queer." Theory of Psychoanalysis

This chapter concerns Sigmund Freud's concept of sublimation. For reasons to be explained below, Freud's remarks on sublimation remained fragmentary, and any attempt to reconstruct a consistent theory from these scattered fragments must adhere to strict limits. Therefore, before entering into the convoluted network of tunnels that comprise Freud's writings, it seems advisable first to lay out briefly the theoretical framework of classical psychoanalysis in which the enigmatic concept of sublimation is to be found. My remarks on psychoanalytic texts will inevitably lead down byways whose connections to the main roads of my argument are not immediately evident. Thus a reconstruction of some basic structures may be helpful as a sort of orientation. At the same time, the following exposition requires a fundamental decision regarding methodology; the reconstruction attempted here approaches Freud's speculations on cultural theory from the point of view of his research on individual psychology, and not the other way around. This preliminary note is important, as at least two narratives of sublimation may be reconstructed from Freud's body of work, depending on whether one begins with the purportedly "scientific" psychology of the individual soul or with Freud's audacious, still controversial speculations concerning cultural history, which reach their impressive climax in his late text on *Moses and Monotheism*, which conceptualizes the history of monotheism as one of "spiritualization".

I have chosen the perspective of individual psychology as a starting point first because Freud's work on cultural history rests on the hypothesis that insights gleaned from individual psychology may be applied to the psychology of groups. Independent of the complicated question as to the conditions that allow for such a generalization—which would have to operate with such concepts as the "unconscious of peoples" [*Unbewusstes der Völker*]—a reconstruction of individual psychology thus logically precedes ethnopsychology. The second reason for beginning with the purportedly "scientific" psychology of the individual is that the notorious twilight in which the concept of sublimation has been obscured can thus more successfully be explained, as will be demonstrated below.

Psychoanalysis, according to its founder, is the name

> "(i) of a procedure for the investigation of mental processes which are almost inaccessible in any other way
> (ii) of a method (based upon that investigation) for the treatment of neurotic disorders and
> (iii) of a collection of psychological information obtained along those lines, which is gradually being accumulated into a new scientific discipline."[1]

Freud's encyclopedia entry makes it clear that, particularly in comparison with the documents of "intellectual history" discussed in the preceding chapters, psychoanalysis marks the beginning of something new and categorically different. This new beginning followed on the heels of Goethe's beautiful literature and romantic natural philosophy, Schopenhauer's obsolete metaphysics, and Nietzsche's forward-looking yet (allegedly) unsystematic observations, and was inaugurated by a neurologist who turned his back on neurons in favor of neuroses. Through his treatment of hysterical patients, Freud gained the fundamental insight that certain physical symptoms (along with neurotic disorders such as compulsions, anxieties, phobias, etc.) have neither somatic nor neurological origins but rather are the result of a mental disorder. Treatment methods thus logically required an elucidation of those "mental processes which are almost inaccessible in any other way". The extensive, years-long conversation between analyst and analysand, otherwise known as the "talking cure", proved to be an effective method of uncovering otherwise inaccessible—unconscious, repressed—mental processes, and a practicable way of curing such afflictions. Inasmuch as psychoanalysis deals with ephemeral phenomena such as dreams (conceived of as wish-fulfillments) and is particularly concerned with sexuality, the infantile dimension of which Freud had demonstrated as early as 1905,[2] the struggle for scientific, medical and social recognition was both difficult and haunted by

---

1 Cited in: Jean Laplanche and Jean-Baptiste Pontalis: *The Language of Psychoanalysis* (trans. Donald Nicholson-Smith, London: Karnac, 2006), p. 367.

2 Sigmund Freud: *Three Essays on the Theory of Sexuality*, in: *The Standard Edition of the Complete Psychological Works of Sigmund Freud* (eds James Strachey and Anna Freud), Vol. 7.

numerous setbacks, many of which were ideologically or politically based.

In the wake of the Nazis' seizure of power, these difficulties culminated in the murder[3] or banishment of the predominantly Jewish psychoanalysts of the first (Sigmund Freud went into exile in 1938) and second generations (Erik H. Erikson, Heinz Hartmann, and David Rapaport, among many others) from the German-speaking world, primarily to England and the United States. Psychoanalysis again returned to Germany after the Second World War. Alexander Mitscherlich,[4] along with those members of the Frankfurt School who were connected with him and who also had returned from exile (Max Horkheimer, Theodor W. Adorno),[5] promoted the process both institutionally and editorially. In Germany today, psychoanalysis is a widespread form of therapy for which health insurance policies frequently assume the cost, demonstrating that it has indeed achieved both medical and social recognition.

What was and sometimes still is suspect is the basic method of psychoanalysis, namely the conversation between analyst and analysand based on transference and countertransference. The analyst is no longer necessarily a physician, since he or she generally does not administer medicine. There have been female analysts almost since the beginning—an underappreciated, socio-politically emancipatory aspect of the new discipline. Analysis is a dialogue that tends to take the form of the analyst listening with evenly suspended attention, intervening only rarely and for a maieutic purpose: "More specifically, it is the participant-observation variant of the method of interpersonal relation; in particular, [analysis] applies the nondirective (free association), the interpretative-genetic, and the defense-analysis techniques of participant observation."[6]

Alongside Laplanche and Pontalis' monumental work on *The Language of Psychoanalysis*, David Rapaport's 1960 essay outlining the scientific structure of psychoanalytic theory can be counted among the most clear and complete surveys of the field. The following overview serves as a summary of Rapaport's dense 150-page piece, although

---

3 The Jewish psychoanalyst Sabina Spielrein, whose major 1912 essay *Destruction as a Cause of Coming into Being* introduced to psychoanalysis the concept of the destructive drive, was abducted and killed by German troops in the Soviet Union in the summer of 1942.

4 Cf. Martin Dehli: *Leben als Konflikt. Zur Biographie Alexander Mitscherlichs* (Göttingen: Wallstein Verlag, 2007).

5 Cf. ibid., p. 227ff.

6 David Rapaport: *The Structure of Psychoanalytic Theory: A Systematizing Attempt* (New York: International Universities, 1960), p. 125.

certain passages will largely be ignored.[7] Rapaport himself offers the shortest version of his study by pointing to Kurt Lewin's structural formula: B = f(P,E), which states that Behavior is a function of the Person and his or her Environment.[8] Psychoanalysis is the attempt to shed light upon this function, which according to Rapaport leads to a set of ten "points of view" from which human behavior may be analyzed. In order to illustrate these psychoanalytic perspectives, I will draw on the example of an embarrassing slip of the tongue employed by Rapaport himself.

The context is a board meeting in which the most important roles are played by the redoubtable chairman and his treasurer, who is being questioned about obscure financial issues. One of the participants in the meeting, responding to certain clarifications made on the part of the chairman in order to exonerate the treasurer, states: "Now things are becoming queer." The speaker is utterly surprised by the shocked reaction of the other participants in the meeting. He had intended to say, "Now things are becoming clear," and he could have sworn that he said "clear" rather than "queer"—meaning strange, weird, dubious or, in American slang as early as 1960, homosexual.[9] A person (P) exhibits a particular behavior (B) in a particular environment (E), and this behavior reveals an abnormality (*f*) whose origins psychoanalysis undertakes to elucidate.

Psychoanalysis is a science whose object is the *empirical behavior* of human beings: this is the first point of view (1). Its particular interest concerns the elucidation of abnormalities, deviations from the norm. In the case of the "queer" slip of the tongue, the question arises as to why this slip occurred. Obviously—and here psychoanalysis can be linked to everyday psychology—the substitution of "queer" for "clear" is due to the fact that the speaker, against his conscious will, uttered something which he did not want to say but which occurred to him as a thought, however vague and "censored." This slip of the tongue allows for the supposition that all empirical behavior is determined by conflicts between various tendencies in the psyche, which is why the starting point of analysis is the individual.

The *Gestalt point of view* (2) posits that in every concrete behavior there is present an amalgam of various aspects of the person—traditionally: affects, emotions, thoughts—a conglomeration made up of some portion of the id, ego and superego along with influences from

7 Such a summary cannot take the place of a thorough study of Rapaport's work, which is to be encouraged here. My overview is concerned primarily with pages 39–72, "The Structure of the System".

8 David Rapaport: *The Structure of Psychoanalytic Theory* (note 6), p. 86f.

9 Ibid., pp. 80ff.

reality; behavior is always "overdetermined." This proposition is complemented by the *organismic point of view* (3): the elements of a behavior do not stand in isolation but are intertwined with the entire personality, for which reason the hermeneutic circle asserts itself within analysis as an equalizing swing of the pendulum between assessments of the whole person and his or her character traits. The *genetic point of view* (4) asserts that a current behavior is determined by an individual's personal history, and particularly by the developmental phases of sexuality. "Complemental series" must thus be reconstructed in order to illuminate the specific origin of a behavior. According to the *topographic point of view* (5), critical determinants of behavior are unconscious; a slip of the tongue thus turns out to be evidence of a confrontation between a conscious behavior in line with reality (a result of the "secondary process") and an urge that is subject to the laws of the archaic "primary process". The *dynamic point of view* (6) emphasizes that all behavior is ultimately determined by the drives, where "drive" (*Trieb*) is defined as a causal agent, inherent to all organisms, whose traces can be found in "representatives" (*Repräsentanzen*) such as the linguistic slip "queer". Behavior is determined by the drives and, at the same time, by control and defense mechanisms, which fail in the case of a *lapsus linguae*. The *economic point of view* (7) complements drive theory: all behavior involves a discharge of energy (the "pleasure/unpleasure principle") and is regulated by mental energy—this is the hydraulic model of drives. The person develops modes of behavior—forms of neutralization, of deferral, of repression, of sublimation—that regulate the mass of drives which unremittingly urge immediate discharge. The neurotic symptom can be understood as a compromise between the demands of the drives and their denial on the part of reality, which admittedly generates suffering. Against this background, the *structural point of view* (8) describes the structure of the personality. In 1923, Freud substituted his old topography of conscious-preconscious-unconscious with a new structural model: the ego stands between the id, representing the dimension of the drives, and the superego, the introjected norms etc. of a particular reality. All behavior is determined by this structure and is thus characterized *throughout* by conflicts—between libidinal and ego drives, drives and censorship, drives and reality. Behavior is the continuous formation of compromises. The remark, "Now things are becoming queer," may be approached both as a compromise and, at the same time, as the trace of a conflict, inasmuch as one part of the person acts in such a way that is consistent with reality, while another part desires to act out a criticism that is inappropriate to the environment, or possibly a genetically-determined emotion (i.e. determined by personal history): the recurrence of a triangulation (chairman and treasurer as father and elder brother; the suspicion that a homosexual relationship exists between the two men, etc.). This insight into the structured nature of the person points to the extent to which behavior is determined by reality, which may be studied from the *adaptive perspective* (9). The person is subject to both internal stimuli (the drives) and external stimuli (reality). The relevant research concerns how objects *emerge* for a small child, particularly *external drive-objects* as a precondition for discharge. Also investigated is the formation of the reality principle, which enables the person to test reality and adjust his or her behavior accordingly. Finally, just as crucial to an understanding of the person, is the *psychosocial dimension* (10), which is analyzed both with respect to one's personal history (the epigenesis of the ego, parents and guardians, phase-specific experiences, etc.) and with a view to one's current situation within a society that is thought to be constitutive:

> "Society is not merely a prohibitor or provider; it is the necessary matrix of the development of all behavior. Indeed, the development and maintenance of the ego, of the superego, and perhaps of all structures are dependent on the social matrix; behavior is determined by it and is possible only within it."[10]

Since the beginnings of psychoanalysis, this psychosocial dimension has remained the subject of intense and open controversies that have often concerned the social function of psychoanalytic therapy itself, which must constantly define and redefine its place between criticism and adaptation, dissidence and the establishment. As is demonstrated below, this controversy has repeatedly been reignited over Freud's proposition regarding man's capacity for instinctual sublimation, the structural location of which between instinctual renunciation and transformation has not actually been clarified.

In 1930 Richard Sterba published the text of a lecture titled "A Contribution to the Theory of Sublimation", which he had delivered to representatives of the Vienna Psychoanalytic Society. Sterba suggests "that any deviation of an object libidinal striving from its original goal, insofar as it takes place without repression and is ego-syntonic, be primarily and explicitly termed a sublimation."[11] In his conclusion—and here one can hear the legacy of the *Symposium*—he outlines a "scale"[12] that, as in Plato, culminates in pure thought. In 1930, the path to the top still leads from the inhibition of sensual tendencies in favor

10 David Rapaport: *The Sturcture of Psychoanalytic Theory* (note 6), p. 65.

11 Richard Sterba: "A Contribution to the Theory of Sublimation" (1930), in: *The Collected Papers* (Croton-on-Hudson, NY: North River, 1987), p. 21.

12 Ibid., p. 26.

of tender ones (1), through primitive symbolism (2), to artistic work (3). These points on Sterba's scale are followed by the altruism of the social aid worker (4) and the work of the researcher (5). Sublimation ultimately achieves its highest form through the attainment of "indifferent displaceable cathexis energy, in which we can no longer recognize the connection with the original instinctual goal", and which has left behind even the concrete objects of the individual sciences.[13]

As in Plato's *Symposium*, the path leads from sensual love to friendship, and from there to art and service to the *polis*, which for its part achieves its highest form in scientific work. At the end, however, stands that form of thought which is free of all cathexes, known throughout the history of philosophy as the ideal of *theoria*: "The process of thought can be called the purest manifestation of the usage of indifferent instinctual energy resulting from sublimation."[14]

The two endpoints of the new science of the soul converge in the concept of sublimation. One the one hand, Sterba concedes that "our therapy rests upon the capacity of the Ego for such extreme sublimation",[15] which for its part, having been attained, is elevated to the *theoria* of the twentieth century. In the light of its central position, it is astonishing that sublimation remains one of the most obscure concepts of psychoanalytic theory; this is more than enough motivation to examine further Freud's remarks on the subject.

An Obscurity at the Center of Metapsychology

In examining the corpus of Freud's writings with respect to his fragmentary theory of sublimation, it is first of all striking that, despite every contradiction and modification, two elements stand out as constants, from the *Three Essays on the Theory of Sexuality* in 1905 through to the 1930s study of *Civilization and Its Discontents*.

Throughout this period, Freud insists first that the process of sublimation is carried out not via the ego drives, the self-preservative drives, nor even the destructive drives, but rather via the *sexual drives*: "The erotic instincts appear to be altogether more plastic, more readily diverted and displaced than the destructive instincts."[16] Just as emphatically, Freud declares that the process of sublimation supplies "powerful components [...] for *every kind* of cultural achievement."[17]

13 Ibid., p. 26f.

14 Ibid., p. 27.

15 Ibid., p. 27f.

16 Sigmund Freud: *The Ego and the Id*, in: *The Standard Edition* (London: Hogarth, 1956–74), Vol. 19, p. 44f.

17 Sigmund Freud: *Three Essays on the Theory of Sexuality* (note 2), p. 178. Emphasis E. G.

These assertions falter, however, with respect to the question of what portion of sublimation may be attributed to the process of civilization. Furthermore, it remains unclear *which* cultural achievements—art,[18] science,[19] ethical norms,[20] fantasies,[21] or simply every form of instinct substitution: institutions, even "labor"[22]—ought to be considered sublimations in the strict sense, whether only a certain few or "every kind" of them.

Thus in his 1931 study of sublimation, Siegfried Bernfeld fundamentally combines both aspects, sexuality and culture. The theory of sublimation appears to him as an attempt to reconstruct "the origin of civilization itself"[23] in sexuality, or, more precisely: in the libidinal cathexis of non-sexual objects:

> "From the beginning, Freud connected [the concept of sublimation] with a theory of the significance of culture. The value given to art, technology, science and religion is sexual in origin – this is the simplified, generalized formulation of the extremely radical and far-reaching theory that the word sublimation carries within itself in a condensed form."[24]

One sometimes gets the impression that Freud largely identifies the process of sublimation with the process of civilization in general. In the same breath, then, it is once again a *prior* culture which compels the sublimations that form culture, and the question thus arises as to where or in what *this* culture-compelling culture originated. A puzzling circularity runs through this description: a culture (1) generates or compels another culture (2):

> "Sublimation of instinct is an especially conspicuous feature of cultural development; it is what makes it possible for higher

18 Cf. ibid., p. 238.

19 Sigmund Freud: "A Special Type of Choice of Object Made by Men (Contributions to the Psychology of Love I)", in: *The Standard Edition* (London: Hogarth, 1956–74), Vol. 11, p. 165.

20 Sigmund Freud: *Beyond the Pleasure Principle*, in: *The Standard Edition* (London: Hogarth, 1956–74), Vol. 18, p. 42.

21 Sigmund Freud: *Introductory Lectures on Psychoanalysis*, in: *The Standard Edition* (London: Hogarth, 1956-1974), Vol. 15/16, p. 272.

22 Sigmund Freud: *Leonardo da Vinci and a Memory of His Childhood*, in: *The Standard Edition* (London: Hogarth, 1956–74), Vol. 11, p. 122.

23 Siegfried Bernfeld: "Zur Sublimierungstheorie" (1931), in: *Antiautoritäre Erziehung und Psychoanalyse*, Bd. 2 (Hg. Lutz von Werder u. Reinhart Wolff, Frankfurt am Main: März Verlag, 1974), pp. 225–35, here: p. 232. Translation JCW.

24 Ibid., p. 226. Translation JCW.

> psychical activities, scientific, artistic or ideological, to play such an important part in civilized life. If one were to yield to a first impression, one would say that sublimation is a vicissitude which has been forced upon the instincts entirely by civilization. But it would be wiser to reflect upon this a little longer."[25]

The vacillation and illogical circularity of this and other passages are consequences of Freud's modifications to the topography of the psyche in the wake of his introduction of narcissism and then of the death drive, which he juxtaposes with Eros. In particular, from the opposition between Eros and the death drive, the question arises as to whether aggressive drives can likewise be sublimated—for example, as Nietzsche claimed, through ritual, cathartic discharge, war games, sport, etc.—or whether they ought primarily to be inhibited. For the sake of clarity, the following reconstruction will for the moment largely avoid the unsettling question of aggression. What first must be discussed is the theory of the admixture of the drives. To the extent that it is the sexual drives which best lend themselves to sublimation, the sublimation of aggression becomes possible primarily when aggression is joined with the libido, a view that became the theoretical standard for, among others, Alexander Mitscherlich. Regarding pedagogy, he postulated that "adaptation must promote the admixture of drives", since as he observed through therapeutic practice "[t]he exsolution of the drives makes it abundantly clear that aggression, as an object-destroying force untempered by the libido, possesses no capacity for sublimation."[26] One can hear the echo of Nietzsche when Mitscherlich, in his study of the concept of aggression, warns against the danger of "false sublimation":

> "The total expulsion of every natural, sexual expression, e.g. into the realms of the worthless, the immoral, the 'base'—to this extent an exaggerated demand for sublimation and neutralization in, for example, Calvinism and Puritanism—has led not only to a life-destroying collective neuroticization with an effective moral double standard but also to a form of unbridled

25 Sigmund Freud: *Civilization and Its Discontents*, in: *The Standard Edition* (London: Hogarth, 1956–74), Vol. 21, p. 97.

26 Alexander Mitscherlich: *Die Idee des Friedens und die menschliche Aggression. Vier Versuche* (Frankfurt am Main: Suhrkamp, 1970), p. 87. Cf. as well ibid. p. 114: "If all power lives by virtue of the utilization of potential aggression, then rational forms of power may be recognized by their fusion of this aggression with another drive, namely the libido. Libido tempers behavior when it is closely linked with aggression." Translation JCW.

> aggression (separated out and emancipated from its true libidinal connection)."[27]

The terminological and factual ambiguities expressed here are the result both of modifications made to the psychical topography and, above all, of the deficient nature of the explanations offered for the process of individual sublimation itself, which Freud nonetheless repeatedly claims is evident:

> "The evidence of analytic experience shows that it is an undoubted fact that instinctual impulses from one source attach themselves to those from other sources and share their further vicissitudes, and that in general one instinctual satisfaction can be replaced by another. But it must be admitted that we do not understand this very well."[28]

In order to be able to clarify sublimation's role in the process of civilization, the psychology of individual sublimation would first have to be elaborated, which—as evidenced by the above quotation, among others—has not been done. From a therapeutic, empirical perspective, what is initially clear is this: that sublimation *exists*, namely as an independent phenomenon to be distinguished from stable repression, neurotic symptoms, inhibitions and reaction formations.

Yet it is difficult for Freud to define sublimation clearly, particularly in its contrast to reaction formation. In his *Three Essays on Sexual Theory*, reaction formation is even made subordinate to sublimation: "A sub-species of sublimation is to be found in suppression by reaction-formation."[29] These relationships become somewhat clearer in Freud's later study of *Character and Anal Erotism*, in which he briefly outlines a stage model that has led to the widespread assumption that sublimation is a kind of defense mechanism.[30] The following passage argues

---

27 Ibid.: "Wesensbestimmung der Aggression", in: *Die Motivation menschlichen Handelns*. (Hg. Hans Thomae, Köln/Berlin: Kiepenheuer & Witsch, 1966), p. 210–15, here: p. 213. Translation JCW.

28 Sigmund Freud: *New Introductory Lectures on Psychoanalysis*, in: *The Standard Edition* (London: Hogarth, 1956–74), Vol. 22, p. 96.

29 Sigmund Freud: *Three Essays on the Theory of Sexuality* (note 2), p. 238.

30 Cf. Anna Freud: *The Ego and the Mechanisms of Defense* (New York: International Universities, 1966), which categorizes sublimation as the tenth defense mechanism, as "displacement of instinctual aims" (p. 44), as well as: Hans W. Loewald: *Sublimation: Inquiries into Theoretical Psychoanalysis* (New Haven: Yale University Press, 1988), pp. 36–44: "The Traditional Theory of Sublimation and Defense". Loewald's investigation is one of the few clinical contributions in recent times to take up sublimation as a subject worthy of its own monograph.

that negative reactions, acquired during childhood, to sexual arousal of the genitals, mouth or anus without intent to procreate—i.e. reactions such as shame, disgust, morality, etc.—are formed over the course of an individual's development into fixed character traits that for their part should then be considered true sublimations:

> "Generally speaking, only a part of them [contributions to the production of sexual excitation, E. G.] is made use of in sexual life; another part is deflected from sexual aims and directed towards others—a process which deserves the name of 'sublimation.' During the period of life which may be called the period of 'sexual latency'—i.e. from the completion of the fifth year to the first manifestations of puberty (round about the eleventh year)—reaction-formations, or counter-forces, such as shame, disgust and morality, are created in the mind. They are actually formed at the expense of the excitations proceeding from the erotogenic zones, and they rise like dams to oppose the later activity of the sexual instincts. Now anal erotism is one of the components of the [sexual] instinct which, in the course of development and in accordance with the education demanded by our present civilization, have become unserviceable for sexual aims. It is therefore plausible to suppose that these character-traits of orderliness, parsimony and obstinacy, which are so often prominent in people who were formerly anal erotics, are to be regarded as the first and most constant results of the sublimation of anal erotism."[31]

For Freud, it is first of all clear that sublimation *exists*. Furthermore, it is clear to him that it is the sexual drives which are sublimated and that sublimation is a potent factor for cultural development. What remains unclear, on the other hand, is how sublimation is to be conceived specifically in a metapsychological sense, as well as what role sublimation plays in civilization. Wilhelm Reich, in his *Character Analysis*, was the first to recognize an opposition between sublimation that has been diverted and yet continues to flow in a similar direction, and reaction formation that has been dammed up and suppressed and thus puts more and more stress on the ego:

Loewald calls attention to the crucial, narcissistic intermediate stage—noted, too, by Adorno—that Freud introduces in his study of *The Ego and the Id* (see below), though his reflections remain on the level of the subject who is to undergo therapy. As a result, the concept of sublimation is divided in half, with the social dimension cut out completely.

31 Sigmund Freud: "Character and Anal Erotism", in: *The Standard Edition* (London: Hogarth, 1956–74), Vol. 9, p. 171.

> "In the case of sublimation, there is no inversion of the drive's direction: the drive is simply taken over by the ego and diverted to another goal. In the case of reaction formation, on the other hand, an inversion of the drive's direction does take place. The drive is turned against the self and is taken over by the ego only insofar as this inversion takes place. In the process of this inversion, the drive's cathexis is turned into a counter-cathexis against the drive's unconscious goal. [...] In reaction formation, the ego is continually occupied with itself; it is its own strict monitor. In sublimation, the ego's energies are free for achievement."[32]

From the beginning, sublimation is assigned a key role in clarifying the nexus between psychoanalysis of the individual and general cultural theory. As Siegfried Bernfeld notes, through the concept of sublimation, psychoanalysis becomes an empirical "science of civilization", a science "that aims beyond the conventional definitions and practices of biology, physiology, psychology and the social sciences, and seeks laws that may be applied generally."[33] And it is precisely in relation to *this* theoretical point, the question of the relationship between the individual and society (and then nature), that so much remains obscure even today. Freud's remarks are fragmentary to the point that the authors of *The Language of Psychoanalysis* were forced to conclude that a theory of sublimation could not be derived from his few references to the subject. Nonetheless, Laplanche and Pontalis ultimately underscore the concept's importance:

> "In the psycho-analytic literature the concept of sublimation is frequently called upon; the idea indeed answers a basic need of the Freudian doctrine and it is hard to see how it could be dispensed with. The lack of a coherent theory of sublimation remains one of the lacunae in psycho-analytic thought."[34]

The question of what the process of sublimation involves, is as pressing as the drive that it redirects, overcomes, refines, spiritualizes or even merely inhibits, as we are faced with the astonishing fact that sublimation's major role in the construction of psychoanalytic theory and in therapy is vigorously asserted here even though it has never been appropriately pinned down or elaborated. This scandal of an obscurity

---

32 Wilhelm Reich: *Character Analysis* (trans. Vincent R. Carfagno, New York: Farrar, Straus and Giroux, 1972), p. 189.

33 Bernfeld: "Zur Sublimierungstheorie" (note 23), p. 234. Translation JCW.

34 Laplanche/Pontalis: *The Language of Psychoanalysis* (note 1), p. 433.

at the center of psychoanalytic theory has had significant consequences for metapsychology and therapy even in recent times.

Otto F. Kernberg, for example, in his influential book on borderline disorders, referred to insufficient sublimations as a "crucial prognostic factor", though he nonetheless concedes, in recognition of the problems outlined by classical psychoanalysis, that this factor is frequently "difficult to evaluate".[35] This unsolved problem returns like something which has been repressed: as a concept of great significance whose theoretical definition and application present eminent difficulties in diagnostic practice. The origin in Freud's writings of what Kernberg calls the signs of sublimatory capacity is apparent, including to the extent that here various different practices are once again and without much ado elevated to the level of a concept:

> "Enjoyment of work and life and the capacity for creative achievement are the main indicators of sublimatory capacity; they have to be distinguished from efficiency, which may reflect the patient's particular defenses, capacities or natural talents rather than sublimatory development."[36]

In its two constant elements, Freud's theory of sublimation is concerned with the relation of the subject to himself, particularly to his sexual drives, and furthermore with the relation of the subject to nature and to other people. In this way, there survive in the concept of sublimation two classic problems of both philosophy and anthropology which are moreover linked to each other in a complicated way: the relationship between body and spirit on the one hand, and that between the individual and society/nature on the other. "[T]he concept of sublimation is an attempt to relate not only body and spirit, but also individual and society; but again it raises problems which it does not solve."[37]

From the perspective of the history of philosophy, the doctrine of sublimation, as a theory of the *individual*, reformulates the chain of thought of German Idealism,[38] including Schopenhauer's metaphysics of the will. At the same time, it updates Nietzsche's theory of self-overcoming: it was Nietzsche, not Freud, who introduced the concept

---

35 Otto F. Kernberg: *Borderline Conditions and Pathological Narcissism* (Northvale, NJ: Jason Aronson, 1985), p. 133.

36 Ibid.

37 Norman O. Brown: *Life Against Death: The Psychoanalytical Meaning of History* (Middletown, CT: Wesleyan University Press, 1985), p. 139.

38 Cf. Odo Marquard: *Transzendentaler Idealismus. Romantische Naturphilosophie. Psychoanalyse* (Köln: Verlag für Philosophie Jürgen Dinter, 1987), pp. 239–48 and passim.

of sublimation to psychology.[39] As a *social* theory, Freud's blueprint presents itself, though admittedly not explicitly, as a revision of Hobbes' theory of the state in the light of the discovery of the unconscious. In its connection to the question of the state and its institutions, the problem of aggression bursts forth. As a concept denoting a project for research, "sublimation" refers to "a strong impression" that, according to Siegfried Bernfeld, marks "one of the fundamental experiences of the psychoanalyst [...]: that something persists unchanged within the constant flow of mental functioning." This "perception of identity in change" makes it tempting to see in psychoanalysis a theoretical apparatus that contributes to the overcoming of traditional dualisms, that is supposed to sublate the division between body and spirit, as well as that between the individual and society. In contrast to the philosophically reserved Freud, Bernfeld explicitly articulates psychoanalysis' claim to dissolve genetically classic dualisms. As demonstrated in the previous chapter, psychoanalysis here inherits the historically-minded thought of Friedrich Nietzsche:

> "Identity of form is interpreted as *genetic* identity when it is defined as 'sublimation.' The spheres of life which are in general highly valued and considered important for our self-esteem are, according to the theory of sublimation, derivative phenomena; the identity of forms is taken as a sign of the identity of the libido. Identity of form is not symbolic but constitutes a real *transposition.*"[40]

There are two dimensions to sublimation, one individual, the other social. The theory of sublimation is the attempt to define more precisely the position of the ego and its character between the drives that compel from within and the necessities of life (*Lebensnot*) that arise from without. Self-preservation of the ego must be established in opposition to overpowering nature, both internal and external, as well as in confrontation with others who themselves are likewise in conflict, whereby problems only increase. With respect to its body, the ego, whose drive towards self-preservation is developed into an orientation towards the reality principle, must assert itself in opposition to the drives. The fragile ego must preserve itself against the pleasure principle, which *sensu stricto* underlies both the partial drives as well as the sex drive, and against the nirvana principle, the aggressive or

39 Cf. Walter Kaufmann: *Nietzsche: Philosopher, Psychologist, Antichrist*, 4th ed. (Princeton: Princeton University, 1974), pp. 211–56, as well as the chapters on Schopenhauer and Nietzsche in this book.

40 Bernfeld: "Zur Sublimierungstheorie", (note 23), p. 226f. Translation JCW.

depressive desire to dissolve into inorganic nature. The complexity of the concept of sublimation is the result of this multilayered challenge.

Working on oneself is the precondition for survival in a world defined by *Lebensnot* and denial. An ego that is incapable of sublimating its erotic drives or inhibiting its aggressive drives (or likewise sublimating them *qua* the admixture of the drives) is, in its conflicts with nature and with others, inferior; the mortal danger, which constantly threatens it as it is, is thereby multiplied. Several of the difficulties involved in elaborating the concept of sublimation follow from the necessary yet still unexplained mediation between interiority and exteriority, the subjective aspect of which Freud ultimately provided with a structural solution through his analysis of melancholia. Nevertheless, it remains unresolved whether sublimation is to be understood as a self-executing internal "program", "as a quasi-biological process undergone by the human race in the course of evolution"[41] similar to the development toward sexual maturity experienced during puberty, or whether sublimation represents a "forced vicissitude of the drives" [*erzwungenes Triebschicksal*], an octroi that comes purely from without: "If sublimations are imposed by society on the individual, then sublimation is the result of repression."[42]

Any attempt at a precise reconstruction of the concept of sublimation, considered here from two different perspectives, must thus methodically dismantle what Freud has soldered together, beginning with his understanding of the mechanisms of sublimation with respect to the individual and his conflict with the ensemble of his drives.

The Individual Dimension of Sublimation

Sublimation and Evolution

If we are to be able to answer the question of whether sublimation is a forced vicissitude of the drives or "a quasi-biological process", we must first break out of the circle in which Freud repeatedly finds himself trapped: How does that culture (1) emerge which is then able to wrest from or instill in its new members—i.e. subsequent generations—sublimations, culture (2)? A plausible link between evolutionary theory and sublimation must be constructed if we wish to be able to assert the existence of those integrated adults who make it possible for "human beings—who, as creatures of their own drives on a par with chimpanzees, must be detached from the bodies of their mothers (through weaning)—to become incorporated into the culture of the community into which they were born."[43] Freud establishes this

---

41 Loewald: *Sublimation* (note 30), p. 6.

42 Brown: *Life Against Death* (note 37), p. 139.

43 Bernfeld: "Zur Sublimierungstheorie", (note 23), p. 231.

connection in an easily overlooked passage from his *Three Essays on Sexual Theory*. From the perspective of evolutionary history, the origins of sublimation in human beings may be traced to our upright gait, which obscures the genitals, as well as to the covering of the body necessitated by our lack of body hair:

> "The progressive concealment of the body which goes along with civilization keeps sexual curiosity awake. This curiosity seeks to complete the sexual object by revealing its hidden parts. It can, however, be diverted ('sublimated') in the direction of art, if its interest can be shifted away from the genitals on to the shape of the body as a whole."[44]

Winfried Menninghaus reconstructed the link between evolutionary theory and sublimation—hardly recognizable in its major significance—primarily with respect to aesthetic theory, resolving Freud's notorious circularity in the process. His reading elucidates not only the evolutionary origins of aesthetic sublimation but also sublimation in general:

> "The specifically human modification of those secondary sex characteristics to which 'beauty clings' promotes a diversionary sublimation in the field of sexual 'stimuli' by virtue of its own conditions. This is what makes the oft-invoked disinterestedness of the aesthetic disposition a genuinely human possibility. What is new, what is specifically human about aesthetic perception is this sublimation unknown in the animal kingdom; it thus justifiably constitutes the core of Freud's theory of beauty. Its evolutionary possibility is inextricably linked with the peculiar caprices of human sexual fashion: the denuding of the skin (with its dual consequences of civilized covering-up and the imagined completion of what has been thus concealed) and the relative devaluation of the intense stimuli that periodically proceed from genital signals in favour of 'milder' and more enduring optical stimuli. [...] Only since Freud is it possible to understand this sublimation from the perspective of its evolutionary improbability rather than perceiving it as an *anthropologicum* that is simply given. Only Freud is capable of demonstrating how sexual selection, in pursuing its own mechanisms, could lead to the development of 'ornaments' (the naked skin, the decoupling of feminine charms from any and all signs of ovulation) that by their very nature promote a civilized sublimation of the sexual drive [...]. Evolutionary theory and psychoanalysis thus deliver a

44 Sigmund Freud: *Three Essays on the Theory of Sexuality* (note 2), p. 156.

> narrative of the emergence of aesthetic disinterestedness from the evolutionary modification of its sexual 'origin.'"[45]

Two evolutionary steps—our upright gait and the covering of the body as a result of our extensive loss of body hair—favor sublimation to the extent that the sexual drive is literally "diverted" from its primary objects, which are now hidden. Other aspects, secondary sex characteristics or the entire *Gestalt* (culturally specified attributes, articles of clothing, jewelry, behavior), become exciting; the imagination completes what has been hidden from view. The *grand récit* of cultural sublimations, Menninghaus notes, can find its origins here.

From the perspective of drive theory, this evolutionary insight is endorsed by Freud's further discovery that the sexual drives are obviously not necessarily tied to their "original" objects, i.e. to the sight or smell of the primary sex characteristics. Sexual excitement is not exclusively linked to a specific situation, and not even to an external "object." It is more comprehensive; if it is directed towards procreation, this is a special case. This notion of the plasticity of the sexual drives is, according to drive theory, the foundation of the doctrine of sublimation:

> "It has been brought to our notice that we have been in the habit of regarding the connection between the sexual instincts and the sexual object as more intimate than it in fact is. Experience of the cases that are considered abnormal has shown us that in them the sexual instinct and the sexual object are merely soldered together—a fact which we have been in danger of overlooking in consequence of the uniformity of the normal picture, where the object appears to form part and parcel of the instinct. We are thus warned to loosen the bond that exists in our thoughts between instinct and object. It seems probable that the sexual instinct is in the first instance independent of its object; nor is its origin likely to be due to its object's attractions."[46]

This basic principle of the sexual drives' plasticity and their ability to become detached from an "object" is articulated repeatedly by Freud and then generalized, as in his 1915 essay on *Instincts and Their Vicissitudes*:

> "The *object* of an instinct is the thing in regard to which or through which the instinct is able to achieve its aim. It is what is most variable about an instinct and is not originally connected

---

45 Winfried Menninghaus: *Das Versprechen der Schönheit* (Frankfurt am Main: Suhrkamp, 2003), p. 210f. Translation JCW.

46 Sigmund Freud: *Three Essays on the Theory of Sexuality* (note 2), p. 147f.

> with it, but becomes assigned to it only in consequence of being peculiarly fitted to make satisfaction possible."[47]

This observation is critical to understanding the mechanics of sublimation as an exchange of objects, from one sexual object to the next, and as the move to non-sexual, "higher" objects. Here it is already apparent that the process of sublimation does not manipulate the drive itself; it is rather concerned with the substitution of objects, whereby the problem of the surrogate is inscribed in the doctrine. The suspicion that sublimation provides only a surrogate falls upon this process like the shadow of the lost object upon the melancholic subject and potentially triggers more than just discontent: the outbreak of aggression from its amalgamation with frustrated desire. That we cannot actually renounce anything and yet must do so—this melancholic insight has hung over the doctrine of sublimation as its emblem since Freud's lecture on the poet and his dreams of another life:

> "As people grow up, then, they cease to play, and they seem to give up the yield of pleasure which they gained from playing. But whoever understands the human mind knows that hardly anything is harder for a man than to give up a pleasure which he has once experienced. Actually, we can never give anything up; we only exchange one thing for another. What appears to be a renunciation is really the formation of a substitute or surrogate."[48]

An understanding of the "normal development" of genital sexuality as a widespread special case implies the next step. Sublimation is carried out on the one hand via *excess* sexual energy, via "excessively strong excitations arising from particular sources of sexuality"[49] that are difficult to qualify, and on the other hand via the *perverse* partial drives of sexual excitement that are dispensable when it comes to procreation. Before we can examine this last differentiation, which overtly presupposes not only a "normal" but also a normative understanding of a given culture, we must first take a look at Freud's model of drives.

The Hydraulic Model of Drives

In its current common usage, sublimation appears as a change *in the drive itself*, as its "spiritualization" or self-sublimation. This is a

---

47 Sigmund Freud: *Instincts and Their Vicissitudes*, in: *The Standard Edition* (London: Hogarth, 1956–74), Vol. 14, p. 122.

48 Sigmund Freud: "Creative Writers and Daydreaming", in: *The Standard Edition* (London: Hogarth, 1956–74), Vol. 9, p. 145.

49 Sigmund Freud: *Three Essays on the Theory of Sexuality* (note 2), p. 238.

misunderstanding of major consequence, and not just for readings of Freud—though Herbert Marcuse, under the banner of Plato and Schiller, undertook the bold attempt to outline a theory of the self-sublimation of Eros, starting from Freud. However, there is no change in the substance of drives according to Freud; this is the theoretical basis for his brusque rejection of the idea of an historical teleology, which assumes a kind of "drive towards perfection". This is why authors such as Herbert Marcuse, Norman O. Brown and Theodor W. Adorno, who were interested in theorizing the process of history, concerned themselves so extensively with Freud's doctrine of sublimation. There is no direct path leading from Freud to the philosophy of history; moreover, Freud's refusal to consider human beings' eccentric position makes possible the onset of Arnold Gehlen's anthropology, which, in defining man as a deficient being with an excess of impulses, contradicts Freud's own Darwinism:

> "The present development of human beings requires, as it seems to me, no different explanation from that of animals. What appears in a minority of human individuals as an untiring impulsion towards further perfection can easily be understood as a result of the instinctual repression upon which is based all that is most precious in human civilization."[50]

The urging of the drives—and we will return to this point in examining Freud's skeptical theory of civilization as a discreet reformulation of the *Leviathan*—remains constant and aims inexorably towards direct discharge. This is also true for the partial, sexual and aggressive drives. In Freud, the drive is a teleologically blind absolute, ineluctable in the sense that, as a continual urging, it cannot itself be "switched off" as long as its bearer lives. This character of permanent urging survives through every modification of drive theory and psychical topography. The drive always remains the drive, a constant current that at best may ebb temporarily as a result of fatigue or recede with the increasing age of the organism. "Maturity" is accordingly an amalgam of experience and diminished pressure from the drives.

As has been frequently noted, Freud's rhetoric "follows a hydraulic metaphorics of the affects, even if not entirely consciously."[51] The current of the drives can be inhibited, dammed, diverted or channeled

---

50 Sigmund Freud: *Beyond the Pleasure Principle* (note 20), p. 42.

51 Glenn W. Most: "Freuds Narziß: Reflexionen über einen Selbstbezug", in: *Narcissus. Ein Mythos von der Antike bis zum Cyberspace* (Hg. Almut-Barbara Renger, Stuttgart: J. B. Metzler Verlag, 2002), pp. 117–31, here: p. 127. Translation JCW.

but cannot *itself* be entirely sublated unless and until its bearer dies. Initially, then, sublimation can *only* mean managing the urge. Freud's model of the drives is explicitly mechanical, as the subject is to be perceived as being under pressure, as an engine at high speed charged with a certain quantum of energy. This quantum is initially high, for which reason

> "[m]astering it by sublimation, by deflecting the sexual instinctual forces away from their sexual aim to higher cultural aims, can be achieved by a minority and then only intermittently, and least easily during the period of ardent and vigorous youth."[52]

Freud's therapeutic work led him to the discovery of a discrepancy between the primary drives. The drive employed for sublimation is not a destructive drive, an ego drive nor a drive for self-preservation, but rather is sexual in nature:

> "A certain kind of modification of the aim and change of the object, in which our social valuation is taken into account, is described by us as 'sublimation.' [...] The sexual instincts are noticeable to us for their plasticity, their capacity for altering their aims, their replaceability, which admits of one instinctual satisfaction being replaced by another, and their readiness for being deferred, of which we have just given a good example in the aim-inhibited instincts. We should be glad to deny these characteristics to the self-preservative instincts, and to say of them that they are inflexible, admit of no delay, are imperative in a very different sense and have a quite other relation to repression and to anxiety."[53]

Inasmuch as it is the sexual drives that are directed towards sublimation, we are faced with a constraint that Jacques Lacan would later seize upon in his work on the subject.[54] The sexual drive is not simply a general, aimless urge; rather, it pushes on towards a goal, a sexual "object." To the extent that this drive is not indeterminate, the quantum of possible sublimation is individually variable, depending on the strength of the individual's sex drive:

> "It seems to us that it is the innate constitution of each individual which decides in the first instance how large a part of his

52 Sigmund Freud: "'Civilized' Sexual Morality and Modern Nervousness", in: *The Standard Edition* (London: Hogarth, 1956–74), Vol. 9, p. 193.

53 Sigmund Freud: *New Introductory Lectures on Psychoanalysis* (note 28), p. 97.

54 Cf. the comments on Lacan's theory of sublimation below.

> sexual instinct it will be possible to sublimate and make use of. In addition to this, the effects of experience and the intellectual influences upon his mental apparatus succeed in bringing about the sublimation of a further portion of it. To extend this process of displacement indefinitely is, however, certainly not possible, any more than is the case with the transformation of heat into mechanical energy in our machines. A certain amount of direct sexual satisfaction seems to be indispensable for most organizations, and a deficiency in this amount, which varies from individual to individual, is visited by phenomena which, on account of their detrimental effects on functioning and their subjective quality of unpleasure, must be regarded as an illness."[55]

The evolutionary "origin" of sublimation is thus clarified, with the sexual drive—as the plastic drive, in contrast to the destructive and self-preservative drives—marked as that which encourages sublimation. In his analysis of the sexual drive, Freud now differentiates sublimation in three respects. First, sublimation is carried out via an *excess* of sexual energy for the discharge of which an object is not available (whether permanently or only temporarily), whereby a certain quantum of direct discharge must nonetheless be allowed if illness is to be avoided. On the basis of the following passage, among others, one might assume that Freud conceives of sublimation as a conscious act, a project that one can resolve to undertake or a task that a therapist can "urge" his or her patient to take up.[56] He thus establishes a latent connection between psychoanalysis and asceticism:

> "There are only two possibilities for remaining healthy when there is a persistent frustration of satisfaction in the real world. The first is by transforming the psychical tension into active energy which remains directed towards the external world and eventually extorts a real satisfaction of the libido from it. The second is by renouncing libidinal satisfaction, sublimating the dammed-up libido and turning it to the attainment of aims which

---

55 Sigmund Freud: "'Civilized' Sexual Morality and Modern Nervousness" (note 52), p. 188.

56 Cf. Sigmund Freud: "Recommendations to Physicians Practising Psychoanalysis", in: *The Standard Edition* (London: Hogarth, 1956–74), Vol. 12, p. 119, as well as Anna Freud: "Sublimation, i.e. the displacement of the instinctual aim in conformity with higher social values, presupposes the acceptance or at least the knowledge of such values, that is to say, presupposes the existence of the superego. Accordingly, the defense mechanisms of repression and sublimation could not be employed until relatively late in the process of development." *The Ego and the Mechanisms of Defense* (note 30), p. 52.

are no longer erotic and which escape frustration. That these two possibilities are realized in men's lives proves that unhappiness does not coincide with neurosis and that frustration does not alone decide whether its victim remains healthy or falls ill."[57]

Second, sublimation is carried out via the *partial drives*, which protrude as perversely or rather uneconomically valued drives into the world of the subject who has matured into heterosexual genitality. Third, sublimation is necessary when one sexual object must be replaced by another, or by something else entirely, whereby the complicated transition to the outside world is fulfilled. Thus with respect to the individual there exists an *ontogenetic* sublimation which concerns the development of the partial drives towards genital sexuality: the sublimation of perversions. There exists as well a *social* sublimation, "since each individual who makes a fresh entry into human society repeats this sacrifice of instinctual satisfaction for the benefit of the whole community."[58] Finally, there exists a sublimation which the socialized, sexually mature subject must carry out on a case-by-case basis with as little regression as possible: the *exchange* of objects, the management of frustration: the sublimation of excess and, if possible, of desire.

Sublimation of the Partial Drives

Freud emphasizes repeatedly that it is primarily the perverse elements of our sexuality that are directed towards sublimation, at which point drive theory begins to move in the direction of normativity. This tendency may be understood as the result of a lack of reflection on Freud's part in operating with social realities. Women are regarded "as having less capacity for sublimating their instincts than men."[59] Homosexual men function as the preferred example of those subjects who turn to artistic pursuits or to the ideals of humanity,[60] while the life of the working heterosexual man finds its solemn fulfillment in "science" (as an occupation or as a "sober attitude" of profound disillusion), which grants him a stoic bearing in the face of life's adversities.

In terms of the history of civilization, there arises a division of emotional labor that the dominant and sober man alone has at his disposal; woman bears the fate of being able to sublimate only poorly.

57 Sigmund Freud: "Types of Onset of Neurogenesis", in: *The Standard Edition* (London: Hogarth, 1956–74), Vol. 12, p. 232.

58 Sigmund Freud: *Introductory Lectures on Psychoanalysis* (note 21), p. 23.

59 Sigmund Freud: *New Introductory Lectures on Psychoanalysis* (note 28), p. 134.

60 Cf. Sigmund Freud: *Psychoanalytic Notes Upon an Autobiographical Account of a Case of Paranoia (Dementia Paranoides)*, in: *The Standard Edition* (London: Hogarth, 1956–74), Vol. 12, p. 61f.

For this reason, she appears to the stoic man as potentially hysterical; around 1900 this was in fact the consequence of ongoing oppression. Thus the scientist is called upon for a cure, who then turns to the neurotics, i.e. those men who are similar to women, who have only a poor mastery of the art of sublimation. It is clear why the neurotic is later elevated to the status of witness against the doctrine of sublimation's repressive elements, as in Adorno's critique of second-generation psychoanalysis. Neurotics, women and perverts: all are potentially distinguished by a keen awareness that civilization compels sublimations.

The difference between sublimation of the drives and renunciation of the drives, never clarified by Freud, can thus only be regarded as plausible with recourse to the distinction between the libidinal neurotic and the plain and modest man as expressed in *On Narcissism: An Introduction*. While the neurotic, whom Freud also calls an "idealist" (he could also have written, as he did in his lecture *On the Poet and his Relation to Daydreaming*: intellectual, philosopher, artist), suffers from the tension between ideal and reality, the simple mind resigns himself to renunciation:

> "We are naturally led to examine the relation between this [narcissistic, E. G.] forming of an ideal and sublimation. Sublimation is a process that concerns object-libido and consists in the instinct's directing itself towards an aim other than, and remote from, that of sexual satisfaction; in this process the accent falls upon deflection from sexuality. [...] [S]ublimation remains a special process which may be prompted by the ideal but the execution of which is entirely independent of any such prompting. It is precisely in neurotics that we find the highest differences of potential between the development of their ego ideal and the amount of sublimation of their primitive libidinal instincts; and in general it is far harder to convince an idealist of the inexpedient location of his libido than a plain man whose pretensions have remained more moderate. Further, the formation of an ego ideal and sublimation are quite different related to the causation of neurosis. As we have learnt, the formation of an ideal heightens the demands of the ego and is the most powerful factor favouring repression; sublimation is a way out, a way by which those demands can be met *without* involving repression."[61]

Intellectuality, or creativity, and wild desire here seem to converge in an astonishing sleight of hand. Freud inverts the expected line of

61 Sigmund Freud: *On Narcissism: An Introduction*, in: *The Standard Edition* (London: Hogarth, 1956–74), Vol. 14, p. 94f.

thought. It is not the primitive but the refined man who has a problem with sublimation and who is only with difficulty convinced of the need to divert his libido. While the "simple" man, with his moderate demands, is easily satisified by his "day job" and quickly adapts to the reality principle of the stoic analyst, the intellectual, the "idealist", insists upon realizing the desires of his drives. The demand of the drive evidently increases in proportion to the subject's capacity for ideal formation. The better he has developed his ability to form ideals, the more keenly he is aware that those ideals must be renounced, so that in the end the relationships are reversed: the higher the ideal, the greater the desire for an uninhibited life; the "degree of tension" increases. Thus in Freud, too, the vanishing point of this double-edged, latently dialectical doctrine of sublimation consists in protest against "reality" itself, the awareness of a repressivity inherent in the reality principle and in the sublimations advanced by it. In the end, this differentiation generates a recurrence of the archaic, that which belongs to the primary process, and in this way the doctrine of sublimation shows itself to be a preliminary form of the notion of a dialectic of enlightenment. As Freud brings neurosis and ideal together, and differentiates them from sublimation—ideals potentially lead to neuroticism, neurotics cling to ideals—the ideal's content is cast into twilight. In the context of psychoanalysis, the ideal can only mean reconciliation between body and soul as well as between the individual and society: the healing of the wound, the overcoming of *Lebensnot*. Stoicism, on the other hand, would mean knowledge of the ideal as well as a simultaneous awareness of its illusionary character; the ideal encourages sublimation, yet one must identify the ideal as a consequence of repressions, so that sublimation may succeed and accordingly leave behind both the ideal and the desire that announces itself in what has been repressed.

One potential way out of this dilemma is offered by the sharp distinction that Freud draws in *On Narcissism* between the formation of ego ideals and the sublimation of the drives, which are "often confused" with each other "to the detriment of our understanding of the facts", though their relationship is effectively one of scale.[62] When Freud notes that "[a] man who has exchanged his narcissism for homage to a high ego ideal has not necessarily on that account succeeded in sublimating his libidinal instincts,"[63] he is announcing a distinction whose full relevance is discernable only in the context of group psychology. Freud's argument is complemented by his explicit distinction between a dubious ideal emanating from a deferred narcissism and an authentic

62 Ibid., p. 94.
63 Ibid.

ideal representing the result of sublimations that then, paradoxically, leave every ideal behind.

According to this theory of narcissism, the subject is able to maintain successfully his all too quickly frustrated narcissism either by deferring it to an ego ideal or by projecting it onto an object that is then courted as an ideal. In his essay on *Group Psychology and the Analysis of the Ego*, Freud applies this mechanism to the formation of groups, thereby explaining their emergence: "*A primary group of this kind is a number of individuals who have put one and the same object in the place of their ego ideal and have consequently identified themselves with one another in their ego.*"[64] In contrast to this primary group formation, Freud conceives of a culture's great old institutions as the result not of a narcissism that has been acted out through identification and idealization, but of sublimations. This becomes particularly clear when, in the postscript to his treatise on group psychology, he distinguishes between traditional and modern forms of social ties. While archaic forms of socialization founded in religion "offered those who were bound by them the most powerful protection against the danger of neurosis", Freud writes of modern social ties:

> "Nor is it hard to discern that all the ties that bind people to mystico-religious or philosophico-religious sects and communities are expressions of crooked cures of all kinds of neuroses. All of this is correlated with the contrast between directly sexual impulsions and those which are inhibited in their aims."[65]

According to Freud, traditional forms of social ties are gone forever, as history has made evident; the crooked cure of narcissistic idealism, as the product of repressions, is constantly subject to the danger of regression. With this astute remark, Freud has explained *en passant* the sudden, notorious shift in cultural history, and particularly in the history of literature, from neurotic isolation to enthusiastic identification with mass movements. The ideal that, unlike its narcissistic counterpart, would not be neurotic thus turns out to be the ideal of utter soberness, the Nietzschean pathos of distance possessed by great individuals.

For their part, however, the social feelings of the stoic, distant man likewise have their origins in perversity. They are to be regarded "as a sublimation of homosexual attitudes towards objects",[66] into which they

---

64 Sigmund Freud: *Group Psychology and the Analysis of the Ego*, in: *The Standard Edition* (London: Hogarth, 1956–74), Vol. 18, p. 116.

65 Ibid., p. 95f.

66 Sigmund Freud: "Some Neurotic Mechanisms in Jealousy, Paranoia and Homosexuality", in: *The Standard Edition* (London: Hogarth, 1956–74), Vol. 18, p. 232.

occasionally revert, whether "what is left of a homosexuality that has run its course"[67] manifests itself in delusional jealousy or simply bursts forth openly. The potential for affectionate, companionable, "sublimated" feelings to revert into openly passionate emotions becomes one of Freud's major arguments in the context of his analysis of sublimation as a vicissitude of the drives enforced by society that must be borne stoically and maintained via severe penalties, as in the army. One of the foundations of homophobia consists in the fact that the melancholic man[68] experiences his own latent homosexuality as a form of paranoia, as a threat to the "scientific attitude" he has ostentatiously assumed:

> "We are justified in saying that they [affectionate emotional ties] have been diverted from these sexual aims, even though there is some difficulty in giving a description of such a diversion of aim which will conform to the requirements of metapsychology. [...] The inhibited instincts are capable of any degree of admixture with the uninhibited; they can be transformed back into them, just as they arose out of them."[69]

Freud's dated typology of women who are incapable of sublimation, artistic or philanthropic perverts, hysterical idealists and stoic, misanthropic men is frustrated by his enthusiastic analysis of the homosexual scientist *and* artist Leonardo da Vinci, who according to Freud achieved the highest level of sublimation possible to man. Freud is quite familiar with the authentic ideal, but only as an individual one.

A ranking of the various forms of sublimation thus begins to take shape here. The path leads from immediate desire through work and daydreaming to religion and finally to science. Freud's doctrine of sublimation reproduces exactly—and probably without his actually having been familiar with the book—the structure of Hegel's

---

67 Ibid., p. 225.

68 "In the case of the melancholic heterosexual male, he never loved another man, he *is* a man, and he can seek recourse to the empirical facts that will prove it. But the literalization of anatomy not only proves nothing, but is a literalizing restriction of pleasure in the very organ that is championed as the sign of masculine identity. The love for the father is stored in the penis, safeguarded through an impervious denial, and the desire which now centers on that penis has that continual denial as its structure and its task. Indeed, the woman-as-object must be the sign that he not only never felt homosexual desire, but never felt the grief over its loss. Indeed, the woman-as-sign must effectively displace and conceal that preheterosexual history in favor of one that consecrates a seamless heterosexuality." Judith Butler: *Gender Trouble* (New York: Routledge, 1990), p. 97.

69 Sigmund Freud: *Group Psychology and the Analysis of the Ego* (note 64), p. 138f.

Phenomenology of Spirit. The simple person sublimates his frustrated desire through work; daydreams and other fantasies compensate for lingering instinctual desires; fantasies are sometimes sublimated by talented individuals into works of art that ultimately allow for a realization of their creators' frustrated desires, if those works are socially recognized and honored. In the realm of religion, individual daydreams and fantasies are shared by the collective and formed into socially powerful illusions about the meaning of the world and the object of desire. Finally, science is characterized by its reflexive and sublime emancipation from all these steps, by its clear insight into reality beyond fantasy and illusion. Science is in fact reconceived here as absolute knowledge, as a radical renunciation of precisely that pleasure principle which inspires the production of dreams, fantasies and illusions. As Freud articulates in his study of Leonardo, at the apex of sublimation, a circle is closed; sublation is achieved. In science, the infantile, pre-oedipal immediacy of desire beyond all authority is, on the one hand, expressed as *Zugreifen* (grasping). On the other hand, it has gone through the comprehensive reflection of all modifications of desire; it has been sublimated into consummate *Begreifen* (reasoning). "[T]he almighty and just God, and kindly Nature [in Leonardo, E. G.], appear to us as grand sublimations of father and mother, or rather as revivals and restorations of the young child's ideas of them."[70]

Before we look more closely at the Hegelian structure of sublimation, it should be added "that [civilization] originates mainly at the cost of the sexual component instincts, and that these must be suppressed, restricted, transformed and directed to higher aims."[71] In his *Fragment of an Analysis of a Case of Hysteria*, Freud writes of the perversions:

> "The perversions are neither bestial nor degenerate in the emotional sense of the word. They are a development of germs all of which are contained in the undifferentiated sexual predisposition of the child, and which, by being suppressed or by being diverted to higher, asexual aims—by being *sublimated*—are destined to provide the energy for a great number of our cultural achievements."[72]

---

70 Sigmund Freud: *Leonardo da Vinci and a Memory of his Childhood* (note 22), p. 123.

71 Sigmund Freud: "The Psychoanalytic View of Psychogenic Disturbance of Vision", in: *The Standard Edition* (London: Hogarth, 1956–74), Vol. 11, p. 215.

72 Sigmund Freud: *Fragment of an Analysis of a Case of Hysteria*, in: *The Standard Edition* (London, Hogarth, 1956–74), Vol. 7, p. 50.

And similarly, in his survey of *"Civilized" Sexual Morality and Modern Nervousness*:

> "Further prospects are opened up when we take into consideration the fact that in man the sexual instinct does not originally serve the purposes of reproduction at all, but has as its aim the gaining of particular kinds of pleasure. [...] During this development a part of the sexual excitation which is provided by the subject's own body is inhibited as being unserviceable for the reproductive function and in favourable cases is brought to sublimation. The forces that can be employed for cultural activities are thus to a great extent obtained through the suppression of what are known as the *perverse* elements of sexual excitation."[73]

From this description of sublimation as the putting to use of perverse organ-pleasure, Freud also draws the contours of a theory of character, according to which *neurosis*, however "characteristic" of an individual it may at first glance appear to be, is precisely *not* to be understood as a character trait: "In the formation of character either repression is not at work at all or it easily attains its aim, which is to replace the repressed impulses by reaction-formations and sublimations."[74] This is an important point for therapy, the goal of which is to allow patients to recognize their neurosis as something that does not actually belong to their character but is merely an introjection. Freud considers sublimation to be so important with regard to the development of neuroses that he assumes of many neurotics "that they would never have fallen ill had they possessed the art of sublimating their impulses."[75] He thus demonstrates the importance of sublimation both for his theory of neurosis as well as for his theory of character:

> "What we describe as a person's 'character' is built up to a considerable extent from the material of sexual excitations and is composed of instincts that have been fixed since childhood, of constructions achieved by means of sublimation, and of other constructions, employed for effectively holding in check perverse impulses which have been recognized as being unutilizable."[76]

---

73 Sigmund Freud: "'Civilized' Sexual Morality and Modern Nervousness" (note 52), p. 188f.

74 Sigmund Freud: "The Disposition to Obsessional Neurosis (A Contribution to the Problem of the Choice of Neurosis)," in: *The Standard Edition* (London: Hogarth, 1956–74), Vol. 12, p. 323.

75 Sigmund Freud: "Recommendations to Physicians Practising Psychoanalysis" (note 56), p. 119.

76 Sigmund Freud: *Three Essays on the Theory of Sexuality* (note 2), p. 238f.

The Ego and the World of Objects

In the wake of his introduction of narcissism, Freud finds himself compelled to deal with sublimation—given its key role in the formation of character—in the context of his theory of the ego, as "with the formulation and elaboration of the narcissism concept, ego psychology began to come into its own."[77] He is compelled to do this as well in consideration of the already mentioned fact that sublimation not only bears on the *genesis* of the ego and its character (sublimation 1), but also, in the context of an *already-established social* context (sublimation 2), continually remains a project with which the adult ego, at times compelled to *change its object*, finds itself confronted (sublimation 3). In accordance with this logic, Freud attempts to bring ego theory and the theory of sublimation into harmony:

> "The concept of sublimation is essentially an attempt to relate the organic and superorganic levels, as part of the general effort of psychoanalysis to rediscover the animal in man and to heal the war between body and soul."[78]

In his first theory of drives, Freud differentiates between the self-preservative drives and the sexual drives, which come together out of the polymorphically perverse partial drives. The innovation to the theory of sublimation in the wake of the development of ego psychology consists first in Freud's claim that during childhood a certain number of the sexual drives follow from the ego drives, whereby the latter are themselves substantially changed. The result is an amalgamation of the sexual and ego drives, as well as an analytical answer to one of the classic problems of philosophy, namely the question of the relation between body and spirit.[79] The split between the two is rearticulated according to drive theory, and Freud succeeds in clarifying why the ego libidinally cathects objects as such in the first place. This insight is important, as libidinal cathexis from the start stands in contradiction to the self-preservative drive. As soon as the ego desires something, it may potentially act against its own interests, as it becomes dependent

---

77 Loewald: *Sublimation* (note 30), p. 16.

78 Brown: *Life Against Death* (note 37), p. 137.

79 David Rapaport explained the genesis of this process in a valuable footnote. The objects of primary desire are simultaneously those which make self-preservation possible. One could almost invert Freud's insight and say that it is the sexual tendencies which follow from the self-preservative drives: "Anaclitic: leaning upon. The implication is that the first objects of the sexual drive are the people who take care of the infant and guarantee his survival, i.e. who are the objects of his self-preservative drives." David Rapaport: *The Structure of Psychoanalytic Theory* (note 6), p. 62, footnote.

on the object of its desire. Libidinal cathexis of objects becomes possible because the drive for self-preservation does not remain "pure"; rather, the sexual drives have clung to it and ultimately fused with it:

> "The aim which each of them [the sexual drives, E. G.] strives for is the attainment of 'organ-pleasure'; only when synthesis is achieved do they enter the service of the reproductive function and thereupon become generally recognizable as sexual instincts. At their first appearance they are attached to the instincts of self-preservation, from which they only gradually become separated; in their choice of object, too, they follow the paths that are indicated to them by the ego-instincts. A portion of them remains associated with the ego-instincts throughout life and furnishes them with libidinal components, which in normal functioning easily escape notice and are revealed clearly only by the onset of illness. They are distinguished by possessing the capacity to act vicariously for one another to a wide extent and by being able to change their objects readily. In consequence of the latter properties they are capable of functions which are far removed from their original purposive actions—capable, that is, of *sublimation*."[80]

Through the unification of the sexual and self-preservative drives, the ego first becomes "social" in the fundamental sense that objects begin to emerge (first erotic, then non-sexual objects). The self-preservative drive desires more than just itself. It wants an object—although of course self-interest remains as an undercurrent—from which arises the potentially disruptive double-edged character of love (and of the social fabric), which wants to assimilate its object even as it desires to *maintain* it *as* an other in order to strengthen the narcissism of the ego, which only thus feels truly loved.[81] We can see here why the theory of the admixture of drives becomes so critical to the question of coping with aggression. Thus, just as the opposition between Eros and the death drive replaces the opposition between the sexual and the ego drives, the doctrine of mitigating aggression through its amalgamation with the libido supercedes the theory of the amalgamation of the sexual and ego drives. In introducing his second theory of drives,

---

80 Sigmund Freud: *Instincts and Their Vicissitudes* (note 47), p. 125f.

81 Cf. Eckart Goebel: *Der engagierte Solitär. Die Gewinnung des Begriffs Einsamkeit aus der Phänomenologie der Liebe im Frühwerk Jean-Paul Sartres* (Berlin: Oldenbourg Akademieverlag, 2001), pp. 60–96. Sartre reconstructs the hopeless circle of passion from the double-edged character of love, which wants egoistically to assimilate its object while simultaneously desiring it as the other who is to love in freedom. This double character applies to both involved parties; the result is the pre-structured drama of passion.

Freud clearly brings together the ego and destruction. Even before it permits or consciously acts out aggression, the ego *as a unit* is already something aggressive, both outwardly and inwardly. In light of the new distinction between Eros and the destructive drive, the ego seems to be a consequence of subjection[82] that for its part practices violence against itself, against others and against nature: self-preservation is, strictly according to Freud's text, aggressive. This insight into the structural connection between the ego and violence on the level of the ego's very constitution marks the point of departure for Theodor W. Adorno's theory of sublimation.[83]

From the fact that the ego drives acquire a libidinal component that is by definition "other" than them, it further becomes possible to conceive of sublimation as a conscious project, as first and foremost an intention of the ego. On the other hand, through its merging with the ego drive, the sexual drive too is transformed into the ability to desire *a specific object* and not just the fulfillment of organ-pleasure itself. By merging with the ego, the sexual drive begins to *see*. The ego becomes the eye of sexuality. In its amalgamation with the ego, desire becomes transitive, becomes the possibility of desiring "love." As Freud explains, employing a semantics of "love" that is as brilliant as it is problematic:

> "Thus the word 'to love' moves further and further into the sphere of the pure pleasure-relation of the ego to the object and finally becomes fixed to sexual objects in the narrower sense and to those which satisfy the needs of sublimated sexual instincts. The distinction between the ego-instincts and the sexual instincts which we have imposed upon our psychology is thus seen to be in conformity with the spirit of our language. The fact that we are not in the habit of saying of a single sexual instinct that it loves its object, but regards the relation of the ego to its sexual object as the most appropriate case in which to employ the word 'love'—this fact teaches us that the word can only begin to be applied in this relation after there has been a synthesis of all the component instincts of sexuality under the primacy of the genitals and in the service of the reproductive function."[84]

Freud's argumentation here is based on linguistic usage. We do not say, of course, that our drive loves something, but rather that he, she or I—as a person—love(s) this or that. The above passage sheds light upon this issue at the same time as it obscures it. Here Freud equates love and

---

82 Cf. the chapter on Nietzsche in this book.

83 Cf. the chapter on Adorno below.

84 Sigmund Freud: *Instincts and Their Vicissitudes* (note 47), p. 137f.

desire. For him, the semantic content of "I love you" is "I desire you." And the statement, "I love you", is only possible if the ego is suffused with the sexual drives; otherwise, it would be nonsensical to demand of the ego what goes against its interests, i.e. that it love something other than itself. With this equation, Freud is serving the psychoanalytic ethic, that permits no illusions about love. Yet the semantic argument is skewed, as it is precisely on the level of linguistic usage that love and desire are differentiated. Language itself here protests against its analyst.

What Freud fails to consider here, what can be read from linguistic usage that is indeed contrary to his hypothesis, is the fact that the *tension* between the ego drives and the sexual drives becomes fully apparent only with the advent of genital sexuality. And linguistic usage registers precisely this. What returns here, and what Freud does not want to allow, is the ancient distinction between love and desire. We experience exactly that difference which Freud here establishes and then strangely revokes. We indeed say that we strongly desire someone yet do not love them, or the reverse: that we love someone but are not desirous of them. Semantically, Freud wants to construct a unity at exactly the place where he has established a difference according to his own theory of drives. I love someone; for Freud, this means solely: I desire someone. The difference between the ego drives and the sexual drives, which erupts as a result of the development of both the ego and its sexuality, is lost precisely because of this. Freud ought to have formulated the exact opposite hypothesis, as linguistic usage and drive theory are both in agreement here: it is only *through* genital sexuality, which allows the split between ego and sexuality to become fully apparent, that it becomes reasonable to differentiate between desire and love. Only thus does love become conceivable as a result of sublimation. If I say, "*I* love someone", the accent must thus first fall on the "I" in order to illustrate the problem. If there is a division between the ego drives (the drives toward preservation) and the sexual drives (the potential surrender of the ego), then it makes absolutely no sense at all to say, "I love you." This would be a contradiction in itself, inasmuch as the ego is, by definition, that which shields itself from love as self-abandonment, that which subsists *by isolating itself*. The ego, as the agent of the self-preservative drive, can only say, "*I, I, I*"; or, broken down narcissistically: "I love *me*."

If we turn Freud's argument about the discrepancy between ego and sexuality established during puberty against his semantics, then the statement "I love you" can be meaningfully elucidated only as follows. When I say, "I love you", I am saying either (1) that I am breaking down the barrier between my ego drives and my sexual drives, i.e. that I am to a certain extent abandoning my ego: "I *love* you"; or (2) that my ego (following the proposition that my sexual drives have been unwittingly sublimated and thus become part of my ego drives) has directed its sublimated sexuality towards another person. "I love *you*" would then mean: I cathect you with sublimated sexuality; my desire for you is mediated. This would be Platonic love, according to the popular understanding of the term. Or I am saying, and this would once again be the ideal, (3) *"I love you"*, i.e. the opposition between the sexual and the ego drives has been overcome, the subject is no longer divided within itself. Everything that I want, my sexuality wants too: you, and you alone. This is the ecstatic experience that has been described exhaustively under the name of "great love". By taking seriously Freud's theory of drives, his semantic argument is flipped upside down. Of course we do not say that our drive loves an object. We express it differently: we say, "I desire this object", in order to place the accent on the drive. Yet when we say "I love you", we bring to light that complicated tripartite phenomenon that I have attempted to outline here.

Melancholia and Sublimation

The semantic knot in which Freud becomes tangled conceals the breakthrough in the theory of sublimation that was achieved with the recognition of the id. The success of this breakthrough was prepared by Freud's analysis of melancholia as identification, which led him to the insight that the shadow of the lost object of desire falls upon the ego, which only seemingly degrades itself. In effect, the ego reconstitutes the lost object internally and is thus faced with the task of surviving this risky identification:

> "[O]wing to a real slight or disappointment coming from this loved person, the object relationship was shattered. The result was not the normal one of a withdrawal of the libido from this object and a displacement of it on to a new one, but something different, for whose coming about various conditions seem to be necessary. The object-cathexis proved to have little power of resistance and was brought to an end. But the free libido was not displaced on to another object; it was withdrawn into the ego. There, however, it was not employed in any unspecificed way, but served to establish an *identification* of the ego with the abandoned object. Thus the shadow of the object fell upon the ego, and the latter could henceforth be judged by a special agency, as though it were an object, the forsaken object. In this way an object-loss was transformed into an ego-loss and the conflict between the ego and the loved person into a cleavage between the critical activity of the ego and the ego as altered by identification."[85]

85 Sigmund Freud: "Mourning and Melancholia," in: *The Standard Edition* (London: Hogarth, 1956–74), Vol. 14, p. 249.

The process of sublimation may now be conceived as a constructive perspective on identification, as the *antithesis of melancholia*: not an impoverishment, but an enrichment. What Freud articulates in 1923's *The Ego and the Id* is the notion that the process of identification should be generalized, while melancholia should not. Freud moves beyond melancholia and arrives at the insight "that the character of the ego is a precipitate of abandoned object-cathexes and that it contains the history of those object-choices."[86] According to this conception, melancholia would be a bleak exceptional case, in which what otherwise could have been an enrichment of the ego fails catastrophically, whether because the underwhelming object of desire turns out to be no good or because the ego has a delicate constitution; the latter point would later provide the spark for Melanie Klein's astute research. In the case of productive identification, too, the ego itself changes by relinquishing its objects, identifying itself with them, transforming object-libido into narcissistic libido—originally, in order to provide itself with a substitute in the form of the id. Through this identification, the ego effectively becomes richer, more complex; in common parlance: it gains experience.

Freud offers a science of the experience of consciousness. He offers, as mentioned above, an analytical revision of Hegel's *Phenomenology of Spirit*. Walter Kaufmann's suggestion that Nietzsche's discourse of sublimation could be mapped onto the trinity of Hegelian sublation—"a simultaneous preserving, canceling, and lifting up"[87]—turns out to be strikingly consistent with Freud's reconstruction of the history of object-choices: if not with the drive itself, then with the ego and its objects, which are lost (negated) and integrated (preserved), whereby the ego itself is further developed (attaining a higher level). Freud updates the structure of "sublation" in 1923 as follows:

> "From another point of view it may be said that this transformation of an erotic object-choice into an alteration of the ego is also a method by which the ego can obtain control over the id and deepen its relations with it—at the cost, it is true, of acquiescing to a large extent in the id's experiences. When the ego assumes the features of the object, it is forcing itself, so to speak, upon the id as a love-object and is trying to make good the id's loss by saying: 'Look, you can love me too—I am so like the object.' The transformation of object-libido into narcissistic libido which thus takes place obviously implies an abandonment of sexual aims, a desexualization—a kind of sublimation, therefore. Indeed, the question arises, and deserves careful consideration, whether this

86 Sigmund Freud: *The Ego and the Id* (note 16), p. 29.
87 Cf. Walter Kaufmann: *Nietzsche* (note 39), p. 236.

> is not the universal road to sublimation, whether all sublimation does not take place through the mediation of the ego, which begins by changing sexual object-libido into narcissistic libido and then, perhaps, goes on to give it another aim."[88]

It is this structure of experience that Adorno uncovers with his meticulous reading of Freud in his *Aesthetic Theory*. Hans-Georg Gadamer, too, elaborates the concept of experience starting from Hegel's *Phenomenology of Spirit*, though without discussing Freud and with a different slant from that of Adorno. Less relevant for a reading of Freud is Gadamer's suggestion, borrowed from Nietzsche, that all experience is "bad experience," the processing of a false assessment: "This [...]—'experience' in the genuine sense—is always negative."[89] Rather, Gadamer's hermeneutics is instructive because it deals extensively with the question, left open by Freud, of why it is the gaining of experience that opens the path to sublimation, even beyond sexual object-choice, which by means of being negative paves the way to general knowledge. Gadamer's phenomenology of experience cannot be reconstructed in detail here. We should, however, point to his elucidation of how experience, if it does not paralyze us with melancholia thanks to its quasi-traumatic nature, paves the way for science as research, thus potentially leading to the "desexualization" of which Freud writes. Experience, thought of not as melancholic but as negative, amends both knowledge *and* its object. However, when knowledge is amended, along with knowledge of oneself, the desire then arises for more experience, better knowledge and ultimately research. To understand an experience *as* experience means to want to have new experiences:

> "[E]xperience itself can never be science [in the ultimate Hegelian sense, E. G.]. Experience stands in an ineluctable opposition to knowledge and to the kind of instruction that follows from general theoretical or technical knowledge. The truth of experience always implies an orientation towards new experience. That is why a person who is called experienced has become so not only *through* experiences but is also open *to* new experiences. The consummation of his experience, the perfection that we called 'being experienced', does not consist in the fact that someone already knows everything and knows better than anyone else. Rather, the experienced person proves to be, on the contrary, someone

---

88 Sigmund Freud: *The Ego and the Id* (note 16), p. 30.

89 Hans-Georg Gadamer: *Truth and Method*, 2nd revised edition (trans. Joel Weinsheimer and Donald G. Marshall, New York: Continuum, 1989), p. 353.

> who is radically undogmatic; who, because of the many experiences he has had and the knowledge he has drawn from them, is particularly well equipped to have new experiences and to learn from them. The dialectic of experience has its proper fulfillment not in definitive knowledge but in the openness to experience that is made possible by experience itself."[90]

A discussion of the significance of Gadamer's readings of Freud would be the subject of its own book. In this instance, he successfully builds a connection between psychoanalytic drive theory and a logic of experience. Gadamer succeeds as well in explaining Freud's theory that the melancholic subject has become narcissistic in his object-choices. Narcissism as a syndrome is the incapacity for reflection, the inability to apply one's experiences to oneself. Frustration would mean the collapse of the narcissistic aggrandized self and thus must be avoided at all costs. Narcissus does not know experience, except as catastrophe. Ego and world remain poor, without experience.

Gadamer's transformation of individual experience into general sublimation is confirmed by Freud directly. In his essay on Leonardo, Freud articulates his ideal of sublimation, which, as in Gadamer, finds its culmination in not allowing any authority to challenge one's right to new, concrete experiences:

> "[Leonardo] dared to utter the bold assertion which contains within itself the justification for all independent research: '*He who appeals to authority when there is a difference of opinion works with his memory rather than with his reason*.' Thus he became the first modern natural scientist, and an abundance of discoveries and suggestive ideas rewarded his courage for being the first man since the time of the Greeks to probe the secrets of nature while relying solely on observation and his own judgment. But in teaching that authority should be looked down on and that imitation of the 'ancients' should be repudiated, and in constantly urging that the study of nature was the source of all truth, he was merely repeating—in the highest sublimation attainable by man—the one-sided point of view which had already forced itself on the little boy as he gazed in wonder at the world. If we translate scientific abstraction back again into concrete individual experience, we see that the 'ancients' and authority simply correspond to his father, and nature once more becomes the tender and kindly mother who nourished him."[91]

90 Ibid., p. 355.

91 Sigmund Freud: *Leonardo da Vinci and a Memory of His Childhood* (note 22), p. 122.

Freud's doctrine of the concrete experience of consciousness as the condition of the possibility of research, his own included, anticipates the theoretical content of Melanie Klein's great essays on the so-called depressive position. Klein develops Freud's discovery into a prehistory of ego formation, whereby actual sublimation as a productive experience is made subordinate to a "melancholia in *statu nascendi*"[92] that first must be successfully overcome. According to Klein, the tiny infant internalizes aspects of external objects (beginning with the breast that nourishes it) and then constructs an inner world of good and evil objects (its own aggressions and feelings of hate). During weaning, the infant passes through a quasi-psychotic phase, in which it must not only process the loss of the breast but also accomplish the transformation, essential in promoting ego formation, of object-aspects into whole objects:

> "the all important process of bringing together more closely the various aspects of objects (external, internal, 'good' and 'bad', loved and hated), and thus for hatred to become actually mitigated by love—which means a decrease of ambivalence."[93]

The emergence of a world of whole objects, both within and without, corresponds—if the depressive position has been successfully worked through—with a stable ego constituted by processed experiences. One's future ability to internalize productively lost objects, i.e. to sublimate, is made possible on the basis of an early childhood depression that has been well overcome. Kernberg accepts the relevance of this concept for borderline disorders, as well, whereby it becomes clear that pathological narcissism, as an exemplary borderline case, marks a major challenge for sublimation. Against the backdrop of Klein's elaboration of Freud, Kernberg notes:

> "The implication of all these observations is that [...] sublimation does not reflect simply an economic change in the direction and utilization of instinctual drive derivatives under the influence of ego and superego functions, but a direct outcome of the vicissitudes of internalized object relationships. The capacity for developing a total object relationship, for integrating loving and hateful aspects of the relationship with others and with one's own self, is a prerequisite for full development of sublimation.

92 Melanie Klein: "Mourning and its Relation to Manic-Depressive States" (1940), in: *Love, Guilt and Reparation and Other Works 1921–1945* (New York: Free Press, 1984), p. 345.

93 Ibid., p. 349, footnote.

> When borderline patients in some area of their life basically trust something good and valuable in their relationships with others (or with work, leisure, art, science or religion) this is of important, positive prognostic value."[94]

With this analysis of a form of identification that productively enriches the ego, the individual dimension of sublimation has thus been extensively described. In the light of this panorama—and with a view to the structure of experience, a distant echo of Hegelian philosophy—Loewald goes so far as to speak of "reconciliation":

> "Sublimation is a kind of reconciliation of the subject-object dichotomy—an atonement for that polarization (the word atone derives from a tone) and a narrowing of the gulf between object libido and narcissistic libido, between object world and self."[95]

Loewald is able to gain this perspective on reconciliation because he, unlike Freud, is of the opinion that "the term sublimation implies transformation of instincts."[96] As I have attempted to demonstrate, this view of sublimation makes understanding Freud impossible. In Freud, the drives themselves are not transformed, but rather their objects are changed. The richness and consistency of Freud's remarks, not to mention the phenomenon of an enduring discontent within civilization, become clear only when one recognizes that the aim of sublimation is substitution. Through the theory of the sexual drives' plasticity, the theory of the amalgamation of the sexual and ego drives, and finally through the doctrine of productive identification, it becomes both possible and plausible to conceive of sublimation as *work on the object of the drive*. To think of sublimation as a transformation of the drive itself would render incomprehensible Freud's lifelong concern with the fact of desublimation, of regression. Any study of the objective dimension of sublimation must take into account the fact that Freud energetically—and after the First World War with increasing poignancy—advocates maintaining subjective sublimations through social sanctions, whereby the concept of sublimation begins to waver between a "quasi-biological developmental process" and a compulsion. Because the object of a drive is its most variable element, regression always remains a possibility if the object should become lost or be flung from the drive like a cork from a champagne bottle. In the case of Schreber, Freud notes that even the mere consumption of alcohol may suffice to bring this delicate

---

94 Kernberg: *Borderline Conditions and Pathological Narcissism* (note 35), p. 134.
95 Hans W. Loewald: *Sublimation* (note 30), p. 20.
96 Ibid., p. 5.

building to the point of collapse: "We know that that source of pleasure removes inhibitions and undoes sublimations."[97]

Loewald is able to gain his perspective on reconciliation because he places his hopes in a transformation of the drive. He can keep reconciliation in view because he is able to point to Freud's Leonardo model, which appears to stand in contradiction to the danger of desublimation. Loewald writes:

> "As Freud said of Leonardo, passion is not absent in sublimation, and it is especially active and experienced in creative work, be it of a scientific, artistic, therapeutic or religious nature, or of any other kind. [...] In its most developed form in creative work it culminates in celebration. This 'manic' element of sublimation is not a denial, or not only that, but an affirmation of unity as well. Yet the organization of the ego itself, to the extent to which it is nonrepressive, is such celebration already."[98]

This overview of Freud's remarks on sublimation ought to demonstrate that the obscurity which shrouds this concept has two primary causes. First, gaining an understanding of the term becomes difficult if one understands sublimation as a manipulation of the drives. Secondly, the roots of the enduring obscurity of the theory of sublimation lie above all in the fact that Freud thinks of sublimation in elitist terms, yet uses the same term both for compulsion and for the ever-fragile ideal:

> "Mastering [the sexual instinct] by sublimation, by deflecting the sexual instinctual forces away from their sexual aim to higher cultural aims, can be achieved by a minority and then only intermittently."[99]

As the notion of the individual's reconciliation with himself and with society, sublimation is an ideal; as a technique for the upbringing of children and the adaptation of adults, this doctrine is repressive. Both sides are articulated by Freud, with the ideal coming to stand on the side of great individuals. Leonardo da Vinci appears as the embodiment of this. For society, on the other hand, Freud emphasizes the repressive moment, so that his argument boils down to an elitist compromise: for certain individuals, culminating in the figure of the

---

97 Sigmund Freud: *Psychoanalytic Notes on an Autobiographical Account of a Case of Paranoia (Dementia paranoides)* (note 60), p. 64.

98 Loewald: *Sublimation* (note 30), p. 21f.

99 Sigmund Freud: "'Civilized' Sexual Morality and Modern Nervousness" (note 52), p. 193.

artist-scientist—Leonardo, Goethe and Freud himself—it is possible to approach an ideal, while society remains under the spell of the leviathan: "Science is, after all, the most complete renunciation of the pleasure principle of which our mental activity is capable."[100]

In *Civilization and Its Discontents*, which contains a number of uncited quotations of Hobbes' *Leviathan*, Freud notes, in a sober rewriting of his passionate, psychoanalytic novel about Leonardo:

> "Another technique for fending off suffering is the employment of the displacements of libido which our mental apparatus permits and through which its function gains so much in flexibility. The task here is that of shifting the instinctual aims in such a way that they cannot come up against frustration from the external world. In this, sublimation of the instincts lends its assistance. One gains the most if one can sufficiently heighten the yield of pleasure from the sources of psychical and intellectual work. When that is so, fate can do little against one."[101]

Freud's Leviathan

The question of whether Freud's discoveries have a socially "emancipatory" effect, whether they ultimately have the potential to be "socially revolutionary", or whether psychoanalysis is in effect an oppressive surveillance technique that serves to help neurotic individuals adapt to a widely-accepted form of the reality principle and to existing social relationships—this question presumably is nearly as old as psychoanalysis itself and has frequently been resolved in such a way that the emancipatory potential of psychoanalysis has been played against the established therapy of doctors. We may come closer to answering this difficult question by elucidating the striking similarities maintained between Freud's hydraulic model of drives and the mechanistic worldview of Thomas Hobbes, from which likewise no path leads to a philosophy of history. We would do well to recall Freud's harsh statement on the notion of the perfection of humanity, articulated in *Beyond the Pleasure Principle*. Freud remarks:

> "It may be difficult, too, for many of us, to abandon the belief that there is an instinct towards perfection at work in human beings, which has brought them to their present high level of intellectual achievement and ethical sublimation and which may be expected to watch over their development into supermen. I have

---

100 Sigmund Freud: "A Special Type of Choice of Object Made by Men (Contributions to the Psychology of Love I)" (note 19), p. 165.

101 Sigmund Freud: *Civilization and Its Discontents* (note 25), p. 79.

> no faith, however, in the existence of any such internal instinct and I cannot see how this benevolent illusion is to be preserved. The present development of human beings requires, it seems to me, no different explanation from that of animals. What appears in a minority of human individuals as an untiring impulsion towards further perfection can easily be understood as a result of the instinctual repression upon which is based all that is most precious in human civilization. The repressed instinct never ceases to strive for complete satisfaction, which would consist in the repetition of a primary experience of satisfaction. No substitutive or reactive formations and no sublimations will suffice to remove the repressed instinct's persisting tension; and it is the difference in amount between the pleasure of satisfaction which is *demanded* and that which is actually *achieved* that provides the driving factor that will permit of no halting at any position attained, but, in the poet's words, *'ungebändigt immer vorwärts drängt'* ['presses ever forward unsubdued'; Mephistopheles in *Faust*, Part I, scene 4]. The backward path that leads to complete satisfaction is as a rule obstructed by the resistances which maintain the repressions. So there is no alternative but to advance in the direction in which growth is still free—though with no prospect of bringing the process to a conclusion or of being able to reach the goal."[102]

Once again, Freud strictly follows the hydraulic model of drives. Their constant urging cannot be suppressed, and in the cited passage Freud amends this concept at three important moments. First, it is only a few individuals who give themselves over to the drive towards ever-increasing perfection in the sense of an elitist concept of experience, though they, too, remain subject to the drives' urging. Second, any and all individual "valves" discovered through psychoanalysis are still insufficient against the ever-pressing force of the drives. Every substitution, every form of surrogate or sublimation, is suffered and is at best accepted with discomfort and discontent; accordingly, the frustrated desire can cast its lot with aggression in order to commit violence against its denials. The drive urges, and because the path towards regression is blocked by resistance "as a rule", the drive pushes "forward", not because a Hegelian spirit wants it to, but because it must. This illusion-nurturing "push forward", according to the passage above, is motivated *solely* by the vague notion that reaction formation, substitution, sublimation inhibition and deferral will eventually have a happy ending, that some day an unrestricted restitution of the pleasure principle, "full gratification"—complete regression—will be possible.

---

102 Sigmund Freud: *Beyond the Pleasure Principle* (note 20), p. 42.

There is no change in the drive itself, which "never gives up" striving towards immediate discharge. What appeared to some philosophers of history as a "drive towards perfection" was merely the eternal conflict between the pleasure principle and the reality principle. Humanity remains the same; to assume a substantial change from the cultural achievements impelled by the force of diverted drives would be illusionary. "Need [is] the mother of all inventions", as Hobbes writes in the *Leviathan*.[103] Yet it would be an error, according to Freud, to conclude from the abundance of human inventions that human urges themselves have been significantly refined. The exsolution of the drives, a reversion to the state of nature, as though civilization had never existed, is still possible at any time. Thus in his first essay on war in 1915, Freud writes:

> "The earlier mental state may not have manifested itself for years, but none the less it is so far present that it may at any time again become the mode of expression of the forces in the mind, and indeed the only one, as though all later developments had been annulled or undone. This extraordinary plasticity of mental developments is not unrestricted as regards direction; it may be described as a special capacity for involution—for regression—since it may well happen that a later and higher stage of development, once abandoned, cannot be reached again. But the primitive stages can always be re-established; the primitive mind is, in the fullest meaning of the word, imperishable."[104]

The fact of historical change in no way allows Freud, who saw no reason to differentiate between the history of human beings and that of animals, to draw an upward-pointing arrow of development through the ups and downs of history. Everything remains essentially the same; the conflict remains on *one* level. The pressing drive is the blind absolute, that which is imperishable "in the fullest meaning of the word", which psychoanalysis has inherited from religion and its secularization, the philosophy of history. Viewed analytically, religion is infantile, as the philosophy of history is. This is the source of Freud's open elitism, which prescribes sublimation as an ideal for the few and as a compulsion towards the renunciation of the drives for the rest, and which in this way casts the obscurity of sublimation emphasized at the start of this chapter into twilight:

---

103 Thomas Hobbes: *Leviathan* (Oxford, UK: Oxford University, 1998), p. 21.

104 Sigmund Freud: *Thoughts for the Times on War and Death*, in: *The Standard Edition* (London: Hogarth, 1956–74), Vol. 14, p. 285f.

> "It is just as impossible to do without control of the mass by a minority as it is to dispense with coercion in the work of civilization. For masses are lazy and unintelligent; they have no love for instinctual renunciation, and they are not to be convinced by argument of its inevitability; and the individuals composing them support one another in giving free rein to their indiscipline. It is only through the influence of individuals who can set an example and who masses recognize as their leaders that they can be induced to perform the work and undergo the renunciations on which the existence of civilization depends. All is well if these leaders are persons who possess superior insight into the necessities of life and who have risen to the height of mastering their own instinctual wishes."[105]

It is nothing new to point out the pessimism of Freud, who in *Beyond the Pleasure Principle* made no secret of the fact that "[w]e have unwittingly steered our course into the harbor of Schopenhauer's philosophy."[106] What is astonishing, however, is that neither a conceptual historian like Marquard, who created a detailed reconstruction of the prehistory of psychoanalysis, nor social philosophers such as Adorno, Horkheimer and Marcuse, ever placed at the center of their studies and reflections the affinity of Freud and Hobbes.[107]

As Herfried Münkler and others have shown, Hobbes' theoretical breakthrough in political philosophy consists in his substituting the ever-controversial question of "justice", which has been continually haunted by religious convictions that as such cannot be rationally accounted for, with his theory of sovereignty. In a radical move, the old, pre-modern opposition between "just" and "unjust", "good" and "evil", is replaced by the ahistorical opposition between the state of

105 Sigmund Freud: *The Future of an Illusion*, in: *The Standard Edition* (London: Hogarth, 1956–74), Vol. 21, p. 7f.

106 Sigmund Freud: *Beyond the Pleasure Principle* (note 20), p. 50.

107 It was the cultural historian and Freud expert Peter Gay who first became aware of the references to Hobbes in Freud, though he never studied this connection more closely. With reference to *Civilization and Its Discontents*, Gay writes: "Prostheses do not always work, and their malfunctioning may be disconcerting. But these failures fade before the unhappiness generated by the relationship of persons to one another: *homo homini lupus*—'man is as a wolf to other men.' Hence mankind must be tamed by institutions. Here Freud linked up with the tough-minded political thought of Thomas Hobbes. [...] The Freud of *Civilization and Its Discontents* was writing in the Hobbesian tradition: the momentous step into culture had come when the community took power, when individuals eschewed the right to take violence into their own hands." Peter Gay: *Freud: A Life For Our Time* (New York: Norton, 1988), p. 546.

nature and the political state.[108] This is the beginning of the modern theory of the political, consistently nominalistic and thus beyond good and evil. Both Nietzsche and Wittgenstein turn out to be administrators of the Hobbesian state:

> "For these words of good, evil and contemptible are ever used with relation to the person that useth them: there being nothing simply and absolutely so; nor any common rule of good and evil, to be taken from the nature of the objects themselves; but from the person of the man (where there is no commonwealth); or (in a commonwealth) from the person that representeth it; or from an arbitrator or judge, whom men disagreeing shall by consent set up, and make his sentence the rule thereof."[109]

If one considers the distinction between the state of nature and the political state developed by Hobbes in the first two parts of the *Leviathan* as a conceptual precursor to the difference between the pleasure principle and the reality principle introduced by Freud in his *Formulations on the Two Principles of Mental Functioning* from 1911, the affinity between Hobbes and Freud becomes clearer and may be detected in a variety of instances. Thus in the already-cited passage from Freud's essay on war, we see the recurrence of Hobbes' warning that it is always possible for man to revert to his natural state. In the *Leviathan*, Hobbes writes:

> "For as to the strength of the body, the weakest has strength enough to kill the strongest, either by secret machination, or by confederacy with others, that are in the same danger with himself. [...] Hereby it is manifest that during the time men live without a common power to keep them all in awe, they are in that condition which is called war; and such a war, as is of every man, against every man."[110]

In Freud's antireligious polemic *The Future of an Illusion*, we find the following reformulation of this fundamental insight:

> "[The strong murderer] would not enjoy his revenge or his robbery for long, but would have every prospect of soon being killed himself. Even if he protected himself against his single foes by extraordinary strength and caution, he would be bound to succumb

---

108 Cf. Herfried Münkler: *Thomas Hobbes*, 2. Revised edition. (Frankfurt am Main: Campus Verlag, 2001).

109 Hobbes: *Leviathan* (note 103), p. 35.

110 Ibid., pp. 82 and 84.

to a combination of weaker men. If a combination of this sort did not take place, the murdering would continue endlessly and the final outcome would be that men would exterminate one another."[111]

Apart from the additional remark about the total destruction of humanity, which surpasses even Hobbes' infinite *bellum omnium contra omnes* in its pessimism, this passage from Freud could almost be said to have been copied directly out of the *Leviathan*. In *Civilization and Its Discontents* as well, references to the *Leviathan* extend even into the details of Freud's vocabulary. Following are but a few examples that may serve as evidence in support of the hypothesis that Freud can indeed be read as a confirmation of Hobbes from the perspective of modern psychological expertise. In the *Leviathan*, for instance, Hobbes writes:

> "For though they obtain a victory by their unanimous endeavour against a foreign enemy; yet afterwards, when either they have no common enemy, or he that by one part is held for an enemy, is by another part held for a friend, they must needs by the difference of their interests dissolve, and fall again into a war amongst themselves."[112]

The corresponding passage in Freud, elegantly abbreviated, reads: "It is always possible to bind together a considerable number of people in love, so long as there are other people left over to receive the manifestations of their aggressiveness."[113]

In 1651, Hobbes writes that what is common to all men is

> "the want of curiosity to search natural causes; and their placing felicity, in the acquisition of the gross pleasures of the senses, and the things that most immediately conduce thereto."[114]

"Felicity is a continual progress of the desire, from one object to another; the attaining of the former, being still but the way to the latter."[115]

Nearly 300 years later, Freud notes:

> "They strive after happiness; they want to become happy and to remain so."[116]

---

111 Sigmund Freud: *The Future of an Illusion* (note 105), p. 40.
112 Hobbes: *Leviathan* (note 103), p. 112.
113 Sigmund Freud: *Civilization and Its Discontents* (note 25), p. 114.
114 Hobbes: *Leviathan* (note 103), p. 52.
115 Ibid., p. 65f.
116 Sigmund Freud: *Civilization and Its Discontents* (note 25), p. 76.

> "As we see, what decides the purpose of life is simply the program of the pleasure principle."[117]
>
> Hobbes writes of religion, to cite just two of his many variations on this theme:
>
> "[F]or the worship which naturally men exhibit to powers invisible, it can be no other, but such expressions of their reverence, as they would towards men."[118]
>
> "And therefore the first founders, and legislators of commonwealths among the Gentiles, whose ends were only to keep the people in obedience and peace, have in all places taken care; first to imprint in their minds a belief that those precepts which they gave concerning religion might not be thought to proceed from their own device, but from the dictates of some god, or other spirit; or else that they themselves were of a higher nature than mere mortals, that their laws might the more easily be received."[119]

The authority of 1930 laments: "[Religion] is so patently infantile, so foreign to reality, that to anyone with a friendly attitude to humanity it is painful to think that the great majority of mortals will never be able to rise above this view of life."[120] As early as 1927, in his treatise on *The Future of an Illusion*, Freud had nonetheless agreed with his imagined opponent that the various religious doctrines "make it possible to avoid the cleft between the uneducated masses and the philosophic thinker, and to preserve the common bond between them which is so important for the safeguarding of civilization."[121]

Hobbes articulates the agreement leading to the emergence of the state as follows:

> "*I authorize and give up my right of governing myself, to this man, or to this assembly of men, on this condition, that thou give up thy right to him, and authorize all his actions in like manner.* This done, the multitude so united in one person, is called a COMMONWEALTH, in Latin CIVITAS. This is the generation of that great LEVIATHAN, or rather (to speak more reverently) of that Mortal God."[122]

The psychologist of the bellicose twentieth century ennobles this idea

117 Ibid.

118 Hobbes: *Leviathan* (note 103), p. 74.

119 Ibid., p. 77.

120 Sigmund Freud: *Civilization and Its Discontents* (note 25), p. 74.

121 Sigmund Freud: *The Future of an Illusion* (note 105), p. 52.

122 Hobbes: *Leviathan* (note 103), p. 114.

by deeming it the founding act of cultural history: "This replacement of the power of the individual by the power of a community constitutes the decisive step of civilization."[123] He further notes:

> "The liberty of the individual is no gift of civilization. It was greatest before there was any civilization, though then, it is true, it had for the most part no value, since the individual was scarcely in a position to defend it."[124]

Hobbes writes that "[i]t may seem strange to some man, that has not well weighed these things; that nature should thus dissociate, and render men apt to invade, and destroy one another: and [yet] this inference, made from the passions, [is] confirmed by experience."[125] Freud alludes to this statement in a passage that would later be both crucial for and quoted by Jacques Lacan:

> "The element of truth behind all this, which people are so ready to disavow, is that men are not gentle creatures who want to be loved, and who at the most can defend themselves if they are attacked; they are, on the contrary, creatures among whose instinctual endowments is to be reckoned a powerful share of aggressiveness. As a result, their neighbor is for them not only a potential helper or sexual object, but also someone who tempts them to satisfy their aggressiveness on him, to exploit his capacity for work without compensation, to use him sexually without his consent, to seize his possessions, to humiliate him, to cause him pain, to torture and to kill him. *Homo homini lupus*."[126]

The proposition of man-as-wolf is commonly accepted as a quotation from the *Leviathan*, which includes such elegant aphorisms as the one describing the state of nature as a *bellum omnium contra omnes*, or the one on the law as determined by power, here meaning power over the army and police force: *auctoritas non veritas facit legem*. As the well-read Freud knew and remarked, however, the quote which defines man as a wolf to his fellow man comes not from Hobbes, who doesn't even use it, but from Plautus. Freud thus subtly, almost amusingly acknowledges his reading of the *Leviathan*, as he had already done with his pessimistic trumping of Hobbes' theory of eternal war. He does not quote Hobbes directly but instead, through

---

123 Sigmund Freud: *Civilization and Its Discontents* (note 25), p. 95.
124 Ibid.
125 Hobbes: *Leviathan* (note 103), p. 84.
126 Sigmund Freud: *Civilization and Its Discontents* (note 25), p. 111.

his allusion to Plautus, corrects a widespread error among the educated bourgeoisie. And through the wolf-man's analyst's allusion to the fact that "*Homo homini lupus*" does not originate in Hobbes' work, this bourgeoisie, whose existence in 1930 was being seriously threatened, was first confronted with the fact that the *Leviathan* had emerged at the center of psychoanalysis.

With this illustration of Sigmund Freud's reading of Hobbes, our elucidation of the doctrine of sublimation from the perspective of individual psychology is largely complete. The obscurities that plague this concept arose in part from Freud's changes to the psychical topography, in part from Freud's twofold usage of the term sublimation, which is never made explicit. One the one hand, sublimation is the name of an individual ideal that Freud sees embodied in figures such as Leonardo or Goethe; on the other hand, it designates the project of a suppression of the drives that Freud considers to be necessary for the safeguarding of civilization. It is thus urgent that we turn to the metacritiques of Freud, in order to determine whether affirmation of the authoritarian state—which within the framework of its powerful institutions nonetheless confers upon a certain small minority the privilege of gaining new experiences—necessarily follows from classical psychoanalysis.

An examination of Lacan's working through of the doctrine of sublimation is important for yet another reason. In breaking down Freud's fragmentary writings on sublimation in this chapter, we have omitted, among other things, a problem that, in the context of the study of aggression, would later become a central issue for Lacanian psychoanalysis. In his investigations of the problem of the sublimation of drives, Freud develops the theory of an entity that arises from the internalization of external compulsions to become the intrapsychic embodiment of sublimation: the superego. Freud had established the structure of sublimation on the basis of his theory of melancholia, via the concept of identification. The ego arises from a history of object-choices that have been successfully endured, yet there *also* emerges the agent of the death drive, the superego. The relationship of the ego to the id, which not only desires but also desires to destroy and to terminate, turns out to be no less dire:

> "Through its work of identification and sublimation [the ego] gives the death instincts in the id assistance in gaining control over the libido, but in so doing it runs the risk of becoming the object of the death instincts and of itself perishing."[127]

---

127 Sigmund Freud: *The Ego and the Id* (note 16), p. 56.

The problem at the root of all of Freud's efforts to conceptualize sublimation—i.e. the problem of defining and in fact strengthening the position of the ego between interiority and exteriority—returns at the theory's apex, the doctrine of productive identification. The ego is on the one hand crushed by the superego, while on the other hand it faces the threat of being destroyed the moment it offers itself to the id as an object of desire. The doctrine of sublimation thus offers no escape from life's adversities; rather, it confirms them. While sublimation announces itself as a *theoria* that transcends the world, that upon which it rests—namely the body, the bearer of the fragile ego—is under threat of perishing.

In his late work on *Moses and Monotheism*, Freud ultimately offers a deeply unsettling suggestion that illuminates why the problem of narcissism increasingly became the focus of his attention. Freud reconstructs the history of monotheism over the course of its development "into a religion of instinctual renunciations."[128] Independent of the already noted fact that Freud's theory of sublimation could well be rewritten proceeding from his historico-cultural speculations, which admittedly would require a background in theology, the treatise on Moses is, with respect to the problem of narcissism, also significant for the doctrine of sublimation considered from the perspective of the individual: Freud observes the phenomenon that human beings, through every instance of cultural progress from sensuality to intellectuality, feel not only restricted and thus discontented, but also "proud and uplifted by each such step in progress". In attempting to explain this surprising phenomenon, which is yet outpaced by the triumph of belief over intellectuality, Freud provides an answer that ultimately calls into question the ideal of individual sublimation itself. Freud poses the question – and leaves it unanswered, as this chapter does – of whether it is not "simply" narcissism that has been behind every advance in the restriction of the drives and thus in intellectuality:

> "Still later it happens that spirituality itself is overpowered by the altogether mysterious emotional phenomenon of belief. This is the famous *credo quia absurdum*, and whoever has compassed this regards it as the highest achievement. Perhaps what is common to all these psychological situations is something else. Perhaps man declares simply that the higher achievement is what is more difficult to attain, and his pride in it is only narcissism heightened by his consciousness of having overcome difficulty."[129]

128 Sigmund Freud: *Moses and Monotheism*, in: *The Standard Edition* (London: Hogarth, 1956–74), Vol. 23, p. 118.

129 Ibid., p. 151.

5. Walking the Dog: Creaturely Transcendence in Thomas Mann

Wer das Konzert zu End' gehört,
das war ein junger Hund,
und als der Hund nach Hause kam,
da war er nicht gesund.

(Echo in Dr. Faustus)[1]

The Pleasure of the Word

A book on sublimation without a chapter on Thomas Mann would be as unlikely as a Thomas Mann portrait without a cigarette or cigar. As is the case with the other authors discussed in this book, an entire monograph could be devoted solely to a consideration of Mann's perspective, drawn from Nietzsche's psychology and later from Schopenhauer's concept of asceticism, on "das Läben."[2] The sublimation, transformation and refinement of the drives on the one hand, along with the fastidious depiction of the disastrous consequences of *inhibition* on the other, remain the focus of his attention, thematically as well as poetologically, from *Buddenbrooks* through *The Black Swan*. Poignantly, Hermann Kurzke gave his biography of Mann the evocative subtitle *Life as a Work of Art*.[3]

One could with relative ease develop the hypothesis that Thomas Mann's work delivers a far-reaching phenomenology of sublimation and inhibition. His practice of thinking in productive antitheses based

1 Thomas Mann: *Doktor Faustus*, in: *Gesammelte Werke*, Bd. 5 (Frankfurt am Main: S. Fischer Verlag, 1990), p. 617.

2 Thomas Mann's ironic misspelling of *das Leben*: "life". Cf. the caption to Mann's well-known drawing depicting a hopeless drunk, reproduced in: *Thomas Mann. Ein Leben in Bildern* (Hg. Hans Wysling und Yvonne Schmidlin, Frankfurt am Main: Artemis & Winkler Verlag, 1997), p. 84.

3 Hermann Kurzke: *Thomas Mann: Life as a Work of Art. A Biography* (trans. Leslie Willson, Princeton: Princeton University Press, 2002).

on the opposition between life and spirit may be traced to the formative influence of Schiller, who described man as that "unfortunate creature halfway between beast and angel". Yet Thomas Mann documents over and over again the historical collapse of the syntheses Schiller formulated, whose ideal of an aesthetic education culminating in grace and play was in effect an early expression of the ideal of successful sublimation.[4] Tonio Kröger, partly overcoming his disgust with knowledge and alienation from life, is still able to find a compromise under the rubric of *Bürgerlichkeit* ("bourgeois existence") that was later devoured by the First World War. Yet as early as 1911, in the prophetic *Death in Venice*, spirit loses its grace; grace, its spirit.[5]

Beginning in the 1920s, Mann supplemented his early educational experiences with Schiller, Nietzsche, Wagner and Schopenhauer by studying Freud, and he was later able rightly to claim for himself the distinction of being one of the first to point out the straight line leading from Schopenhauer's will to Freud's assumption of unconscious drives.[6] Finally, we should recall that Mann's increasing identification with Goethe also involves a commitment, however couched in irony, to Goethe's poetics of a sublimational processing of experiences as outlined in his autobiography, *Poetry and Truth*. Indeed, Thomas Mann addressed this dimension directly in his own work. As we now know, the set of ideas out of which the novel *Lotte in Weimar* ultimately crystallized included the idea of working out in an epic context Goethe's last love for Ulrike von Levetzow.[7]

The past few decades have produced a great number of studies describing Thomas Mann's work as a sublimation of passion, particularly with respect to the author's homosexual tendencies.[8] Put briefly, this research demonstrates the theory that Mann himself succeeded where his protagonists so often horribly and fatally failed, namely in sublating his harrowing erotic experiences through his writing. From Thomas Buddenbrook to Gustav von Aschenbach to Adrian Leverkühn, Mann's body of work presents a series of autobiographically determined figures who lead their lives under the banner of asceticism or the prohibition of love and as a result must pay a terrible price. In his late novel about the German composer Leverkühn, Mann develops a

---

4 Cf. Eckart Goebel: *Charis und Charisma. Grazie und Gewalt von Winckelmann bis Heidegger* (Berlin: Kulturverlag Kadmos, 2006), pp. 35–56.

5 Cf. ibid., pp. 95–117 on Tadzio's grace and Aschenbach's dignity.

6 Cf. Thomas Mann: Schopenhauer (1938), in: *Essays of Three Decades* (trans. H. T. Lowe-Porter, New York: Knopf, 1965), pp. 372–410, here p. 408.

7 Cf. Werner Frizen: "Kommentar zu *Lotte in Weimar*," in: *Große kommentierte Frankfurter Ausgabe*, Bd. 9.2 (Frankfurt am Main: S. Fischer Verlag, 2003), p. 11f.

8 Cf. Karl Werner Böhm: *Zwischen Selbstzucht und Verlangen. Thomas Mann und das Stigma Homosexualität* (Würzburg: Verlag Königshausen & Neumann, 1991).

constellation polar to that of *Death in Venice*. The inhibited hero of *Dr. Faustus* at first survives, while those characters meet their deaths who approach him with love, e.g. the violinist Rudi Schwerdtfeger, modeled after Mann's childhood friend Paul Ehrenberg. From the perspective of biographical research, Mann's corpus appears to be an update of the Werther formula: Werther and Aschenbach die, while – or rather, *so that*—Goethe and Thomas Mann may successfully carry out their lives and their writing.

Yet there exists a significant difference between Goethe and Mann: in the case of the latter, not only is the sublimational processing of frustrated instinctual desires carried out *through* his work, it is also depicted and analyzed *in* his work. Sublimation *qua* the portrayal of sublimation: this is Thomas Mann's epic reflexity, that is, if one would even want to claim that Mann achieved sublimation through the process of writing. The uncovering of the homoerotic dimension in Mann's work opened up new terrain and is of sociopolitical significance. A biographically focused investigation of Thomas Mann's *poetics*, however, runs the risk of falling behind its modernity. Already in his early works, Mann had abandoned naïve writing, which may be conceived as the acting out of deferred instinctual energy; rather, he discovered through his exploration of naïve writing one of the major themes of his works, which as a result are on a par with psychoanalysis and even trump it artistically—in my view, as early as *Death in Venice*. Freud's 1908 lecture *On the Poet and His Relation to Daydreaming* may illuminate our view of Gustav von Aschenbach and his uptight classicism, but it does not approach the text in which he figures.

The famous scene involving Aschenbach and Tadzio on the beach offers a paradigmatic enactment of the orthodox doctrine of sublimation. The "primal drive-object" of having sexual contact with the young boy, for Aschenbach still a preconscious aim, is "deferred". Unlike Goethe, who in his *Roman Elegies*—likewise a beautiful refutation *avant la lettre* of Freud's doctrine, too narrow and restrictive for poetry, of sublimation—counts off poetic meter on the back of his naked beloved, Aschenbach's hand does not travel along Tadzio's body. Rather,

> "he longed to work in Tadzio's presence, to model his writing on the boy's physique, to let his style follow the lines of that body, which he saw as godlike, and bear its beauty to the realm of the intellect, as the eagle had once borne the Trojan shepherd to the ether. Never had he experienced the pleasure of the word to be sweeter, never had he known with such certitude that Eros is in the word than during those dangerously delightful hours when […] he formulated that little essay—a page and half of sublime prose […]. It is surely as well that the world knows only

> a beautiful work itself and not its origins, the conditions under which it comes into being, for if people had knowledge of the sources from which the artist derives his inspiration they would oftentimes be confused and alarmed and thus vitiate the effects the artist had achieved. How strange those hours were! How oddly enervating the effort! How curiously fruitful the intercourse of mind with body! When Aschenbach put away his work and quit the beach, he felt exhausted and, yes, spent, as if his conscience were reproaching him after a debauch."[9]

Thomas Mann here brings together the Platonic theory of sublimation and that of Nietzsche, blending the ancient doctrine of borrowing aesthetic forms from the concrete body with the modern psychology of intellectual work's sexual roots. At the same time, the passage is inscribed with the line along which Aschenbach's life will shatter. He conceives of himself as a second Zeus, seducing Ganymede once again. In terms of literary history, Aschenbach wishes to be the prince of poets, to be a new Goethe, author of the hymn "Ganymede". Yet Aschenbach leaps over a crucial rung of Plato's ladder, according to which the experience of sensuous love represents a necessary precondition for the free contemplation of the Platonic idea. The text discounts the ideology of classicism that it stages in apparent accord with Aschenbach. The novella-like aspect here, the unheard-of event, consists precisely in *exhibiting* the libidinal conditions of the work's genesis. What is worth communicating here is not the content of Aschenbach's page and a half of sublime prose (its subject is not even mentioned), but rather the unnerving intercourse between a spirit and a body, to wit: debauchery. Freud's model of sublimation is both staged and critically reflected upon here. Clearly, Thomas Mann's "sublimation" does not consist simply in writing about, of all people, Wagner[10]—who sowed the suspicion that Nietzsche was a pederast—in the face of a beautiful Polish boy; rather, it consists in depicting the process of sublimation, in marking it as unsuccessful. The fourth chapter of *Death in Venice*, which includes this scene of writing, famously ends with the eruption of unmediated desire, culminating in an "I love you!" and commencing Aschenbach's downfall. Aschenbach's sublimation founders because, in terms of the fictional hero's life, it is no sublimation but only a surrogate, an impenetrable narcissistic reflection. Sublimation is only the preparation of catastrophe. By staring at Tadzio both while he

---

9 Thomas Mann: *Death in Venice* (trans. Michael Henry Heim, New York: Ecco, 2004), p. 85f.

10 While in Venice, Thomas Mann wrote a short text on Richard Wagner.

writes and afterwards, Aschenbach brings the boy's narcisstic reaction on himself:

> "It was the smile of Narcissus bending over the water mirror, the deep, enchanted, protracted smile with which he stretched out his arms to the reflection of his own beauty, an ever so slightly contorted smile—contorted by the hopelessness of his endeavor to kiss the lovely lips of his shadow—and coquettish, inquisitive and mildly pained, beguiled and beguiling."[11]

That the pretty youth feels flattered by the adoration that serves to intensify his adolescent narcissism is psychologically to be expected and thus not particularly surprising. More interesting is the poet's misreading of Tadzio's smile, which leads to his outburst of passion. Aschenbach reads this narcissistic smile narcissistically, imagining it is directed at him, the new Zeus and prince of poets. The psychological lynchpin of the erotic pantomime acted out between Aschenbach and the young boy is Aschenbach's own narcissistic disorder, the escalation of which leads to the collapse of the *Praeceptor Germaniae*'s grandiose self-image. Three years before Freud officially introduced the concept of narcissism, *Death in Venice* had already established its mechanism. Tadzio, as Aschenbach's "object," exemplifies a narcissistic ideal formation in which the repressed is projected. And Freud had drawn a sharp distinction between this questionable formation of an ideal and sublimation, which may indeed be motivated by an ideal but which also must leave that ideal behind if it is to be truly successful.

Death in Venice already makes clear that, when it comes to the depiction of artists who pursue sublimation or who have given themselves over—whether consciously or compulsively—to asceticism, the pressing question of the extent to which producing art requires inhibiting the drives is up for debate. Thomas Mann is moreover clearly concerned with the identity of the true and therefore justified artist, as well as with the justification of his own life.[12] A direct comparison

---

11 Thomas Mann: *Death in Venice*, (note 9), p. 95.

12 "If it is Christian to perceive life, one's own life, as a liability, as a debt, as guilt, as the object of religious discomfort, as something that urgently requires atonement, salvation and justification, then those theologians who have taken the position that I am the archetype of an a-Christian author are not entirely right. For only rarely has the product of a life [...], from its beginning to its approaching end, sprung so entirely from precisely this anxious need for atonement, purification and justification as my own personal and so limited exemplary attempt to practise art." Thomas Mann: *Meine Zeit* (1950), in: *Gesammelte Werke*, Bd. 11 (Frankfurt am Main: S. Fischer Verlag. 1990), p. 302 (translation JCW). Thomas Mann probably had his American Christian

between *Lotte in Weimar* and *Dr Faustus* would demonstrate that these two later works also take as their theme a narcissistic artist who haunts his surroundings. In *Lotte in Weimar*, the road leads past the ranks of the narcissistically aggrieved—Goethe's discarded lovers, his untalented contemporaries, his disciples, his son—in order ultimately to reveal at the center of the novel's hall of mirrors a priapic and simultaneously androgynous Olympian who is deeply satisfied with himself. Similarly, *Dr Faustus* depicts how Leverkühn uses or destroys the people who surround him. Yet while Leverkühn ultimately descends into the hell of madness because his "big break" is the work of the devil, Goethe's life is justified in *Lotte*'s dreamlike closing chapter as that of a veritable genius. With a view to the theory of sublimation, the problem at the center of Mann's work could potentially be reformulated thus: there is something amiss about a work of art whose genesis requires a "bedeviled" sublimation understood as inhibition; art is dignified and metaphysically justified only when it claims a different victim, namely the artist's own life. The true artist does not sublimate in the sense of a purely narcissistic idealization but rather abandons himself. Expressed in psychoanalytic terms, Thomas Mann writes with a clear awareness of the difference between ideal formation and sublimation articulated by Freud. His work surveys the abyss that lies between these two forms of confronting desire. His careful depiction of artistic production represents a phenomenology of sublimation in the sense that narcissistic ideal formation is repudiated because, at its core, it has to do with the frustrations of the dilettante. In contrast, the true artist, exemplified by Goethe, succeeds in leaving behind his individual fate, in allowing permanent transformation to supersede addiction to individual fulfillment and thereby achieving "objectivity" of representation, the pathos of distance. According to Thomas Mann's poetics, art becomes dignified only when it is no longer the product of deferred narcissism but rather that of sublimation as the relinquishment of particularity. Only against this backdrop does it become clear why the parade of the narcissistically, bitterly aggrieved is depicted before Goethe himself enters the scene. Goethe appears to be narcissistic, but this is the case only *from the perspective* of the narcissistically aggrieved. The conclusion of *Lotte in Weimar* poignantly illustrates this connection.

Charlotte Kestner reproaches her childhood friend with disgust, alleging that Goethe's world reeks of "human sacrifices": "[I]t is almost like a battlefield and the kingdom of a wicked emperor." Hidden in

---

audience in mind during his lecture in Chicago. In my view, however, this self-characterization is an underappreciated key to understanding an author who both suffered the guilt of the living and attempted to sublate it through an eroticization of the world realized as the eroticization of language.

shadow, Goethe seizes upon the metaphor of sacrifice and turns it around:

> "They sacrificed to the gods, and in the end the sacrifice was God. You used a figure dear and familiar to me; long since, it took possession of my soul. I mean the parable of the moth and the fatal luring flame. Say, if you will, that I am the flame, and into me the poor moth flings itself. Yet in the chance and change of things I am the candle too, giving my body that the light may burn. And finally, I am the drunken butterfly that falls to the flame – figure of the eternal sacrifice, body transmuted into soul, and life to spirit. Dear soul, dear child, dear childlike old soul, I, first and last, am the sacrifice, and he that offers it. Once I burned you, ever I burn you, into spirit and light. Know that metamorphosis is the dearest and most inward of thy friends, his great hope, his deepest craving: the play of transformation, changing face, greybeard to youth, to youth the boy, yet ever the human countenance with traits of its proper stage, youth like a miracle shining out in age, age out of youth."[13]

This dark confession delivered in the dark of a carriage is a late revision of Tonio Kröger's lament that he is infinitely tired of depicting life without actually partaking in it. Thomas Mann's Goethe does partake in life, he suffers through it, *er badet das Lebendige aus*, to use Mann's phrase. In contrast to the typical person, however, it is not possible for the artist to construct a stable identity, nor would this be desirable, as it would amount to a regression into narrow-minded narcissism. There arises the paradox, difficult to grasp conceptually, of a full life that yet stands at a distance from life as a whole. Goethe's victims can name a perpetrator, namely Goethe, who paradoxically becomes the negative ego ideal—and it is precisely this ideal that stabilizes their lives of narcissistic grievance. Goethe himself, however, suffers everything and nothing. Under the rubric of sacrifice and metamorphosis, the end of *Lotte in Weimar* establishes a mystical conception of sublimation that anticipates Lacan, whose own vision of sublimation likewise oscillates between mysticism and analysis. Biographically speaking, the solution to the problem of protean identity consists in the dispersion of desire, in the realization of patterns. In the succession of Goethe's lovers, a stable idea is figured which is then articulated by the artwork. In all these lovers it is the image of the beloved that advances to the position of the "Thing"; for this reason, it is wrong to say that what Thomas

13 Thomas Mann: *The Beloved Returns: Lotte in Weimar* (trans. H. T. Lowe-Porter, New York: Knopf, 1940), p. 451.

Mann offers is a poetics of the sublimation of sexual frustrations. All that remains to an unstable identity subject to a constant metamorphosis between man and woman, old and young, is successful artistic expression, the "pleasure of the word" as the path to fulfillment. The objects are fleeting, Eros is enduring, and it is the word, the ever new *Wort-Laut*, that causes him to appear. Aschenbach's "mistake" lies in the fact that he does not recognize Tadzio for what he is, namely the announcement of the poet's pending metamorphosis, an ideal that encourages sublimation. Aschenbach confuses the messenger with the message. From the perspective of constant transformation—to which the young boy, who will inexorably grow old, is also subject—there "is" no Tadzio. Overflowing Eros is attained only through the attempt to eroticize the flood of language and thus prepare an eroticization of the world.

On the one hand, it is characteristic of Thomas Mann to depict the Freudian mechanism of sublimation ironically, in which tendency we might identify his contribution to the modern self-reflexivity of art. Against the backdrop of erotic mysticism, however, this illuminating attempt to make transparent the allegedly sexual substratum of supposed sublimations falls short. Thomas Mann's writing unfolds a pan-erotic worldview. The experience of *tat-tvam-asi* is mediated through the "pleasure of the word", which ascribes an erotic dimension to the world while at the same time extracting it from the world. There is a famous passage in *Buddenbrooks*, for example, that describes Hanno Buddenbrook's passionate piano-playing in such a way that Ludger Lütkehaus was inspired to reprint it in his anthology on the history of self-gratification.[14] As easy as it may be to read Hanno's experience of music as encoded masturbation at his mother's piano, this reading seems overly obvious. It is important to remember that Hanno actually is playing the piano. What Thomas Mann is up to in this and numerous other passages is an attempt to demonstrate that there lives on in cultural artifacts a transformed eroticism that under the circumstances is more fulfilling than the directly sexual—here, masturbatory—act.

Much of what Thomas Mann evokes vanished with the sexual revolution of the late twentieth century, which brought about not only a kind of liberation but also the loss of a certain allure which may be described as morbid, and not only in the style of *décadence*. The liberation of sexuality has impeded the erotic charging of the world, the disclosure of its ubiquitous eroticism. Mann's pan-erotic world is to the sexualized world of the twenty-first century what animism is to the worldview of modern science. Whereas in the age of sexual repression

14 Ludger Lütkehaus: *"O Wollust, o Hölle." Die Onanie. Stationen einer Inquisition* (Frankfurt am Main: Imago Psychosozial-Verlag, 1992), pp. 69–75.

eroticization revealed the magic of a world whose trees were populated by nymphs and whose flowers were actually transmuted youths such as Hyacinth or even Narcissus, to the modern mind, a flower is a flower and a piano a piano. In this context, society's ostracism of homosexuality generated a poetically productive asynchrony. The "love that dare not speak its name" remained dependent on camouflage and ambiguity until well into the twentieth century, thus preserving the secret of erotic experience.

Thomas Mann is a master at detecting the traces of Eros in the world beyond the body or in the depiction of that world's aspects, which also makes him a poet of the fetish, of, for example, the famously exposed underarm of a beautiful woman in *The Black Swan*, or of the exposed, muscular, masculine upper arm in the same novella. With the liberation of sexuality—or, to cite Foucault, with the coronation of "King Sex"—there arises a new order of things that complicates our access to Thomas Mann. Literature and its reception have lost a great reservoir of allusions, motifs and masks. Though Thomas Mann's world is slipping from our grasp, it nevertheless remains readable to each new generation, in whose sexual development the animistic world is renewed. It establishes itself again and again in the context of youth, which must discover its sexuality and ultimately bring the archaic eroticization of the world into sexual focus. Attempts to reduce Mann's efforts toward such an eroticization—which ultimately is nothing less than a form of puberty, made perpetual and fertile for literature—to the level of mere "inhibitedness" or its depiction thus seem to be in error.

In his book *Eros & Civilization*, which attempts to rehabilitate primary narcissism, again with recourse to Plato and Schiller, Herbert Marcuse achieved a theoretical analysis of the idea of Narcissus as a figure who sacrifices himself to Eros and thereby leaves "false" ideal formation behind him. Marcuse rethinks Freud's concept. Primary narcissism, he argues, is not only the atavistic delusion that the world revolves around me; rather, it consists essentially in the feeling that no separation exists between me and the world, in the inalienable experience of "being one": "Primary narcissism is more than autoeroticism; it engulfs the 'environment', integrating the narcissistic ego with the objective world."[15] Marcuse recalls the difference between a love that encompasses the whole world and a sexuality that is restricted to genitality and then to reproduction: "Eros signifies a quantitative and qualitative aggrandizement of sexuality. And the aggrandized concept seems to demand a correspondingly modified concept of sublimation."[16]

---

15 Herbert Marcuse: *Eros and Civilization* (New York: Vintage, 1962), p. 153.

16 Ibid., p. 187f.

To the extent that, beyond the fact that the genitals and the ego desire something, the subject also recognizes that the entirety of existence, being and thought can be eroticized so that all aspects of the world bring pleasure to him, and the biological drive becomes more than just the drive to procreate. According to Marcuse, it is formative of civilization. Under the influence of Plato's *Symposium*, he posits that there exists "an inherent trend in the libido itself towards 'cultural' expression, *without* external repressive modification."[17] Body and spirit, the separated substances, flow into each other, coming together as a creative force, as the self-sublimation of Eros:

> "The biological drive becomes a cultural drive. The pleasure principle reveals its own dialectic. The erotic aim of sustaining the entire body as subject-object of pleasure calls for the continual refinement of the organism, the intensification of its receptivity, the growth of its sensuousness."
>
> "The culture-building power of Eros is non-repressive sublimation: sexuality is neither deflected from nor blocked in its objective; rather, in attaining its objective, it transcends it to others, searching for fuller gratification."
>
> "If this is the case, then all sublimation would begin with the reactivation of narcissistic libido, which somehow overflows and extends to objects. The hypothesis all but revolutionizes the idea of sublimation: it hints at a non-repressive mode of sublimation which results from an extension rather than from a constraining deflection of the libido."[18]

The result of this revaluation of primary narcissism is a view of the world not only as a site of deficiency, danger and lethal hostility, but also as the entirety of that which brings us "holistic" joy if we open up all our organs and sensors: "Non-repressive order is essentially an order of *abundance*."[19] Thomas Mann's project of eroticizing language under the rubric of the true poet's justified narcissism is inscribed in Marcuse's project of overcoming that division for which, as discussed above, Mann rebuked Schopenhauer:

> "But suppose [Schopenhauer] had learned to reconcile [the unity of world and representation, E. G.] in his genius, in his creative life. Suppose he had understood that genius does not at all consist in sensuality put out of action and will unhinged, that art is not

17 Ibid., p. 190.
18 Ibid., p. 193, p. 193, p. 154.
19 Ibid., p. 177.

> mere objectivation of spirit, but the fruitful union and interpenetration of both spheres, immensely heightening to life and more fascinating than either can be by itself! [...] But in Schopenhauer genius intensified both spheres until they took refuge in the ascetic. To him, sex is of the Devil, a diabolic distraction from pure contemplation; knowledge is that denial of sex which says: 'If thine eye offend thee, pluck it out.' "[20]

Gottfried Benn at the Academy

On 29 January 1932—exactly one year before the Nazis seized power, the literature department at the Prussian Academy of Arts appointed six new members, among them the poet Gottfried Benn. The new members of the academy were assigned the task of giving a short presentation describing the character of their own work. On 5 April Benn delivered his inaugural address. It was met with a celebratory reception and on 14 May was published in the *Frankfurter Zeitung*, a highly visible forum. As Benn himself assures us, his speech to the academy in fact consists of "ten minutes of Belleallliancestraße-model schrapnel; those who hear it will be gobsmacked."[21]

The speech is striking not only as a thoroughly typical "document of the time" borne of "heroic nihilism", as it was advertised in the FZ,[22] but also and especially because Benn cites Thomas Mann as the source of his aggressively melancholic poetics, which seeks to counteract the continued "brainification" [*Verhirnung*] of man by positing a "deeper organic basis" for him and binding him "to an older and more dependable reality."[23] Benn hopes for renewed access to "a supraindividual sphere",[24] and by this he does not at all mean modern democratic society but rather a pre-cultural, "creaturely" stage. And the bourgeois individualist Thomas Mann, of all people, who in the crisis year of 1932 had campaigned publicly for social democracy,[25] is

---

20 Thomas Mann: "Schopenhauer" (1938), in: *Essays of Three Decades* (trans. H. T. Lowe-Porter, New York: Knopf, 1965), pp. 372–410, here p. 406.

21 "[Z]ehn Minuten Schrapnell Modell Belleallliancestraße, den Zuhörern bleibt die Spucke weg." So writes Benn in a letter, cited in: Gottfried Benn: *Sämtliche Werke*, Bd. 3 (Hg. Gerhard Schuster in Verbindung mit Ilse Benn, Stuttgart: Klett-Cotta-Verlag, 1987), p. 568. Translation JCW.

22 Cited in: ibid. p. 569. Translation JCW.

23 Gottfried Benn: "Akademie-Rede", in: *Sämtliche Werke* (note 21), p. 391. Translation JCW.

24 Ibid. Translation JCW.

25 Regarding the disturbance by Nazi hooligans of Thomas Mann's speech in defence of the Weimar Republic in Berlin's Beethoven Hall on 14 September 1930, cf. Martin Dehli: *Leben als Konflikt. Zur Biographie Alexander Mitscherlichs* (Göttingen: Wallstein Verlag, 2007), p. 40f.

supposed to have provided the slogan for Benn's desired regression to the "creaturely". Given the Nobel Prize winner's oft-ridiculed distinguished appearance, Benn's punch line is certainly witty, yet it loses its humorous aspect in light of the Weimar Republic's imminent demise. An engagement with Thomas Mann's supposed predilection for the "creaturely" is pressing also for purely political reasons. Benn writes:

> "One of the classic insights of the post-Nietzschean era comes from Thomas Mann and reads: 'Everything transcendental is creaturely, everything creaturely transcends' – an exceedingly strange expression, it must be said. To wit, if a transcendence still exists, it must be creaturely; if somewhere there still exists a mooring in the supraindividual, it can only be in the organic. This I that lives on loss, frigidity, isolation of the centers, without psychological continuity, without biography, without a history that is viewed as central—this I, if it wishes to ensure its existence, will, from a certain level of organization on, find no other reality remaining but its drives; they alone, the organic mass alone bears a transcendence, the transcendence of its earlier condition. Primitive peoples are once again raised to the level of later civilization. This mystic participation [...] pierces through the era of consciousness. [...] Thus the body, suddenly, is what is creative. What a turn of events: the body transcends the soul—what a paradox, directed against millennia."[26]

In the wake of Nietzsche's psychology, the idea that it is in fact the drives which define the horizon of our experience has become widespread. An apologia of regression, however, does not necessarily follow from the insight that our reason is rooted in the drives, especially considering that the pre-cultural world discloses itself in the first place only to the sentimental mind. Nonetheless, Benn puts his finger on a sore spot, namely the fact that after Nietzsche there no longer exists any transcendental authority on which to anchor a potential morality. Benn points out that the return of the archaic remains a possibility in modernity. As early as in his 1915 essay on war, Freud had also called attention to the fact that regression, radical desublimation is still possible. Thomas Mann, advocate for a self-sublimation of Eros, knows this. In keeping with Freud's warning, he depicts a regression to the creaturely stage in 1925's *The Magic Mountain*, though here as something horrifying. The sophisticated old-European society of the Berghof regresses; towards the end, in a chapter titled "The Great Petulance", the repugnant

---

26 Benn: "Akademie-Rede" (note 21), p. 391. Translation JCW.

anti-Semite Wiedemann[27] and the Jew Sonnenschein "run afoul of each other and [go] at it like savage beasts":

> "What a horrible, wretched sight they were. They scuffled like little boys, but with the desperation of grown men who have come to such a pass. They clawed faces, pinched noses, clutched throats, all the while punching away at one another, grappling, rolling about on the floor in terribly dead earnest; they spat, kicked, grabbed, trounced, whacked and frothed at the mouth. Clerks from the management office came running and with some difficulty separated the two bitten and scratched opponents. Drooling and bleeding, his face doltish with rage, Wiedemann stood there with his hair literally standing on end [...], while Herr Sonnenschein—with one eye turning black now and a bloody patch in the curly black hair that wreathed his head—was led away to the office, where he sat down, hid his face in his hands, and wept bitterly."[28]

This prophetic description would seem to argue against Benn's assumption that Mann favors a regression to the creaturely; the chapter on "The Great Petulance" leaves no doubt that, for Mann, such a regression leads to catastrophe. Benn's insinuation, however—and herein lies its perfidy—raises doubts about *The Magic Mountain*'s moral position, which, to call up a favorite concept of Mann's, appears to be mere "velleity", moralizing against one's better judgment. Gottfried Benn quotes accurately, namely from Thomas Mann's 1921 essay on Goethe and Tolstoy, in which Mann writes:

> "The creaturely in us transcends; and all transcendence is creaturely. The highly irritable sense-equipment of a man who is nature's familiar goes beyond the bounds of the actual senses and issues in the suprasensual, in natural mysticism."[29]

Lurking behind Benn's insinuation is the accusation that Mann had allied himself with the Weimar system and for this paid the price of

27 In marking Wiedemann's anti-Semitism as that which first lends any sort of "identity" to the failed petit bourgeois, Thomas Mann anticipates Jean-Paul Sartre's famous analysis of an anti-Semitic psyche in "The Childhood of a Leader".

28 Thomas Mann: *The Magic Mountain* (trans. John E. Woods, New York: Vintage, 1995), p. 675f.

29 Thomas Mann: "Goethe and Tolstoy" (1921), in: *Essays of Three Decades* (trans. H. T. Lowe-Porter, New York: Knopf, 1965), pp. 93–175, here: p. 153. Translation slightly altered, JCW.

having to renounce the level of knowledge he had attained. We may interpret Benn's invective as suggesting that Thomas Mann in this way squandered an opportunity for a fundamental renewal. The Weimar Republic followed the model of Western, democratic Enlightenment. For Benn, the looming failure of this "system" in 1932 proves that the path of the Enlightenment, "brainification", no longer has a future, so that it seems obvious to him—and not only to him—that a radically different way should be taken, by regressing to the "organic level", or, to be politically correct, by opting for community, the nation, the national, by opting for National Socialism, which promised the path to salvation in a renewal of Germany on the basis of *Blut und Boden*.

Against the backdrop of Nietzsche's concept of sublimation, it becomes clear that the Nietzscheans Benn and Mann react differently to the philosopher's genealogy of civilization. Benn reads in Nietzsche—and then in Thomas Mann—an invitation to wanton regression, while Mann as a novelist utilizes his knowledge of civilization's rootedness in the drives to then develop, in a second step, a concept of sublimation that encompasses both nature and man in equal measure.

Benn repeats Nietzsche's mistake of arguing that earlier history enjoys the privilege of truth compared to later history, thereby forgetting that the concept of a pre-cultural sphere of Being allegedly based in the supraindividual is itself a product of culture. Benn's phantasm of blissful regression is a by-product of cultural sublimation, or possibly its shadow, but it is not something that has always existed; or rather, this is only the case if one assumes a metaphysical perspective, jumping out of the civilization process like a god and claiming for oneself a divinatory ability that allows one to transport oneself into the alogical world of the *apeiron*. It is precisely this anticipation of joy in regression that the conservative avant-gardist art Benn demands is to engender. My reaction to Benn's insistence on holding Thomas Mann in 1932 to something he wrote in 1921 is to go back still further in history, namely to the crisis year 1919. That year, Thomas Mann published an astonishingly underrated text that, surprisingly enough, transforms creaturely transcendence directly into literature according to avant-garde poetics. In 1919, Thomas Mann brings up one of his dogs from the basement and takes him for a walk.

The Avant-Garde in Thomas Mann

Thomas Mann is a son of the great century, the nineteenth. His heroes are Goethe and Tolstoy, Dostoevsky within limits, Nietzsche in the light of recent history and Oscar Wilde only occasionally. Wanting to demonstrate Thomas Mann's avant-gardism thus seems to be from the start a rather hopeless endeavor. Even if one ought to admit that this self-reflective author of the *fin de siècle* clearly fulfills at least one of the criteria of the avant-garde outlined by Peter Bürger—namely, conscious command of the *idea* of artistic means "as artistic means"[30]—one would on the other hand hardly concede that he wanted to abolish the "institution of art", a further avant-garde criterion. An author whose narrative prose notoriously operates with the opposition between the bourgeois and the artist rather stabilizes the separation between everyday life and art that has become an institution, even if in an oft-envied variant which has been so successful that even today the bourgeois enjoy consuming those works in which the artist appears as a stray member of their class. One would thus hesitate to associate Thomas Mann with those avant-garde movements through which the "subsystem that is art enters the stage of self-criticism."[31] Ultimately, "[t]he avant-gardiste protest, whose aim it is to reintegrate art into the praxis of life"[32] appears to be utterly irreconcilable with Thomas Mann, the conservative author of *Reflections of an Unpolitical Man*, which lashed out against the civilized literati [*Zivilisationsliteraten*]; unless, that is, one considers the idea of a conservative revolution to be a variation of the avant-garde, or its black shadow.

This briefly sketched assessment seemingly proves true when, in 1953, the old Mann ridicules the avant-garde movement in the fine arts, not in secret but explicitly. The novella *The Black Swan*, set in the 1920s, ultimately extrapolates from Anna's lack of sexual opportunities as a result of a club foot her chosen path of "extreme intellectualism, which, disdaining mere imitation of nature, transfigured sensory content into the strictly cerebral, the abstractly symbolical, often into the cubistically mathematical."[33] Moreover, her dispute with her sensuous mother turns into a parody of the conversation about aesthetic theory between Adrian Leverkühn and the devil (from whom the intellectual Anna inherits both her club foot and her Adornian vocabulary):[34]

> "'Are those cones and circles against the grayish-yellow background meant to represent trees—and that peculiar spiraling line the wind? [...]'
>
> 'Anna, you don't mean to tell me that, with your talent, you can't paint something [...] to refresh the heart!'
>
> 'You misunderstand me, Mama! It's not a question of whether

30 Peter Bürger: *Theory of the Avant-Garde* (trans. Michael Shaw, Minneapolis: University of Minnesota, 1984), p. 18.

31 Ibid., p. 22.

32 Ibid.

33 Thomas Mann: *The Black Swan* (trans. Willard R. Trask, Berkeley: University of California, 1990), p. 8.

34 Cf. Thomas Mann: *Doctor Faustus* (trans. John E. Woods, New York: Knopf, 1997), p. 254ff.

> I can. Nobody can. The state of the times and of art no longer permits it.'
>
> 'So much the more regrettable for the times and art! No, forgive me, child, I did not mean to say quite that. If it is life and progress that make it impossible, there is no room for regret.' "[35]

That Rosalie von Thümmler, herself ultimately betrayed by life as well, is willing in this conversation to see the progress of life in abstraction—this is admittedly a courtesy that masks a cruelty: Anna cannot progress. Rather, as her mother also comes to think, she finds "in her work—which, if abstract and [...] deadening, was still an active handicraft—[...] [and] in her artist's smock comfort and compensation for much that she was forced to renounce."[36]

Despite this malicious view of the avant-garde, shared also by his own *Dr Faustus*, Thomas Mann can, as a poet of ironic copying and self-copying in an age that views the making of texts from texts as theoretically advanced, claim new interest for himself as a reluctant avant-gardist, and for his famous practice of playful plagiarism, which

> "makes no claim to reproduce reality, but rather simulates it playfully in its interaction with literature. Readers who have grown up with the citationism of postmodern modernity may be sensitized to this, perhaps more so than Thomas Mann's contemporary audience."[37]

The fact that Thomas Mann nonetheless has played no role in and has been almost aggressively ignored by the theoretical literary discourse of the past three decades (particularly in regard to deconstruction), can be only partly explained by his mockery of cubism, by his partial retraction of the claims made in *Dr Faustus*, or by the fact that the appointed custodians of his work sometimes watch over it with the severe dignity of narrow-mindedness, as Nursy watches over Snapper and Ellie.

Aside from his adherence to the idea of the independent work, which as such affirms the independence of the institution of art, the main reason for Mann's being so ignored presumably lies in the fact that he never exorcized the spirit of storytelling, not even in *Lotte in Weimar*, his homage to Joyce and Gide. In the end, at least, this—the spirit of storytelling—becomes his theme, in *The Holy Sinner*, his story of the great Pope Gregory, the Holy Father. The durable and captivating

---

35 Thomas Mann: *The Black Swan*, (note 33), p. 9f.

36 Ibid., p. 10.

37 Frizen: "Kommentar zu *Lotte in Weimar*" (note 7), p. 176. Translation JCW.

thread of storytelling is never cut, neither in his fictional nor in his essayistic works. The entertainingly and instructively unraveled "There was … and then …"[38] maintains its beguiling spell through any and all reflective digressions, allusions and subtle playing with time and myth, elevates the narrator to an authority, to the father who is hearkened to by his children, or at least by his dog, who recognizes "in the man of the house and head of the family his absolute master and overlord, protector of the hearth, […] the basis and value of his own existence."[39] Thomas Mann seduces us into regressing; the theory of the avant-garde, along with other schools of thought, holds this against him and in turn petulantly declares *him* to be backward. According to this conception, Robert Musil is spirit, Thomas Mann drive. We like reading and listening to Mann, we like it a lot, and this is a libidinal behavior, because we give ourselves over to him. In a letter, Sigmund Freud even admitted to Thomas Mann that he envied him.

The spell of storytelling is of an identificatory type; the reader comes along, at once gaining and losing himself. In *A Man and His Dog*, the spell of regression is grasped in the paradoxical concept of an "intoxication with one's own identity"—in fact, identity and intoxication have stood in opposition to each other at least since Nietzsche's writings on tragedy—and demonstrated in the exemplary form of Bauschan the dog. The *poeta doctus* closes the book that he has just been reading, reclining against his favorite tree, and speaks:

> "And what do I say to him? Mostly his own name, the two syllables which are of the utmost personal interest because they refer to himself and have an electric effect upon his whole being. I rouse and stimulate his sense of his own ego by impressing upon him—varying my tone and emphasis—that he *is* Bauschan and that Bauschan is his name. By continuing this for a while I can actually produce in him a state of ecstasy, a sort of intoxication with his own identity, so that he begins to whirl round on himself and send up loud exultant barks to heaven out of the weight of the dignity that lies on his chest" (244f.).

Confronted with a narrator who is closer to the old Fontane than the young Döblin, one can choose from at least three paths in grappling

38 Cf. Eberhard Lämmert: *Bauformen des Erzählens*, 7. Aufl. (Stuttgart: Metzler Verlag, 1980), p. 21.

39 Thomas Mann: *A Man and His Dog* (1919), in: *Death in Venice and Seven Other Stories* (trans. H. T. Lowe-Porter, New York: Vintage, 1936), pp. 217–91, here: p. 229. Citations for *A Man and His Dog* are henceforth indicated by page numbers in parentheses immediately following the quote.

with the question of Thomas Mann's contribution to the avant-garde. One could research his idiosyncratic reception of progressive authors, perhaps shedding light on his underexposed connection with André Gide, to whom he pays tribute by, among other things, imitating the gesture of Gide's *Diary of The Counterfeiters* in publishing his *Genesis of Doctor Faustus*. One could produce entire studies dedicated to examining Mann's "citationism" in detail. Werner Frizen's impressive commentary on the excessively citational novel *Lotte in Weimar* is a great example of such a study, even formally as commentary. Finally, one could turn the entire issue on its head or, as it were, grab it by the throat, by studying more precisely a work that may be any number of things but decidedly does not appear to be an avant-garde text. I shall pursue this third path here through a reading of a text that, published in 1919 at the end of the avant-garde decade, carries its anti-avant-gardism programmatically and provocatively in its title: *A Man and His Dog: An Idyll*.[40]

Erlebniskunst and Allegory

A Man and His Dog produces in its readers a kind of "double blind". Anyone who owns or has ever owned a dog is dazzled by the exceedingly precise description of Bauschan: everything here is simply right. If one possessed Thomas Mann's crystal-clear descriptive talent, which obviously is shaped by real affection, one would describe one's own dog exactly like this, from its strangely grooved and rose-colored palate to the mute rejoicing of its gestures of salutation, the way it writhes in ectsasy and shakes itself off on the lawn, its awkward and embarrassed behavior towards other dogs, the frenzy of the hunt.[41]

Excited by this precision, one may easily overlook the provocation that lies at its heart, namely the fact that this *Idyll* dates from 1919 and that an important episode is missing from this dog's (and not only the dog's) life: sexuality. Unless, that is, we include under this lemma the sheep that is smitten with Bauschan, which may dispose us towards

---

40 In a surprising way, *A Man and His Dog* is in any event a contribution to the avant-garde inasmuch as Thomas Mann, here actually stepping out into the praxis of life, donated his income from the idyll's first printing to the Association for the Protection of German Authors, so that his impoverished colleagues—typically authors with avant-garde leanings—could be given a hand financially.

41 This precision was part of Thomas Mann's program, as he remarks in a letter from 1918: "The issue is precisely this, that to make interesting what in and of itself is trivial, one must be very precise, and such precision requires space." Cited in: *Dichter über ihre Dichtungen*, Bd. 14/II. *Thomas Mann Teil II: 1918–1943* (Hg. Rudolf Hirsch und Werner Vortriede, München/Frankfurt am Main: Heimeran Verlag, 1979), p. 8. Translation JCW.

the idea that in this silly, bleating episode of pursuit Mann is quoting directly from Death in Venice: Aschenbach literally returns as a dumb sheep. Where he foolishly followed after Tadzio, "tied inexitricably to his passion's [...] strings,"[42] now a sheep plods along behind Bauschan, led on "by the string of its passion" (cf. 284, translation altered JCW). Acting as an intermediary between *Death in Venice* and *A Man and His Dog* is the name Bauschan, which may be "traced back to Bastian, that is, to Sebastian",[43] and thus to the "model for homosexuality"[44] invoked in Mann's Nobel prize acceptance speech, in honor of whom Oscar Wilde renamed himself Sebastian Melmoth upon his release from prison. When a Czech translation that incorporated both novellas was prepared in 1932, Thomas Mann noted in a letter their correlation *qua* contrast: "If need be, the volume could be called *Novellas of Life and Death*. That would draw the contrast that exists between *A Man and His Dog and Death in Venice*."[45]

One might also potentially overlook the rather astounding fact that Bauschan is perhaps the only creature aside from Heinrich, Katia, his children and—much later—Bruno Walter, with whom Thomas Mann happily exchanges the informal pronoun *du*. If one were to pick up *A Man and His Dog* immediately after reading *Dr Faustus*, the icy apotheosis of the formal *Sie*, one would cringe. In *Dr Faustus*, it is the devil who says *du*; here it is only a dog, and not even a "circus dog" or "trained clown" (239) but rather a friendly hunting dog. Bauschan can laugh, and it is precisely Thomas Mann's belief that there exist dogs who can laugh, a popular belief as old as it is wrong, which points to the autobiographical dimension of *Dr Faustus*. Conversely, the Faustian dimension of the dog story becomes clear in retrospect: from the acquisition of the pup in a witches' kitchen (p. 225f.); to the interruption of intellectual work; to the dog obliterating its owner's writing in his study and "damag[ing] the carpet with his claws" (231). Through the unusual designation of the dog's extremities—usually called paws—as "claws", the "carpet" in the study scene acquires a function in the text's symbolic network: it is the fabric of the poet that is torn apart by the dog's claws, just as in his day the Doctor Faustus of folk tales was torn apart by the claws of Satan. Thomas Mann can banish Bauschan from his study; Dr. Faustus cannot. Bauschan, a strong Mann despite his

42 Thomas Mann: *Death in Venice* (note 9), p. 134.

43 Hermann Wiegmann: *Die Erzählungen Thomas Manns. Interpretation und Materialien* (Bielefeld: Aisthesis Verlag, 1992), p. 202. Translation JCW.

44 Karl Werner Böhm: *Zwischen Selbstzucht und Verlangen. Thomas Mann und das Stigma Homosexualität* (Würzburg: Verlag Königshausen & Neumann, 1991), p. 339. Translation JCW.

45 *Dichter über ihre Dichtungen*, Bd. 14/II. *Thomas Mann* (note 41), p. 12. Translation JCW.

weak bladder and tendency toward occult hemorrhage, stands exactly in the middle between the "harmless, feeble-minded aristocrat" (224) of Thomas Mann's early work, the *décadent* standard poodle Percy, and the bewitched dog of *Faustus*. The intermediate position—between pastoral remoteness and realistic integration in the world—of the idyll, which marks the incision of the First World War, is repeated on the level of character. Adrian, too, has someone who is his friend and to whom he says *du*, a laughing dog that returns at the end of his life as a laughing "clown" [*Kaschperl*], bewitched by the devil [*Kesperl*]:

> "He had a friend, and so did I, in the farm's dog Suso—that indeed was his somewhat peculiar name—a rather scruffy spaniel, whose face broke into a wide grin when he was brought his meal, but who could prove more than a little dangerous to strangers."[46]

Those who have never owned a dog and take no further interest in these creatures, including so-called cat people, are likewise dazzled by the canine idyll. Among Thomas Mann's novellas, *A Man and His Dog* assumes the role that *Royal Highness* possesses among his novels: it becomes an occasion for self-assertion in the face of the narcissistic writer who, like every writer, imperiously demands that one read everything he has written. One ought to have read *The Magic Mountain* or *Death in Venice*, but *A Man and His Dog* or *Royal Highness*? That is something for scholars who wish to argue from the complete works, or a so-called "treat" for devotees, from whom one may quickly differentiate oneself by asking, "*A Man and His Dog*, I don't really have to read that, do I?"

As a result of this twofold dazzling, *A Man and His Dog* became one of Mann's most successful novellas in dog-loving Great Britain during his lifetime. In the realm of scholarship, however, it has managed only to eke out an existence as a largely overlooked wallflower, attended to—with one notable exception—only in overviews of Mann's complete works, and then only because they are overviews of the complete works; commentaries on the novella are weak.

From the airplane and the factory at its beginning to the modern veterinary clinic and the electric ferryman's bell at its end, *A Man and His Dog* is consistently and ostentatiously constructed around the historical concurrence of virgin landscapes and the industrial age. Thomas Mann's walks with Bauschan lead the pair through a ruined investment of modern capitalism, right through the middle of a failed construction project. Hans R. Vaget thus fails the text miserably when

46 Thomas Mann: *Doctor Faustus* (trans. John E. Woods, New York: Knopf, 1997), p. 27.

he claims that the idyll seems to "play out in a different historical era."[47] Hermann Wiegmann embraces the peculiarly prohibitive gesture of Thomas Mann scholarship when he reduces this highly coded text to the level of banality:

> "Mann's affectionately ironic remarks on canine psychology are play, affectionate play out of joy over his discoveries with Bauschan, an expression of sympathy for an estimable character – no more! No, the suggestion of deeper meanings in the Bauschan story is uncalled for."[48]

No more. The notable exception to the meager state of scholarship on *A Man and His Dog* is a 1965 essay by the author's son Michael Mann, which names in its title two characteristics of modernity: allegory and parody. The younger Mann bases his politicizing allegorical interpretation of the idyll on the topography outlined by the text, which positions Thomas Mann's house midway between the city on the left and nature on the right, and arrives at the following conclusion to his study, rich in subtle individual observations, of a poet caught between left and right:

> "The bourgeois man—and the narrator sees himself as one—has not yet found a connection to the world on his left; yet at the same time he has already taken leave of the dream landscape on his right. An idyll is ruined when it recognizes itself as an 'illusion' (as happens right at the beginning of this novella). This is the crucial insight after the *Reflections*."[49]

This reading, despite or perhaps because of its solid evidence, tends to offend dilletantes in light of the dog story's plasticity and liveliness. Hiding behind this dispute between allegorists and dog lovers is a conflict of opposing values described by Hans-Georg Gadamer in *Truth and Method*. Gadamer differentiates between the aesthetic of *Erlebniskunst* ("art of experience"), which simultaneously "comes *from* experience and is an expression of experience",[50] and an aesthetic according to which it is "the ingenious manipulation of fixed forms and modes of statement that makes something a work of art."[51] In rhetorical

47 Hans R. Vaget in: *Thomas-Mann-Handbuch* (Hg. Helmut Koopmann, Stuttgart: Kröner Verlag, 1990), p. 593. Translation JCW.

48 Wiegmann: *Die Erzählungen Thomas Manns* (note 43), p. 208. Translation JCW.

49 Michael Mann: "Allegorie und Parodie in Thomas Manns Idyll 'Herr und Hund,'" in: Monatshefte 57 (1965), p. 336–42, here: p. 341. Translation JCW.

50 Hans-Georg Gadamer: *Truth and Method* (trans. Joel Weinsheimer and Donald G. Marshall, New York: Continuum, 1989), p. 70.

51 Ibid., p. 71.

terms, these aesthetic options, perceived as a dichotomy since the age of Goethe, correspond to the opposition between symbol and allegory. Allegory assumes "not the kind of original metaphysical affinity that a symbol claims but rather a co-ordination created by convention and dogmatic agreement, which enables one to present in images something that is imageless."[52] In contrast, the symbol represents belonging to a community, initially as a form of identification. Against this social backdrop, the symbol in modernity acquires a "gnostic function"; it is "not an arbitrarily chosen or created sign, but presupposes a metaphysical connection between visible and invisible."[53]

Characteristic of *A Man and His Dog: An Idyll* is a tension that is generated already in its title: the text originates from the author's experiences with Bauschan and narrates these experiences. On the other hand, there is scarcely any literary genre that is more heavily coded or, to use Gadamer's words, more strictly characterized by "the ingenious manipulation of fixed [...] modes of statement" than the idyll, which demands a fixed series of elements that *A Man and His Dog* provides with astounding completeness.

The singular status of this 1919 novella is initially established through its fascinating mixture of concrete *Erlebniskunst* and artistic form. The insufficiency of scholarship on the text can be seen in the way this mixture has been dissolved in one direction or the other instead of being recognized as the avant-garde punch line of a well concealed idyll. The text demonstrates its singularity and radicality by taking both elements to their extremes *and* at the same time blending them together. *Erlebniskunst* is raised to the level of autobiography in order to substantiate it to the highest possible degree. On the other hand, the experience involved is presented in an extremely stylized form. Commentaries on the text have tended to emphasize only either its experiential character or its political allegory. Before the paradox of an extremely stylized *Erlebniskunst* can be discussed, then, we ought first to demonstrate the basics of this stylization, in order to get away from the "No more!" of a Thomas Mann scholarship that without reservation counts among the *novellas* a text whose protagonist is Thomas Mann himself—as far as I can tell, a singular case. One of Goethe's remarks about *Elective Affinities*, that "there is not a touch in it that he had not experienced, and at the same time not a touch just as he had experienced it",[54] applies as well to A Man and His Dog. It becomes apparent that Thomas Mann has elevated the landscape—itself already

52 Ibid., p. 74.

53 Ibid., p. 73.

54 Johann Wolfgang Goethe: *Conversations of Goethe with Johann Peter Eckermann* (trans. John Oxenford, ed. J. K. Moorhead, New York: Da Capo, 1998), p. 351.

sublimated nature – to an idyll, only then again to sublimate the idyll itself into a rewriting of Goethean texts.

Et in Arcadia Ego

The villa's façade faces west. Before it flows a river along a north-south axis. If you go left, towards the south, you will come to the tramway station that leads into the city. If you go right, towards the north, the avenue gives way after a five minute walk to a gravel path, and the hunting ground begins. It is divided into three zones. In the west, it is bordered by the riverbank, in the east by a hillside down which flows a small brook. Between river and hillside extends a forest marked by seemingly tropical vines, the actual hunting ground, about five hundred meters wide. It is crossed by a series of streets that never advanced beyond the first phase of their construction but instead were gradually reclaimed by nature, remnants of a failed investment on the part of the construction industry. To the north, the hunting ground is bordered by a village, at the entrance to which stands an inn, and in front of it a pond. Mann begins his description of the forest with an enumeration of its various tree and plant species, then tells of flushing a pair of lovers out of their nest. He then directs his view towards the eastern zone and the brook which lends it "its idyllic character as landscape" (253). There he finds grazing sheep, tended by a young girl in a red skirt, and a farm. Connected to the inn is an allotment of gardens "that looks rather like a cemetery": "Sometimes I have seen a man with his sleeves rolled up digging his few yards of vegetable plot—he looked as though he were digging his own grave" (255). After a description of the brook itself, Mann's gaze follows the inn that forms the landscape's northern border, before which the brook empties into a pond in which the village women wash their laundry. The gaze then turns, after a description of the forest in the center and the hillside to the east, towards a detailed depiction of the river and its bank to the west. The narrator, having completed his descriptive task, sits down on a bench before the ferryman's house, finding company in a magnificent rooster. The description of the hunting ground ends with a recollection of Venice and a description of the river during rain and flooding. The idyllic dog cannot comprehend the transformation of the beautiful river into raging waters and dumbfounded ponders the unleashing of raw nature with his tongue in the corner of his mouth, an expression that is

> "just what an ordinary simple-minded man might do in face of a surprising situation, very likely scratching his neck at the same time" (262).

This condescending bourgeois view of a man of lower station represented in the form of a dog is sociologically revealing, though not crucial in an idyllic context. Poetologically, the scene marks the idyll's end. Bauschan, as peasant and hunter, is part of the idyllic world in which raw nature is sublimated into landscape. At the moment menacing nature returns, Bauschan loses his position as an element of the landscape:

> "Enjoyment of nature and aesthetic devotion to nature thus presuppose both freedom and the rule of society. Where nature turns violent, breaking its shackles and sweeping away defenseless man, there prevails a dreadful horror that is blind. Freedom is existence above nature which has been subdued. Thus nature can exist as landscape only under the condition of the freedom that underlies modern society."[55]

Even Mann's attempt to convey as succinctly as possible his characterization of the landscape—all the way to its end in the raging river—and to avoid allusions, literary or otherwise, must inevitably take recourse to elements that belong to the genre of the idyll, which Renate Böschenstein notes "possesses no clearly established 'structure', but is rather more characterized by a series of motifs and stylistic features."[56] The use of such motifs generates a characteristic literary or artistic representation, a succinct description of which is provided by Goethe:

> "All artistically rich idyllic depictions thus acquire the highest grace, as the eternally recurring delightful states of life which are natural to man are simply and truly rendered, and freely sequestered from all those bothersome, impure and repulsive cloaks in which we find them draped on earth."[57]

A Man and His Dog follows this very tradition, from its enumeration of plant species, to the pair of lovers hidden in the nest of their *locus amoenus*, the sheep, peasants and washerwomen, to the motif of death in Arcadia, made famous by Erwin Panofsky, with the gardener who appears to dig his own grave: *Et in Arcadia Ego*.[58] Thomas Mann's success in fusing together experience and art can be seen in a further

55 Joachim Ritter: "Landschaft", in: *Subjektivität* (Frankfurt am Main: Suhrkamp, 1989), pp. 141–63, here: p. 162. Translation JCW.

56 Renate Böschenstein: *Idylle* (Stuttgart: Metzler Verlag, 1967), p. 2. Translation JCW.

57 Johann Wolfgang Goethe: "Wilhelm Tischbeins Idyllen (VI)", cited in: Böschenstein (note 56), p. 12. Translation JCW.

58 Erwin Panofsky: "Et in Arcadia Ego", in: *Meaning in the Visual Arts* (Chicago: University of Chicago Press, 1982), pp. 295–320.

detail. Panofsky demonstrated that the discovery of death in Arcadia precedes the discovery of night.[59] Already in the poetry of antiquity, it is night that threatens the idyll. Thus the country dog Bauschan, with his "simple soul", turns out to be incapable of taking walks at night: "[H]e was afraid of the bright lights in the darkness, he shied at every bush, at every human form" (236). Mann not only follows classical guidelines but, in locating his idyll in an *intermediary region*, also adheres to the *modern* bucolic tradition, which imagines Arcadia as one of the conditions of bourgeois society:

> "the possibility of a problematic intermediary region that in its pastoral character is far removed from the world, yet which is so afflicted by the marks of reality that it can only be the reflection of a Golden Age, that unattainable standard to which it always refers in mourning."[60]

Bernhard Buschendorf's description of the fragile Arcadia in Goethe's *Elective Affinities* may be applied as well to Thomas Mann's short idyll, which goes yet another step further within the modern bucolic tradition. The depiction of an Arcadian landscape in 1919 finds itself confronted with the industrial world:

> "Thus in our half-suburban, half-rural seclusion the voice of nature mingles with that of man, and over all lies the bright-eyed freshness of the new day." (220)

Given the care with which Mann inscribes himself into tradition here, this is not a departure from the idyll but rather an attempt to preserve this intermediate realm precisely by weaving in the world of modern industry, from the locomotive factory at the beginning to the ferryman's electric bell pull. The idyll of the twentieth century can be constructed only by including modernity, not by repressing it; nature as "landscape belongs [...] historically and objectively to the dividing structure of modern society, as the visible side of nature in the Ptolemaic age."[61] The following passage concerns the modern ferryman who fears losing his post and at the same time presents the poetics of the modern idyll *in nuce*:

---

59 Cf. ibid., p. 300.

60 Bernhard Buschendorf: *Goethes mythische Denkform. Zur Ikonographie der "Wahlverwandtschaften"* (Frankfurt am Main: Suhrkamp, 1986), p. 79. Translation JCW.

61 Joachim Ritter: "Landschaft" (note 55), p. 161. Translation JCW.

> "[T]he 'Boat ahoy!' is an age-old, picturesque cry, with a poetry not impaired by the fact that the business is done somewhat differently nowadays" (260).

During his stroll through the idyll in the middle of the industrial age, the novella's narrator reads the rusty street signs. Included are the names of a number of authors, yet Goethe, of all people, is missing; he is inscribed in this idyll differently. Thomas Mann is aware of the specific configuration that the idyll assumes in Goethe, a configuration that Renate Böschenstein describes as follows:

> "The peculiar and problematic concept of nature as encompassing even history would have to stand at the center of any interpretation of Goethe's idylls [...] The rift appears in *Tischbein's Idylls* as a component of the idyllic world itself, yet the contradiction between "natural" ways of life oriented towards archaic prototypes and the status of the modern world runs through a number of [Goethe's] works. The actual conflict between an idyllic conception of existence and a historical condition that calls it into question is first presented in *Hermann and Dorothea*."[62]

As we know, at the time that he was writing *A Man and His Dog*, Thomas Mann was also reading *Hermann and Dorothea*, in order to attune himself to the hexameter he would use in *Gesang vom Kindchen*, his other idyll published the same year. What is missing from Mann's canine idyll—most improbably, from an empirical perspective—is a Goethestraße. There must have been a Goethestraße among that unfinished network of streets. Thomas Mann, in the context of a process of reading described as painstaking, omits precisely this reality—the *written name* "Goethestraße"; as a result, this seemingly realistic text is transformed into a self-reflexive work of literary art. Goethe can appear on the level of linguistic representation only when his written name is eliminated from the empirical world. Through this significant defect or rather poetic correction of the empirical world—the deletion of the signifier "Goethestraße"—our attention is directed towards the question of Goethe's role in this idyll insofar as it is a text. It is reported how Thomas Mann painstakingly deciphers the rusted street signs. And the description of this act of deciphering demonstrates, via the omission of the signifier "Goethestraße", that we can begin to decipher the text in which this scene occurs: *A Man and His Dog*. Through the omission of Goethestraße, a look at Goethe becomes the via regia

62 Böschenstein: *Idylle* (note 56), p. 80f. Translation JCW.

towards a reading of the text, and admittedly it is amusing to see that Thomas Mann has already led his readers to Goethe by following the extravagant principles of early Romantic poetry. This subtlety, driven to its extreme in a web of allusions, becomes discernable when one realizes that Goethestraβe is omitted because there *ought* to have been a Claude Lorrain-Straβe:

> "[This is] foliage such as Claude Lorrain used to paint, three centuries ago. Such as he used to paint, did I say? But surely he painted *this*. He was here, he knew this scene, he studied it. If my building-society man had not confined himself to the literary field, one of these rusty street signs might have borne the name of Claude" (252).

The joke of this passage can only be guessed if one recalls the important role Claude Lorrain played in the life not of Thomas Mann but of Goethe, for as Buschendorf has demonstrated, it was Lorrain who provided the blueprints for the landscapes in Goethe's dark idyll *Elective Affinities*. There is no Goethestraβe in *A Man and His Dog* because Goethe's late work and iconography are already installed in the idyll with breathtaking finesse. This work begins with a mere detail. In recalling certain scenes of Claude Lorrain, Goethe remarked to Eckermann that he took great pleasure in the depiction of, among other things,

> "a marshy spot with standing pools, which in the powerful summer heat gives a pleasant impression of coolness—there was always complete unity in the picture; nowhere anything that did not belong to its element."[63]

For his part, Thomas Mann in 1919, describing his wanderings with Bauschan through the Lorrainian landscape, reports on

> "certain low, retired, and rushy spots, relics of the primeval condition of the region, whose damp coolness defies the summer heat and makes them a grateful place wherein to draw a few long breaths" (246).

---

63 Johann Wolfgang Goethe: *Conversations of Goethe with Johann Peter Eckermann*, (note 54), p. 321. I cite here only a few examples of Thomas Mann's rewritings. Those interested in further details should read the entire conversation of 10 April 1829, study the works of Goethe mentioned below and take a look at the writings of Schiller or Johann Joachim Winckelmann. A number of the epithets applied to Bauschan, for example, are taken from Winckelmann's essays.

In his 1925 study of *Elective Affinities*, Mann cites Zelter's famous characterization of the style of Goethe's novels:

> "which is constituted like the clear element, whose nimble inhabitants swim through each other, gleaming or darkening as they dart up and down, never going astray nor becoming lost."[64]

Bauschan and his friend are offered a similar image. The element, the water as well as the style of this modern prose idyll's author, is still clear in 1919, even if it includes debris of the industrial age in addition to the little fish:

> "[The brook] is shallow and candid and makes no bones of betraying that there are old tins and the mouldering remains of a laced shoe in its bed. But it is deep enough to serve as a home for pretty, lively, silver-grey little fish, which dart away in zigzags at our approach" (257).

Alongside such rewritings there appears that famous motif that sublimely opens Goethe's *Novella*, which likewise deals with the relationship between human beings and wild creatures, though Goethe works with a great lion and not with a small hunting dog as his ironic heir does nearly one hundred years later:

> "Here, as you advance along the narrow path through the outer ring to the fortress proper, one of the most massive rocks of the whole mountain rises before you. A tower has been built upon it, yet no one would be able to say where nature ends and art and craftsmanship begin. […] It is a wilderness unlike any other, a unique place, where you can see traces of the long-vanished power of man in tenacious struggle with the ever-living, ever-working power of nature."[65]

Goethe's singular setting returns in Thomas Mann's idyll, and it becomes clear why a Goethestraβe is allowed to go missing:

> "[T]he wood does not remain passive. It does not let the streets stop as they were made, through decade after decade, until at last people come and settle on them. It takes every step to close them

64 Thomas Mann: "Zu Goethe's 'Wahlverwandtschaften'", in: *Gesammelte Werke*, Bd. 9 (Frankfurt am Main: S. Fischer Verlag, 1990), p. 176. Translation JCW.

65 Goethe: *Novella* (trans. Victor Lange), in: *The Sorrows of Young Werther--Elective Affinities – Novella* (New York: Suhrkamp, 1988), p. 266f.

> again; for what grows here does not mind gravel, it flourishes in it. [...] [T]he streets with the poetic names are going back to the wilderness" (252).

It is this description of civilization reclaimed by nature and ultimately rendered unrecognizable that culminates in the above-cited apotheosis of Claude Lorrain.

It isn't possible to pursue here in detail every instance of engagement with literary tradition in *A Man and His Dog*. We must also forego consideration of a scarcely less significant aspect of the text: that here Thomas Mann stages a review of his own work through 1919, in particular *Tonio Kröger* and *Death in Venice*.[66] Before we can move on to an examination of *A Man and His Dog*'s avant-garde poetics, we must first at least point out a reference to *Elective Affinities* in which Mann's practice of paraphrased citation reaches the pinnacle of craftsmanship in its correlation of the sublimation of nature with the sublime.

In *Elective Affinities*, a new house is built atop a mountain. In the fateful thirteenth chapter of the novel's second book, Eduard and the Major see "in the distance the new house on the hill [and catch] sight of its red tiles shining in the sun."[67] Eduard is seized by an irresistible desire to precipitate a violent change in the relationships among the novel's four protagonists. Ottilie, too, finds herself magically drawn to the "mountain house" and boards a rowboat with Charlotte's uncanny child in order to set out across the lake, as she thinks she sees "Charlotte's white dress on the porch."[68] The child drowns, and the novel floats towards its tragic end like the boat towards the plane trees.

Thomas Mann's idyll also features bright red bricks that remain visible after the demolition of a mountain house. In the light of the close connections to Goethe's later works that *A Man and His Dog* maintains, it is tempting to see in the following scene an expression of reverence towards the author of *Elective Affinities*, which Thomas Mann called the greatest German novel. The brook in *A Man and His Dog* establishes the idyllic character of the landscape. At one point, however, it turns red as it runs along the ever-changing hillside:

---

66 It would moreover be possible to discern preludes to Mann's later works in this text, from the sheep of the *Joseph* novels, to the veterinary clinic to which the bleeding and anemic Bauschan is admitted that prefigures the Berghof of *The Magic Mountain*, to the dog in *Dr Faustus*, etc.

67 Goethe: *Elective Affinities* (Trans. Judith Ryan), in: *The Sorrows of Young Werther – Elective Affinities – Novella* (note 65), p. 237.

68 Ibid., p. 239.

> "The first part is shadowed and gloomy and set with pines. Then comes a sand-pit which reflects the warm rays of the sun; then a gravel-pit, then a cataract of bricks, as though a house had been demolished up above and the rubble simply flung down the hill, damming the brook at the bottom. But the brook rises until its waters flow over the obstacle and go on, reddened with brick-dust and dyeing the grass along its edge, to flow all the more blithely and pellucidly further on, with the sun making diamonds sparkle on its surface" (255f.).

Walter Benjamin, in his 1921 study of *Elective Affinities*, called attention to the fact that the landscape in Goethe's novel "nowhere appears in sunlight".[69] Benjamin also dedicates a haunting passage to the ominous nature of the still waters:

> "Water as the chaotic element of life does not threaten here in desolate waves that sink a man; rather, it threatens in the enigmatic calm that lets him go to his ruin. To the extent that fate governs, the lovers go to their ruin. Where they spurn the blessing of firm ground, they succumb to the unfathomable, which in stagnant water appears as something primeval."[70]

With his description of the river in winter, wild and swollen, Thomas Mann underscores the threat to the idyll presented by the return of raw nature. Yet as Benjamin's observations reveal, nature's character is here conceived as a contrast to the blackness of *Elective Affinities*. The "dead plane" of the sinister lake's "mirroring surface" is replaced in *A Man and His Dog* by the cool, babbling brook that washes away the blood-red remains of the mountain house. The water that now once again flows freely glistens in the sunlight; the "pallid light of a solar eclipse",[71] which Benjamin claims pervades the dusky world of *Elective Affinities*, gives way to the brightness of day.

The Water's Course

The above section on the intermediate realm of the modern idyll, which highlights only a few of its elements, ought to illustrate that *A Man and His Dog* possesses a complexity comparable to that of *Death in Venice*, a

---

69 Walter Benjamin: "Goethe's Elective Affinities" (1925), in: *Selected Writings, Volume 1: 1913–1926* (ed. Marcus Bullock and Michael W. Jennings, Cambridge, MA: Belknap Press of Harvard University Press, 2004), p. 303.

70 Ibid.

71 Ibid., p. 305.

complexity deserving of its own monograph, the tasks of which can be outlined here only briefly and by way of conclusion.

First, the accurate depiction of "what is in and of itself trivial" (fn. 40) represents the hard work of reclaiming poetic language in the wake of the First World War, which was also a war of pompous and evil words in which Thomas Mann had taken part. By 1919, the formerly ultranationalistic author no longer cares for the thunder:

> "I could say that he was thunderstruck. But I do not like them, I do not want to use them. The large words are worn out when the great occasion comes they do not describe it. Better use the small ones and put into them every ounce of their weight" (287).

The text offers one of the most precise depictions of canine psychology in literature; the work that goes into Mann's presentation of the animal turns out to be work towards a renewal of poetic language, which having been renewed would at the same time allow for a deeper understanding of him who employs it, of man. This view of the animal, along with the effort to describe it exactly, will, it is hoped, set free once again what has been lost: the literal meaning of words in their original power of naming:

> "Animals are more primitive and less inhibited in giving expression to their mental state—there is a sense in which one might say they are more human: descriptive phrases which to us have become mere metaphor still fit them literally, we get a fresh and diverting sense of their meaning when we see it embodied before our eyes. Bauschan, as we say, 'hung his head'; that is, he did it literally and visibly, till he looked like a worn-out cab-horse, with sores on its legs, standing at the cab-rank, its skin twitching and its poor fly-infested nose weighed down towards the pavement" (276).

This attempt to revive poetic language is accomplished formally in the constitution of the modern idyll under the conditions of the industrial age. Both dimensions need to be examined in detail, as does the allegorical reading begun by Michael Mann. The positioning of the bourgeois subject between right and left in the idyll is developed with great care by, among other things, establishing a relationship between sociological categories and the characterization of natural phenomena, especially living creatures. The story achieves its great humor through this process, which describes Percy on the one hand as a proud but mad aristocrat and Bauschan on the other as a basically healthy but self-pitying peasant. Specifically, what needs to be demonstrated is why the bourgeoisie in *A Man and His Dog* ultimately fares so poorly. I am referring here to the swaying bourgeois ducks in their provocative complacency, satiety and disdainful comfort (cf. 282). Impressed by neither the bourgeois author nor his idyllic hound, one duck ultimately falls victim to poetry become militant, to a hunter who looks like he originated in an opera yet who carries a real weapon. In the uncanny figure of the poacher, we can see an already ironic depiction of the conservative revolutionary or the *Freikorps* volunteer who shoots down the bourgeois subject who in 1919 no longer feels certain about the future of society:

> "The duck—no doubt one of those that had rocked in such pert security on the water in front of our noses—went driving like a wreck on the water, you could not tell which was head and which tail" (288).

A Man and His Dog, as an idyll, is modern; the description of the landscape documents an awareness of the rupture. Yet in what does this text's avant-garde moment consist?

Mann's work generally follows a clear tripartite structure that corresponds to the conventions of nineteenth-century realism. Alongside the actual autobiographical works, such as *On Myself*, there stand on the one hand the literary texts, with their autobiographical dimensions that are veiled to varying degress but never fully burst forth, and on the other the essays, in which Thomas Mann himself speaks, but about the works of other authors. *A Man and His Dog* marks an exception; it does not conform to this tripartite pattern. The text is counted among the novellas, though the author himself is its protagonist. As amazing as it may seem, then, *A Man and His Dog* is a text with avant-garde characteristics that, for a brief moment which may be called a state of exception, leaves the nineteenth century behind. It breaks down aesthetic boundaries while confusing those of genre. Its hero is named neither Hanno Buddenbrook nor Tonio Kröger, nor Gustav von Aschenbach. Like Phorkyas-Mephistopheles at the end of the Helena idyll in *Faust II*, Thomas Mann takes off his mask and appears as himself, accompanied by a dog that likewise actually existed. This move away from fiction occurs in a world that is empirically present; there is no element of the text that could not conceivably be found in the outside world. On the other hand, the elements of the world of objects that appear in *A Man and His Dog* are thus doubled: they actually exist yet are also highly stylized. With this step out of fiction and into real life, the world in its state of exception itself becomes a work of art, even if only in the magic garden of the idyll. *A Man and His Dog* is an articulation of crisis that documents the collapse of the realistic *Erlebniskunst* of the nineteenth century by pushing it towards its formal extreme: the autobiography. The author himself steps out before the curtain, forthright and exposed. At the same time, the text expresses the utopian hope that this act of stepping out could lead to a poeticization of reality, to a reality in which everything is itself and yet means something else. To read this text purely as *Erlebniskunst* is to miss the point. The text's specificity is likewise lost if one views it only as allegory and idyll. Nonetheless, this fragile poetic, political and topographical intermediary region exists only for an instant, in that exceptional moment between dreaming and daytime:

> "You look confidently forward to the day, yet pleasantly hesitate to begin it, being master as you are of this little untroubled span of time between dreaming and daytime, which is your good reward for good behavior. You indulge in the illusion that your life is habitually steady, simple, concentrated and contemplative, that you belong entirely to yourself—and this illusion makes you quite happy" (221).

Shortly after this moment of happy illusion in the magic garden, Thomas Mann takes it all back again, step by step. What had been synthesized for an instant in *A Man and His Dog* soon breaks apart into the familiar forms of the nineteenth century, as demonstrated by those exemplary texts that Mann composed shortly after completing his idyll. *A Man and His Dog* is followed by Mann's studies of *Goethe and Tolstoy* (1921) and *Elective Affinities* (1925), which attempt to clarify conceptually the relationship between man and nature. In terms of narration, the idylls of the dog and of the child are followed by a withdrawal into established realistic prose. The bastard Bauschan is followed in *Disorder and Early Sorrow* (1925) by the young Bolshevik and underdog Xaver, who, like the dog before him, refuses to jump through hoops. For his part, Thomas Mann recedes into fiction, once again taking up his mask to appear as Professor Cornelius, who takes his walks at night alone, dog-less. The child who had been celebrated in hexameter returns in the form of Ellie, and the troubling subtexts of Cornelius' joy at her birth are illuminated, analytically and with an eye towards the abandoned idylls, on the banks of a river immersed in darkness:

> "For the temper of timelessness, the temper of eternity—thus the scholar communes with himself when he takes his walk by the river before supper—that temper broods over the past; and it is a temper much better suited to the nervous system of a history professor than are the excesses of the present. The past is immortalized; that is to say, it is dead; and death is the root of

all godliness and all abiding significance. Dr Cornelius, walking alone in the dark, has a profound insight into this truth. It is this conservative instinct of his, his sense of the eternal, that has found in his love for his little daughter a way to save itself from the wounding inflicted by the times. For father love, and a little child on its mother's breast—are not these timeless, and thus very, very holy and beautiful? Yet Cornelius, pondering there in the dark, descries something not perfectly right and good in his love. [...] There is something ulterior about it, in the nature of it; that something is hostility, hostility against the history of today, which is still in the making and thus not history at all, on behalf of the genuine history that has already happened—that is to say, death."[72]

This passage can also be read as a self-criticism of the celebration of the eternal staged in *A Man and His Dog*. What Dr Cornelius understands in the dark becomes compulsory for Thomas Mann in the light of the mid-1920s: political engagement on the side of democracy and of history yet to come.

An examination of the idyll's avant-garde characteristics would remain incomplete if one didn't also point out that *A Man and His Dog* is inscribed in a modern discourse structured around the concepts of cynicism[73] and the "creaturely":[74]

"The climate of polarization has a complex relation to the ideology of vitalism, which is widespread among intellectuals at the time. The assumption here is that any particular life currents, viewed in sufficient depth, are characterized by absolute continuity, even if what we see on the surface are discontinuous and contradictory rigidified forms."[75]

In *A Man and His Dog*, that subtle recovery of literal meaning, this "life current" appears as the everywhere flowing water that constitutes the true object of courtship. Thomas Mann follows the course of this water, whose bubbling, babbling and flowing, culminating in the surge of the ocean, he again and again compared to epic literature, including in

72 Thomas Mann: *Disorder and Early Sorrow* (1925), in: *Death in Venice and Seven Other Stories* (trans. H. T. Lowe-Porter, New York: Vintage, 1936), p. 189f.

73 Cf. Peter Sloterdijk: *Kritik der zynischen Vernunft*, Bd. 2 (Frankfurt am Main: Suhrkamp, 1983).

74 Cf. Helmut Lethen: *Cool Conduct: The Culture of Distance in Weimar Germany* (trans. Don Reneau, Berkeley: University of California Press, 2002), p. 22ff.

75 Ibid., p. 23f.

1934's *Voyage of Don Quixote*. The walk through the idyll comes to its climax in a celebration of the life current and ultimately leads Thomas Mann in his enthusiasm to say du to his readership—as far as I can tell, a rare, if not singular case:

> "For my part I freely admit that the sight of water in whatever form or shape is my most lively and immediate kind of natural enjoyment; yes, I would even say that only in contemplation of it do I achieve true self-forgetfulness and feel my own limited individuality merge into the universal. [...] I can lean on the rail of a little bridge over a brook and contemplate its currents, its whirlpools, and its steady flow for as long as you [*ihr*, the plural form of *du*] like." (256)

Love of water establishes the most intimate bond between the man and his dog, for Bauschan too "stands there with his ears laid back and a look of virtue on his face and lets the water stream round and over him" (257). Thomas Mann stands above the river, Bauschan halfway in it. Water thus becomes the central symbol of this idyll about man and beast that seeks a universal medium which will guarantee a "metaphysical connection between visible and invisible". The movement of man and beast towards each other is imagined and made evident through the water's course, the epic's flow. The man at the water transcends, in the sense offered by *Goethe and Tolstoy*:

> "The creaturely in us transcends; and all transcendence is creaturely. The highly irritable sense equipment of a man who is nature's familiar goes beyond the bounds of the actual senses and issues in the suprasensual, in natural mysticism."[76]

On the other hand, the dog that yet stands halfway in the water out of which all life once sprang aims toward man, in the sense offered by Mann's study of Goethe's *Elective Affinities*:

> "Striving is not only in the spirit, it is also in that place towards which it strives. Nature, too, is sentimental; its aim is spirtualization."[77]

Under the sign of water, the idyll *A Man and His Dog* pursues the question of how far man and beast can move towards each other

---

76 Thomas Mann: "Goethe and Tolstoy", (note 29), p. 153. Translation slightly altered, JCW.

77 Thomas Mann: "Zu Goethe's 'Wahlverwandtschaften'" (note 64), p. 177f.

according to this metaphysics. Man's treatment of animals elicits from them a longing for spiritualization, just as man's regression brings him closer to the beast and leads into the inner heart of the landscape, as depicted in the chapter on the chase. The sentimental nature of the beast finds its emblem in the dog's laugh, which here is not yet diabolical, but rather moving:

> "It is moving to see how under my teasing his thin animal cheeks and the corners of his mouth will twitch, and over his dark animal mask will pass an expression like a human smile, or at least some ungainly, pathetic semblance of one. It gives way to a look of startled embarrassment, then transforms the face by appearing again ..." (245).

As described above, the conservative avant-gardist Gottfried Benn, in his 1932 speech at the Prussian Academy of Arts, wanted to bind Thomas Mann to the doctrine of creaturely transcendence. As my reading of Mann's underappreciated canine idyll demonstrates, however, Benn, as an aggressive advocate of man's regression to beast, ignores the other side of Mann's doctrine, namely his theory of the sentimental dimension of nature, according to which nature itself strives after spiritualization, sublimation: "A grand encounter between nature and spirit upon their yearning path towards one another: this is man."[78]

What this fascinating concept of a creaturely transcendence might specifically entail, aside from pointing to the animalistic ecstasy of sexuality, is perhaps nowhere made more evident than in the case of the hunt. Thomas Mann's text thus logically follows its description of the idyllic hunting ground with an account of the chase. With great candor the author describes how he allows himself to be infected by his dog's passion for the hunt, how he excitedly helps Bauschan poke around for field mice and how he sticks by him when he chases after other animals in order to develop—as he did politically in 1914—his own "bloodthirstiness" (279). Yet in spite of all this, Gottfried Benn cannot invoke the chapter on the hunt in his attempt to bind Thomas Mann to creaturely transcendence, for at its climax there occurs a sudden turn.

It is the hares which are the objects of Bauschan's greatest passion. In the course of one of his chases, there comes a moment that turns everything upside down. The hounded hare suddenly bears down on Thomas Mann, runs up his overcoat and looks him in the eye:

> "I felt or thought I felt the throbbing of its hunted heart. And it was strange to see it so clearly and have it so close to me, the little

78 Ibid., p. 178.

> genius of the place, the inmost beating heart of our whole region [*Landschaft*]" (281).

Here again, in this seemingly humorous episode, we can observe the care given to the prose of this idyll. The hare is the inmost heart of the landscape, which can come into existence as landscape only when man has already stepped outside of nature. Thomas Mann not only allows the hare to run away but trips up his own dog, as well, so that he gives up the chase; this act documents, among other things, an idiosyncrasy that separates man's mind from the undeveloped mind of the animal: compassion. The blow with the stick that interrupts the "horrid head-tones of [Bauschan's] hue-and-cry" (281) and rescues the hare simultaneously rescues nature as landscape by preserving its heart. The beast can only hunt and kill the landscape's heart, but man can first bring it into view. *A Man and His Dog* thus ultimately stands as a defense not of creaturely transcendence but of the sublimation of nature, of the landscape that, traversed in equal measure by water and allusions to literature, is elevated to the symbol of a potential, reciprocal relationship between man and beast.

6. The Sublimation of Nature: Theodor W. Adorno

No sublimation succeeds that does not guard in itself what it sublimates.

Aesthetic Theory, p. 94

Sils Maria 1966

Departing from St Moritz, the last train station in the Engadin Valley, and traveling via Silvaplana, you will soon arrive at Sils Maria, a short distance from the Maloja Pass that connects the Engadin to the Val Bregaglia. Located just below the tree line, Sils Maria today remains a small village with scarcely more than forty buildings, most of them boarding houses and hotels. We are once again passing through, having stopped for Nietzsche, and will remain for three days, out of our interest in Adorno.

The Upper Engadin, almost perfectly horizontal and traversed by gravel paths, allows for long hikes among the mountains without the difficulties of climbing, an urban stroll nearly two thousand meters above sea level. A walk through the valley is hardly monotonous, however, as with each step the mountain backdrop recedes, disclosing ever new and higher gradations and greater views. The expansive, undeveloped marsh and the glassy lake—on whose shores stands the so-called Zarathustra Rock, in the shadow of which the idea of the "eternal return" allegedly came to Nietzsche—rob the valley, so closely surrounded by mountains, of its claustrophobic qualities and intensify the impression of a wide, silent landscape at the end of the world. We no longer remember, not even in Europe (northern Norway, or perhaps Iceland, excepted), ever having been exposed to such an impenetrable silence. It seems in fact as though, apart from the rivers' relentless seething, every sound is swallowed up. The softly purring automobiles below appear laughably small. Even today, the valley has maintained its character of the technically undisclosed and undisclosable:

> "Cocteau savvily wrote that Nietzsche's judgments of French literature were directed at the inventory of the bookstore in the Sils Maria train station. But in Sils Maria there is no train, no train station, no train station bookstore."[1]

Though it is early summer and the air temperature quite pleasant, the plateau has a cold, dismissive, hostile effect: the crystal clear lake almost entirely free of underwater plants, the green of the meadows and trees with its playful hints of yellow and blue, the leaden grey of the mountains whose peaks are frozen year round. Adorno writes primarily about the lake, whose eye, as beautiful as it is empty, lends the landscape its monstrous expression of inexpressiveness.

Interrupted by the sharing of an anecdote about a ridiculous optical illusion, the lake appears as the river Acheron in Hades, the Upper Engadin not as a vacation paradise but as the kingdom of the dead. It is no hero nor heroine but an animal, the beast that threw off Europa and let her sink beneath the waters, that triumphs here over death, to which all human beings succumb:

> "From a certain distance a cow that meddled in the lake, grazing between boats. Optical illusion caused me to see it as though it were standing in a boat. Truly jaunty mythology: Europa's steer, triumphantly navigating the Acheron."[2]

The subject of Adorno's notes, which begin with the mythological image of the drowned Europa and end with a report of the demise of one of the last people who knew Nietzsche, is death: Europe after the downfall. Death is present for the author himself in the mechanical-sounding whistle of the groundhogs. For Adorno, this whistle—the description of which serves as a prelude to a reflection that was later included almost verbatim in Adorno's *Aethestic Theory*—announces the identity of wholly conquered with wholly unconquered nature, founded via an accordance with death. The sound of nature rings out like a mechanically-produced signal:

> "Whoever has once heard the sound of the groundhogs will not easily forget it. To call it a whistle is to say too little: it sounds

1 Theodor W. Adorno: "Aus Sils Maria", in: *Gesammelte Schriften*, Vol. 10.1. (Hg. Rolf Tiedemann, Frankfurt am Main: Suhrkamp, 1997), p. 328. Translation JCW.

2 Ibid., p. 326. Translation JCW.

> mechanical, as though it were operated by steam. And precisely for this reason as an alarm. The fear that these little animals must have felt from time immemorial is frozen in their throats as a warning signal; what is supposed to protect their lives has lost the expression of the living. In their panic over death, they have trained themselves to mimic death."[3]

Even those who are otherwise indifferent towards the mountain world of the Alps will hardly be able to deny the Upper Engadin in its severity. The air is too thin even for geraniums. It induces the well-known "tipsiness", the slight febrility and the chronic cravings that Thomas Mann describes in *The Magic Mountain*; even Davos sits at a lower elevation than Sils. The philosophy professor Martin Heidegger, along with everything he stands for, is far away from here, down in the lowlands. From the perspective of Sils Maria, looking down from above in 1966, Heidegger's "country road" is nothing more than the "philosophy of culture". Of the Upper Engadin's uninviting mountain landscape, Adorno notes:

> "It does not breathe out any average humanity. This lends it Nietzsche's pathos of distance, who hid himself away there. At the same time, the moraines characteristic of the region resemble industrial waste piles, heaps of rubble from the building of the mountains. Both the scars of civilization and what is untouched beyond the treeline stand contrary to the image of nature as consoling, warming, made for human beings; here already it betrays its appearance as seen from outer space."[4]

Above the village, not even ten minutes from Nietzsche's house, stands a grand hotel erected in 1908 in the style of a medieval castle, "our hotel [...] with its inordinate dimensions",[5] the *Waldhaus*. The guest list, for reasons of discretion available only up until 1978, includes famous names from the worlds of politics, society, culture and economics. At the end of the world, under the spell of Nietzsche, whose memory is evoked by nearly every place here, whether marked by the bronze plaques and heavy bronze eagles commissioned by Frau Foerster or not, the pillars of capitalist society are assembled in concentrate. Rothschild, Thyssen, Siemens, Rockefeller and Bosch all took up residence at the *Waldhaus*, just as Richard Strauss, Clara

3 Ibid., p. 326f. Translation JCW.
4 Ibid., p. 327. Translation JCW.
5 Ibid., p. 326. Translation JCW.

Haskil, Wilhelm Backhaus and Dinu Lipatti did. Léon Blum, Theodor Heuss and Frau von Hindenburg, accompanied by her children, were here, too. The families of Europe's aristocracy spent their vacations at the *Waldhaus* alongside Hermann Hesse, C. G. Jung, André Gide, the family Mann and many others. The secluded hotel represents not the world stage—as, for example, the *Carlton* in Cannes does—but rather an opportunity to retreat from that stage. There is no audience here, not even today. The *Waldhaus* is a spacious and luxurious hideaway for the powerful representatives of Old Europe and the United States. The guest list also includes the names of Theodor and Margarethe Adorno, who regularly spent their summers here between 1955 and 1966 (the year of the publication of *Negative Dialectics*), 394 days in all, more than a full year.

That the residencies of these prominent guests so often overlapped allows us to imagine the strangest possible dinner parties, communal strolls and meetings along the beige gravel paths. A number of stories have circulated of awkward encounters along the trails blazed by Nietzsche and trampled upon by posterity. Georg Lukács' famous 1962 polemic against the "Grand Hotel Abyss" has a strikingly precise empirical foundation, particularly as regards the abysmal character of this part of the Engadin:

> "A considerable part of the leading German intelligentsia, including Adorno, have taken up residence in the 'Grand Hotel Abyss' which I described in connection with my critique of Schopenhauer as 'a beautiful hotel, equipped with every comfort, on the edge of an abyss, of nothingness, of absurdity. And the daily contemplation of the abyss between excellent meals or artistic entertainments, can only heighten the enjoyment of the subtle comforts offered.' "[6]

Adorno, who in 1966 did not begrudge those in either camp,[7] provocatively blends—most likely in reference to Lukács' polemic—the spheres of exclusive society and sublime nature in a further observation that rings true even today. St Moritz, with its ski circus, is chi-chi; Sils, the site of effortless walking and talking, rather chic by comparison:

---

6 Georg Lukács in his preface to the 1962 edition of his *Theory of the Novel*, in: Georg Lukács: *The Theory of the Novel. A Historico-philosophical Essay on the Forms of Great Epic Literature* (trans. Anna Bostock, Cambridge, MA: M.I.T., 1971), p. 22.

7 According to the end of the preface to *Negative Dialectics*. The notes about Sils were first published in the *Süddeutsche Zeitung* on 1 and 2 October 1966, the year of the publication of Adorno's major philsosophical work, which is also widely recognized as a book "*aus Sils Maria*".

> "Peaks that tower above plumes of fog and mist appear incomparably higher than when they rise up in the clear light, unveiled. But when the Margna wears its light shawl of mist, it is a lady, playful yet reserved, of whom one may be sure that she disdains travelling to St Moritz and going shopping."[8]

Grand hotels are discreet, even after their guests have passed away. The family owners and their old employees evidently remember the Adornos even after more than thirty years. They point us to the couple's table in the dining room, to their renovated room as well as to one that has been preserved in its 1908 condition (the suite occupied by Thomas Mann and his daughter Erika). They are also kind enough to reveal that Adorno was an especially taciturn guest who knew exactly what he wanted: peace and quiet. The hotel made every effort to create the appropriate conditions. More than three decades later, Adorno's desire for quiet is still respected; there are no anecdotes told about him here. The night spent on the hotel's rooftop terrace on account of the launch of Sputnik is well remembered, however; the Adornos were probably in attendance. Again appealing to the cosmos—a cipher for solitude and fear of a meaningless death ever since Pascal expressed his horror of the emptiness of space—Adorno later wrote:

> "In the evening, we had to observe Sputnik from the roof. It would not have been distinguishable from any star, nor from Venus, if it had not staggered along its course. That is how it goes with humanity's victories. That with which it dominates the cosmos, a dream realized, is shaky and blurred as in a dream, unconscious, as though it would tumble."[9]

With his notes *Aus Sils Maria*, published in a widely-read newspaper, Adorno exposed himself to accusations of snobbery and invited his opponents to discredit West German Critical Theory through *ad hominem* polemics. Adorno meets Lukács' charge that there exists a scandalous, "decadent" contradiction between leftism and the upper-class lifestyle by disclosing it to the public and literally publishing the address of the "Grand Hotel Abyss". This bold gesture represents an invitation to reflect upon the contradiction thus laid bare, beyond the moral indignation of the Eastern bloc. Here Adorno answers Lukács

8 Adorno: "Aus Sils Maria" (note 1), p. 327. Translation JCW.

9 Ibid., p. 326. Translation JCW. One of the hotel's former night clerks, an avid stargazer, points out that Adorno is mistaken here: *Sputnik* charted its course without staggering. The jittery appearance of the movement of artificial heavenly bodies is a result of the effects of the earth's atmospheric layers.

aesthetically, by transforming his account of the tantalizing "Grand Hotel Abyss" into a fully-realized allegory centered around the stark contrast of an imperial grand hotel in an imperial landscape. Formally, the subtlety of Adorno's response can also be seen in the way he plays off the young Lukács against the late. The young Lukács' Theory of the Novel had emphasized modernity's tendency towards allegory a full decade before Benjamin's treatise on *The Origin of German Tragic Drama*, while the older Lukács held out that a healthy "realism" was once again possible. As Lukács had written in 1916, in the age of "transcendental homelessness",[10] the meaning of life has been concealed and thus life itself has become a problem. The objects of experience no longer reveal a fullness of meaning with joy and awe but rather must be intellectually deciphered by a subject who has become solitary and problematic; they become allegories. The scene Adorno evokes of an eerie assembly of the pillars of society amid a deathly landscape itself allegorizes the following passage on allegory from *The Theory of the Novel*:

> "The problem here is inexpressible because it is the concrete idea of the whole, because only the polyphony of all the voices can carry the full wealth of content concealed in it. For life, the problem is an abstraction; the relationship of a character to a problem can never absorb the whole fullness of that character's life, and every event in the sphere in life can relate only allegorically to the problem."[11]

The grand hotel itself figures the allegory of a concrete idea of the whole. The thought behind Adorno's 1966 allegory may be illuminated by looking at a work first published shortly before the Nazis' seizure of power and then promptly banned. In his 1932 book *The Socialist Decision*, Adorno's academic advisor Paul Tillich, following in the footsteps of Marx and Max Weber, named the principle of Western bourgeois society, which amounts to "an attack on the myth of origin and the bond of origin everywhere on earth".[12]

"Its principle is the radical dissolution of all conditions, bonds and forms related to the origin into elements that are to be rationally mastered, and the rational assemblage of these elements into structures serving the aims of thought and action."[13] Bourgeois society is,

---

10 Lukács: *The Theory of the Novel* (note 6), p. 41.

11 Ibid., p. 54f.

12 Paul Tillich: *The Socialist Decision* (trans. Franklin Sherman, New York: Harper & Row, 1977), p. 47.

13 Ibid., p. 48.

according to its own claims, international and egalitarian, equally accessible to everyone in the world. It thus finds its philosophical expression in Enlightenment thought, in the program of a rational demystification of the world, which is then irrationally combined with what Tillich calls the bourgeois "belief in harmony", "the most profound principle of the Western Enlightenment, though it often remains unrecognized."[14] According to Marxist analysis, the capitalist order leads to a breakdown of human beings' alleged harmonious unity into classes; it leads to the emergence of the proletariat, which confronts the propertied middle class both as its truth and as a threat:

> "To begin with, the proletariat is nothing but a product of bourgeois society and its formation of the world and of society. It is the result of the complete objectification of all existing things in nature and society through the domination of the bourgeois principle. In the proletariat, all bonds to the myth of origin have been completely broken. The individual is left entirely to himself. Immediately supporting powers such as soil, blood, group and community are lacking. While the bourgeoisie disclaimed for itself the radical implications of its own principle and allied itself with prebourgeois forces, it abandoned the proletariat completely to the dynamic of this principle."[15]

The classic grand hotel of the nineteenth century is an architectural manifestation of both the ideal and the ideology of the bourgeoisie. The grand hotel is the sublimation of the bourgeois lifestyle, integrating both architecturally and culinarily its national and international dimensions. A particular nation finds its sublimated entry into the hotel through certain accents in the architectural design, in the flower arrangements and on the dinner menu. A range of international cuisine can regularly be found alongside the selection of "regional specialities" that have been tweaked to appeal better to an international palate. Not coincidentally, a world-renowned salad bears the name of one of the grand hotels of Manhattan: Waldorf. The architectural and social gesture of the grand hotel is the idea of cosmopolitanism. The grand hotel stages a sweeping harmony between regionalism and internationalism through language as well. Knowledge of English and French, as well as the local tongue, is mandatory among the staff, which for its part is also deliberately international. In the grand hotel, with its masterful co-ordination of regionalism and internationalism, the world becomes home. Its exclusivity consists precisely not in condescension, but in conveying a

14 Ibid., p. 51.
15 Ibid., p. 67.

feeling of privateness. A grand hotel that does not elicit from its guest, even for a moment, the fantasy of remaining there forever—as the expatriate Nabokov dreamed in Montreux—is a grand hotel no longer.

At the same time, the alliance between the bourgeoisie and pre-bourgeois powers noted by Tillich is manifested in the classic grand hotel's architecture. The *Carlton* in Cannes resembles a French chateau of the *ancien régime*; the *Waldhaus* in Sils Maria, a medieval castle. Through its pre-modern design the grand hotel assumes a semblance of old substance, as though it were inexchangeable, hence the passionate public discussion that always arises when once again some venerable *Traditionshaus* comes under the hammer. The architecturally branded class structure is further carried out through the regulation of dress, as in the requirement of evening attire at dinner. The stark class difference highlighted by the already intimidating architecture—particularly through the sleekness of the parquet, the marble, the conversation—is complemented by the subtle distinctions that may be observed in the course of living at such a hotel.

In its ponderous grandiosity, the grand hotel thus embodies what Paul Tillich described as the contradiction between utopia and ideology. Grand hotels are a transnational homeland in which one may seek refuge, especially in exile. On the other hand, the grand hotel is financially and sociologically exclusive; it is expensive, or rather, to use a proto-bourgeois term that brings together both Schiller's transcendental pathos of the limit and money, "exorbitant". Adorno's reports of his sojourns at the *Waldhaus* are thus an allegorical indication of the fact that twentieth-century thought carries out the unmediated contradictions that shaped the nineteenth century, as may be seen by considering the paradigm of the hotel as the petrified idea of the whole: the Hegelian system in the form of an old house.

At the same time, these notes on Adorno's annual trips to Switzerland signify a critical turn against the aggressively restorative German Federal Republic of the '50s and early '60s. This voluntary Swiss exile was evidently necessary for a time for the Adornos to be able not just to maintain their productivity, but to endure life in what had formerly been Nazi Germany, to which they had returned very early on after the end of the war. Regarding the other house, the one in which Nietzsche—himself a German exile—had lived, with a view not of the panorama but only of a wet rock face, Adorno notes:

> "It demonstrates with what dignity one could be poor eighty years ago. Today, under similar material conditions, one would be classed out of the bourgeoisie; the spareness was humbling in the light of the general standard of ostentatious grandeur. At that time, the price of intellectual independence was a most humble

> lifestyle. The relation between productitivy and economic footing also underlies history."[16]

The need to seek refuge once a year in the classically contradictory milieu of the Swiss grand hotel makes it clear to the German public that Germany is no homeland. With respect to Lukács, Adorno recognizes that "the socialist decision" had in 1966 been deferred, that philosophy survives only because it missed the moment of its realization. Taking the place of this realization is Critical Theory, which analyzes not only the hotel's interior but also the nature that surrounds it. Unrestrained nature offers no escape from industrial society; it is rather identical to it and thus itself demands the rehabilitation of a category of aesthetics, presumed to be obsolete, that would mediate between the extremes of subjectless imperialism: natural beauty, the sublimation of nature. This reflection, too, is anticipated allegorically in Adorno's notes from Sils Maria:

> "The cows march into the mountains with visible pleasure, and with little regard for the human beings who laid the wide paths on which they walk. Model for how civilization, which oppressed nature, might support the oppressed."[17]

There are many beautiful mountain villages in Switzerland. A philosopher who spends his summers in Sils Maria for over a decade, and then in 1966—the same year he published *Negative Dialectics*, his most important philosophical work—informs the public about his visits there via the *Süddeutsche Zeitung*, is being clear enough in his claim to be Nietzsche's successor in the twentieth century. The writings that emerged between 1955 and 1956—particularly *The Jargon of Authenticity*, inspired by Nietzsche and Karl Kraus—become open letters, sent down from Upper Engadin to those "places where Nietzsche and the Englightenment have not yet been heard of".[18] In the introduction to *Against Epistemology: A Metacritique*, Adorno's central programmatic text after the *Dialectic of Enlightenment*, written together with Max Horkheimer, it is the extensively quoted Nietzsche, far more than Hegel, who serves as the most important witness along the path to articulating a last philosophy that no longer thinks within the confines of these traditions, but looks at them historically, sociologically and

16 Adorno: "Aus Sils Maria" (note 1), p. 328. Translation JCW.

17 Ibid., p. 326. Translation JCW.

18 Adorno: *The Jargon of Authenticity* (trans. Knut Tarnowski and Frederic Will, Evanston, IL: Northwestern University, 1973), p. 26.

psychologically, from the outside, as a play. That Adorno never wrote a book or even a single essay on Nietzsche underscores his claim to successorship (a claim often also raised with respect to Heidegger, an eager exegete of Nietzsche) more than his silence discounts it. In his definition of sublimation, Adorno, taking recourse to the prehistory of subjectivity, draws on Nietzsche's insights into sublimation's origins. The price for man's emancipation from nature is the self-subjection of the subject. According to the *Metacritique*, it is only the philosopher of Sils Maria who has recognized that philosophy since Greek antiquity has hindered the historical thinking—the "theory of residue"—that Nietzsche demands: "Truth is supposed to be the leftover, the dregs, the most thoroughly insipid."[19] Nietzsche's blueprint for a historical philosophy that holds the concept of sublimation as its methodological key is necessary to Adorno's project of combating the fallacy which claims that "what persists is truer than what perishes."[20] In a stunning passage, Adorno brings together the history of Western philosophy, from which he critically distances himself, and the history of domination, which in the twentieth century had developed into totalitarian bureaucracy:

> "To its greater glory, the pure concept abuses the more highly developed individual as impure and decay. No progress of scientific and philosophical rationality without such retrenchment. Totalitarian systems have not contrived that saying out of the historical nowhere, but rather brutally executed what ideology for thousands of years had prepared spiritually as the lordship of spirit. The word 'elementary', however, includes both the scientifically simple and the mythologically original. The equivocation is as little an accident as most. Fascism sought to actualize philosophy of origins."[21]

Adorno succeeds Nietzsche as the creator of genealogy but parts ways with him at the moment when his apologia of coming into being transforms into an apologia of the will to power. As the above citation demonstrates, Adorno shares Nietzsche's diagnosis of the connection between philosophy and domination but rejects the corollary drawn by him that establishes the will to power as the central concept of a new cosmology. Nietzsche ultimately identifies with the aggressor and reverts to metaphysics. On the one hand, he recognizes the will to

19 Adorno: *Against Epistemology. A Metacritique* (trans. Willis Domingo, Cambridge, MA: M.I.T. Press, 1983), p. 15.

20 Ibid., p. 17.

21 Ibid., p. 20.

power that pervades allegedly pure philosophy; in the end, however, he becomes one of its most fierce advocates. From the beginning, philosophy has given theoretical succor to real domination, inasmuch as the constitution of the subject was an act of subjection, a forced identity.

This break from Nietzsche is worked into Adorno's notes from Sils Maria as well. It likewise becomes an element of Adorno's allegory when he reports, seemingly in passing, that he and Herbert Marcuse together had sought out Herr Zuan, "the last person" alive who had known Nietzsche personally. Along with Marcuse, who had endeavored in *Eros and Civilization* to rethink the concept of non-repressive sublimation as the self-sublimation of Eros, Adorno embarked on a pilgrimage to visit Nietzsche's contemporary. At the same time, an anecdote offered by Herr Zuan marks the point at which Marcuse and Adorno break from Nietzsche, whose fetishization of power and rejection of compassion are in turn rejected by Critical Theory:

> "We went there, Herbert Marcuse and I, and were graciously received in a sort of private office. Indeed, Herr Zuan could remember. Asked about particulars, he told us that Nietzsche carried a red umbrella, in rain as in fair weather—one assumes that he hoped it would protect against headaches. A gang of children, Herr Zuan among them, had made an amusement for themselves out of slipping into the folded-up umbrella pebbles which fell upon his head as soon as he opened it. He then chased after them, threatening them with the raised umbrella, but never caught them. We thought: what a difficult situation the suffering man must have come into, who pursued his tormentors in vain and perhaps in the end conceded to them because they represented life against the spirit; unless, that is, the experience of real compassionlessness had confused him about certain philosophemes."[22]

In a clearly ironic conclusion, Adorno remarks that he and Marcuse were not interested in hearing Herr Zuan's anecdotes about a visit to Sils Maria by Queen Victoria, who gave her name to the epoch that Karl Marx had studied in London. They were interested in Nietzsche as a precursor of the idea of non-repressive sublimation and as a critic of the subjected subject in philosophy under the banner of a consistently applied genealogy, not as an apologist for power and mercilessness. Moreover, Adorno's allegory insists that analysis of society take the place of Nietzsche's naïve and elitist alienation from it. Adorno links

22 Adorno: "Aus Sils Maria" (note 1), p. 328f. Translation JCW.

his psychological critique of Nietzsche's power fetish with his demand that society be studied sociologically. His notes *Aus Sils Maria* document the broken nature of Adorno's emulation of Nietzsche. Whereas eighty years earlier Nietzsche had fled society, of which he had formulated no concept, Adorno was now spending his summers among society's leaders. He corrects the solitary philosopher's power fantasies in his reflections upon the pathos of the perspective of "looking down from on high", which he interprets as emanating from Nietzsche's unscrutinized infantile fantasy of being a giant. The timid *Übermensch* confuses the social world with a child's toy; the social philosopher of the twentieth century, on the other hand, from now on finds real society within what in childhood had been a mysterious object of fascination:

> "From this altitude, the villages look as though they were placed there from above with gentle fingers, movable and foundationless. In this way they resemble a toy, with the happy promise offered by the fantasy of being a giant: you could do with them what you will. Our hotel, however, with its inordinate dimensions, is one of those tiny structures adorned with crenellations which in childhood decorated the tunnels through which the model train roared. Now one finally sets foot in them and knows what is inside."[23]

Adorno's allegory culminates in the stark contrast drawn between the grand hotel and the industrial site. The nostalgic notion that raw nature could be Edenic is rejected, and the course of Adorno's thought is thus determined. Its path leads through a consideration of natural beauty, in order to be able to arrive at a striking assertion that disburdens sublimation of the allegation that it harasses the subject and demands sorrowful sacrifice: "[S]ublimation and freedom mutually accord."[24]

That freedom and sublimation are in accordance with each other is apparent neither in the bourgeois world for which the grand hotel stands nor in the world of nature into which the bourgeoisie escapes from itself. Adorno's reflection on the industrial character of the mountain landscape recurs in the corresponding passages of his *Aesthetic Theory*:

> "Natural beauty, such as it is perceived unmediated in appearing nature, is compromised by the Rousseauian *retournons*. The mistakenness of the crude antithesis of technique and nature is

23 Ibid., p. 326. Translation JCW.

24 Adorno: *Aesthetic Theory* (trans. Robert Hullot-Kentor, Minneapolis: University of Minnesota Press, 1997), p. 130.

obvious in the fact that precisely nature that has not been pacified by human civilization, nature over which no human hand has passed—alpine moraines and taluses—resembles those industrial mountains of debris from which the socially lauded aesthetic need for nature flees. Just how industrial it looks in inorganic outer space will someday be clear."[25]

The idea of natural beauty in the form of a landscape, as Thomas Mann exemplarily evoked it in *A Man and His Dog*, calls to mind the fact that the path to freedom is partially blocked if freedom is conceived only as emancipation from nature. Liberation from nature, which demands as its price the self-subjection of the subject, is haunted by the incomprehensibility of nature, which has become ever more mythic. Walter Benjamin had already developed this insight in his essay on Goethe's *Elective Affinities*, with a view towards the novel's ill-fated enlightened personnel:

"Where does their freedom lead those who act thus? Far from opening up new perspectives for them, it blinds them to the reality that inhabits what they fear. And this because these perspectives are unsuited to them. Nothing but strict attachment to ritual—which may be called superstition only when, torn from its context, it survives in rudimentary fashion—can promise these human beings a stay against the nature in which they live. Charged, as only mythic nature is, with superhuman powers, it comes menacingly into play."[26]

The return to raw nature allows for a sigh of relief which for its part refers back to a restrictive society that prohibits such sighing. In a disenchanted world, strict attachment to ritual has become "superstition", or at best possible as a "crooked cure of neuroses", to use Freud's words. The aim of Adorno's reflections is neither to suggest a regression to raw nature nor to demand blind attachment to ritual; their aim is rather the remembrance of nature within the subject. And this remembrance of nature in the subject is prepared through the the experience of natural beauty, which is an experience not of raw nature, like that which surrounds Sils Maria, but of the cultural landscape (Kulturlandschaft) that epitomizes the successful mediation between nature and the world of man. The references to Sils Maria in Adorno's *Aesthetic Theory* serve

25 Ibid., p. 68.

26 Walter Benjamin: "Goethe's Elective Affinities" (1925), in: *Selected Writings, Volume 1: 1913–1926* ((eds) Marcus Bullock and Michael W. Jennings, Cambridge, MA: Belknap Press of Harvard University Press, 2004), p. 303.

to exorcise the notorious nostalgia lurking in the modern notion of being in touch with nature, in order to protect natural beauty from becoming kitsch. One who breathes a sigh of relief in raw nature is in danger of forgetting that this sigh "depends on what is mediated, on the world of conventions".[27] The sigh, however legitimate,

> "fails to perceive that natural grandeur reveals another aspect to its beholder: that aspect in which human domination has its limits and that calls to mind the powerlessness of human bustle. This is why Nietzsche in Sils Maria felt himself to be 'two thousand metres above sea level, but even higher than that above all things human'."[28]

The recollections of Sils Maria in the *Aesthetic Theory* mark the difference between raw nature and the experience of natural beauty, which paves the way for a remembrance of nature within the subject. Yet the fact that sublimation and freedom mutually accord will only become wholly apparent, according to Adorno, if one concerns oneself with what lies furthest away from the concept of nature, namely art. Veneration of natural beauty is thus led astray when it allows itself to grow into a fetishization of raw nature, which Adorno repudiates via his allusion to the industrial character of the cosmos. The experience of natural beauty announces the idea of a concession, what Thomas Mann, in his image of the laughing dog, described as the sentimental side of nature. Yet like Mann's dog, natural beauty ultimately remains silent and resists conceptual penetration, as Adorno makes disarmingly clear in pointing out the failure of any attempt to reproduce, to spiritualize natural beauty; no photograph of a landscape can convey what is felt by the person who sighs within it. Adorno's analysis leads to a limit where what is spiritual in natural beauty silently becomes tangible. In order to be able to develop the concept of sublimation as one of freedom, Adorno correctly follows the opposite path of analyzing precisely that subject who sighs in the landscape. Natural beauty becomes conscious in artistic beauty, which is established the moment the spiritual limit of natural beauty is experienced as an oppressive spell:

> "The song of birds is found beautiful by everyone; no feeling person in whom something of the European tradition survives fails to be moved by the sound of a robin after a rain shower. Yet something frightening lurks in the song of birds precisely because it is not a song but obeys the spell in which it is enmeshed. The

---

27 Adorno: *Aesthetic Theory* (note 24), p. 63.
28 Ibid., p. 70.

> fright appears as well in the threat of migratory flocks, which bespeak ancient divinations, forever presaging ill fortune. With regard to its content, the ambiguity of natural beauty has its origin in mythical ambiguity. This is why genius, once it has become aware of itself, is no longer satisfied with natural beauty. [...] Only what had escaped nature as fate would help nature to its restitution."[29]

Artistic beauty is realized as the spiritualization of the process of civilization, which is already conceived of as an emancipation, a continued sublimation; nature thereby recurs in the beauty of art. So reads Adorno's theory of sublimation. Only the fulfillment of this spiritualization measures up to what nature presumably desires. Only through the total alienation of this spiritualization can the essence from which man is alienated be divined. Adorno rescues Nietzsche in a move as subtle as it is masterly. The path of Nietzsche's thought leads from the aesthetic theory of *The Birth of Tragedy* to an obsessive apologia of the will to power. From this development Adorno draws insight into the history of the origins of thought, the central concept of which for Nietzsche was sublimation. In order to be able to recognize Nietzsche's step towards the affirmation of power as false, however, Adorno returns to Nietzsche's beginnings, to aesthetic theory. Nietzsche survives in Adorno as the critic of a metaphysics that is more oblivious to history than it is to Being. Art, according to Adorno, recalls what has been repressed by a metaphysics blind to history. The experience of art clarifies the sacrifices man had to make in order to subject the world. To become himself, man had to subject himself both to himself and to his fellow man as that which is at all times identifiable and administratively controllable. Thus was instituted the uneasy circle of false sublimation, of constant domination over oneself and others that Freud made famous in his theory of civilization. Art, as the sublimation of cultural sublimation spiritualized as the sublime, objects:

> "Spiritualized, the artwork becomes in itself what was previously attributed to it as its cathartic effect on another spirit: the sublimation of nature. The sublime, which Kant reserved exclusively for nature, later became the historical constituent of art itself. [...] Nature, no longer oppressed by spirit, frees itself from the miserable nexus of rank second nature and subjective sovereignty."[30]

---

29 Ibid., p. 66f.
30 Ibid., p. 196f.

Adorno's *Aesthetic Theory* acquires the concept of a "sublimation of nature" along the path of a detailed critique of two prominent theories of sublimation, that of Kant and that of Freud. The relevant passages now require our attention.

Erschütterung

I recall from seminars and other conversations that Adorno's critique of the Freudian doctrine of sublimation in the first section of his *Aesthetic Theory* is considered a passage to be read through quickly. Compared to other parts of the book, such as Adorno's reflections on *Semblance and Expression*, the dispute with Kant and Freud may appear to be little more than a long-winded treatise on key texts of aesthetic thought that have long been deemed obsolete, a history course that paves the way for Adorno's own project, which begins to be developed in the second section of the text, titled *Situation*.

Despite its wordiness, there is a certain resonance to Adorno's admittedly justified resistance to the popular concept of sublimation promoted by Freud himself in his essay on the relation of the poet to daydreaming and in certain passages of the *Introductory Lectures on Psychoanalysis*,[31] namely the notion that a literary work of art represents little more than the transformation of the artist's own socially unacceptable instinctual impulses into a product that is recognized by society and offers a gentle "fore-pleasure"[32] to its consumers.

Freud generalizes this somewhat condescending concept of the literary work as a marketable product of imagination that, for its part, is already the result of an avoidance of reality and applies it to art as a whole in his *Formulations on the Two Principles of Mental Functioning*—i.e. the reality principle and the pleasure principle—from 1911

> "Art brings about a reconciliation between the two principles in a peculiar way. An artist is originally a man who turns away from reality because he cannot come to terms with the renunciation of instinctual satisfaction which it at first demands, and who allows his erotic and ambitious wishes full play in the life of phantasy. He finds the way back to reality, however, from this world of phantasy by making use of special gifts to mould his phantasies into truths of a new kind, which are valued by men as precious reflections of reality. Thus in a certain fashion he actually becomes

31 Cf. Sigmund Freud: *Introductory Lectures on Psychoanalysis*, in: *The Standard Edition of the Complete Psychological Works of Sigmund Freud* ((eds) James Strachey and Anna Freud, London: Hogarth, 1956–74), vol. 15/16, p. 376f.

32 Freud: "Creative Writers and Daydreaming," in: *The Standard Edition* (London: Hogarth, 1956–74), vol. 9, p. 153.

the hero, the king, the creator or the favourite he desired to be, without following the long roundabout path of making real alterations in the external world. But he can only achieve this because other men feel the same dissatisfaction as he does with the renunciation demanded by reality, and because that dissatisfaction, which results from the replacement of the pleasure principle by the reality principle, is itself a part of reality."[33]

This simple, popular conception—which interprets the work of art as merely a sly means of compensating for instinctual desires *in order* then to be able to realize them immediately—is at odds with the idea of art's negativity. It is compatible neither with the art of modernity, which stresses incompatibility in terms of *form*, nor with the critique frequently articulated via art's *content* of the pathological normativity of a society that restricts, excludes and proscribes even those instinctual impulses not considered deviant. Freud's slightly insulting notion of fore-pleasure, conceptualized historically in terms of Nietzsche, Ibsen and Dostoevsky, is rather unalluring when compared with a concept of art marked by dissonance, the "seal of everything modern",[34] that protests stridently or seductively against the fetishization of the reality principle itself:

> "If successful sublimation and integration are made the be-all and end-all of the artwork, it loses the force by which it exceeds the given, which it renounces by its mere existence."[35]

Freud harmoniously integrates art and artist, potentially as an act of resistance or of envy. He integrates them into reality and thus shifts attention to the description of this reality as an aesthetic phenomenon, a perspective that since Nietzsche has led to an alliance between aesthetic theory and the critique of metaphysics. His concept of creative writing is notably innocuous, "falling strangely short of Freud's own theory of the 'dreamwork'",[36] and not only in terms of formal provocation or (socio)critical content. Freud, the bourgeois advocate of imagination as mere daydreaming, weakens the epistemological impact of a conception of art that sees in the productive power of the imagination a faculty that is equal to the reality principle, that may even precede it, that creates an entire world: the imaginary.

---

33 Freud: *Formulations on the Two Principles of Mental Functioning*, in: *The Standard Edition* (London: Hogarth, 1956–74), vol. 12, p. 224.

34 Adorno: *Aesthetic Theory* (note 24), p. 15.

35 Ibid., p. 12.

36 Ibid., p. 8.

Below, I hope to combat the impression that Adorno's critique of Freud is limited to these insights, which nonetheless are preliminarily articulated as follows:

> "The narrow-mindedness, in spite of all the emphasis on sex, is revealed by the fact that as a result of these studies, [...] artists whose work gave uncensored shape to the negativity of life are dismissed as neurotics. [...] For psychoanalysis, artworks are daydreams; it confuses them with documents."[37]

I wish to demonstrate that Adorno, by boldly integrating theoretical elements that in Freud are unconnected and contradictory, marks the open question of sublimation's mechanism as indispensible to the formulation of a theory of the production and reception of art, thereby calling attention to an ever-acute problem beyond the realm of Freud research. Because neither sublimation's concept nor its object is persuasively defined—Laplanche and Pontalis, as already mentioned, note the lack of a "comprehensive theory of sublimation"[38]—, aesthetic theory itself remains fragmentary. Aesthetic theory is always also a theory of sublimation.

Paradoxically enough, Adorno's critique and theory of sublimation, which culminate in an unanswered question, may be counted among the worked-through and completed sections of his otherwise fragmentary *Aesthetic Theory*. Through the "intrusion of death into the work",[39] Adorno's provocation, likewise present in the works he published during his lifetime, is elevated almost to the level of unreadability. The hermeneutic circle, which constitutes understanding in a pendulum swing between the interpretation of details and the idea of the whole, cannot be closed. The whole, the complete *Aesthetic Theory* does not exist. Nonetheless, individual passages of the posthumously published text exemplify Adorno's intentions: to immerse himself in micrological work on individual problems while always keeping present—yet at the same time always concealing—his central idea that art and its reflection, aesthetics, are indispensable to the critique of society and thus for the undiminished, exhilarating fullness of experience.

Among the passages which exemplify the ruin that has survived as Adorno's *Aesthetic Theory* are those pages that stretch from a critique

---

37 Ibid.

38 J. Laplanche/J.-B. Pontalis: *The Language of Psychoanalysis* (trans. Donald Nicholson-Smith, London: Karnac, 2006), p. 432.

39 Cf. Rolf Tiedemann's editorial afterword in: Adorno: *Ästhetische Theorie*, in: *Gesammelte Schriften*, Vol. 7 (Hg. Rolf Tiedemann, Frankfurt am Main: Suhrkamp, 1997), p. 537. Translation JCW.

of the psychoanalytic theory of art to a discussion of the pleasure of knowledge. A reading of this section can thus not only demonstrate what immanent critique means in Adorno's thought but also offer an idea, however inadequate, of what the book as it exists is missing. The coherent critique of Freud makes clear that aesthetic theory, formulated in terms of pleasure and "unbound possibility",[40] can help rid civilization of the discontent that Freud considers an inescapable fate. Adorno's striking turn of phrase reveals not only the latent complexity of the Freudian doctrine but also—and Marcuse endeavored to develop this line of thought more fully—that a theory of sublimation not only articulates a theory of renunciation, of lack, of self-denial or of compensation, but also always writes a theory of pleasure and abundance.

If we wish to be able to uncover the argument of Adorno's reconstruction, we cannot avoid another brief look at Freud's scattered remarks on sublimation. His notes were never consolidated into a coherent theory; the term's semantic success, which stretches from the name of the most sublime artistic achievement to the reluctant overcoming of everyday frustrations, is perhaps a result of this openness. Three primary meanings nonetheless stand out.

Freud explicates a first Sublimation A through the example of the poet, then of the artist in general. The *production* of art is an exemplary instance of sublimation: "His Majesty the Ego" is "the hero alike of every day-dream and of every story."[41] Beyond this, Freud recognizes a second Sublimation B, the *reception* of art, noting that "our actual enjoyment of an imaginative work proceeds from a liberation of tensions in our minds."[42] Both forms of sublimation are exceptional realizations of a general human talent, given man's estrangement from nature, for a third Sublimation C, which first makes possible the cultural development of humanity, a development that is constantly threatened by three sources of suffering: the hostile natural world, the frail human body, and the not-always-sympathetic Other:

> "Another technique for fending off suffering is the employment of the displacements of libido which our mental apparatus permits and through which its function gains so much in flexibility. The task here is that of shifting the instinctual aims in such a way that they cannot come up against frustration from the external world.

40 Adorno: *Aesthetic Theory* (note 24), p. 12.
41 Freud: "Creative Writers and Daydreaming" (note 32), p. 150.
42 Ibid., p. 153.

> In this, sublimation of the instincts lends its assistance. One gains the most if one can sufficiently heighten the yield of pleasure from the sources of psychical and intellectual work. When that is so, fate can do little against one."[43]

With respect to drive theory, these three prominent forms of sublimation allow for the option of displacing the libido, the ability to substitute one object by another, as Freud explains elsewhere:

> "The object of an instinct is the thing in regard to which or through which the instinct is able to achieve its aim. It is what is most variable about an instinct and is not originally connected with it, but becomes assigned to it only in consequence of being peculiarly fitted to make satisfaction possible."[44]

Since Freud at the very least differentiates between the sexual and the self-preservative drives, it should be emphasized that in his remarks on sublimation Freud's attention is directed primarily toward sexuality, whereby it must be noted that here a certain inconsistency begins to creep in. Sublimation can mean the simple replacement of one sexual object by another, but it can also refer to a desexualization, a qualitative change in relation to the object, and finally that far-reaching renunciation of the drives that makes civilization possible while simultaneously effecting the discontent that endures within it:

> "Sublimation is a process that concerns object-libido and consists in the instinct's directing itself towards an aim other than, and remote from, that of sexual satisfaction; in this process the accent falls upon deflection from sexuality."[45]

As far as I know, there is no explanation in Freud of the relationship of the different forms—different in Adorno, as well—of Sublimations A, B and C to each other, though one may find individual refinements to the structure of libido displacement, which likewise are carried over into Adorno's reconstruction in the form of his crucial observation of a change *in interest itself*. In his study of *The Ego and the Id*, Freud claims that the displacement of the object-libido is always mediated by an

---

43 Freud: *Civilization and Its Discontents*, in: *The Standard Edition* (London: Hogarth, 1956–74), vol. 21, p. 79.

44 Freud: *Instincts and Their Vicissitudes*, in: *The Standard Edition* (London: Hogarth, 1956–74), vol. 14, p. 122.

45 Freud: *On Narcissism: An Introduction*, in: *The Standard Edition* (London: Hogarth, 1956–74), vol. 14, p. 94.

intermediate step, a transitory narcissistic turn, an occasional aversion to the world of things:

> "From another point of view it may be said that this transformation of an erotic object-choice into an alteration of the ego is also a method by which the ego can obtain control over the id and deepen its relations with it—at the cost, it is true, of acquiescing to a large extent in the id's experiences. When the ego assumes the features of the object, it is forcing itself, so to speak, upon the id as a love-object and is trying to make good the id's loss by saying: 'Look, you can love me too—I am so like the object.' The transformation of object-libido into narcissistic libido which thus takes place obviously implies an abandonment of sexual aims, a desexualization—a kind of sublimation, therefore. Indeed, the question arises, and deserves careful consideration, whether this is not the universal road to sublimation, whether all sublimation does not take place through the mediation of the ego, which begins by changing sexual object-libido into narcissistic libido and then, perhaps, goes on to give it another aim."[46]

In this passage, Freud complements the mechanism of libido displacement with the notion of a neutral alteration of the ego itself. The ego can occasionally offer itself to the id as a transitional object only by taking on characteristics of the lost or unattainable object of desire, by qualitatively changing itself, whereby the possibility of a desexualization first begins to take shape. Here Freud outlines a concept of sublimation that distantly recalls Plato's *Symposium*—moving from one body to another produces the idea of the body and of beauty—and that Adorno brilliantly elaborates as a mediating category between philosophy and psychology (here: between Kant and Freud). The ego participates in an experience, undergoes the painful process of internalizing the world, differentiates itself and thus develops an interest that transcends the particular and refines the immediate desire. The original option of libido displacement is the condition of the possibility of differentiation, the psychogenetic origin of aesthetic consciousness, of erotically disinterested delight, which means not "castrated hedonism" but rather the opposite: "[D]isinterestedness immanently reproduces—and transforms—interest."[47]

A reconstruction of the Freudian doctrine of sublimation is made difficult not only by the ambiguity of the term and its complicated relation

46 Freud: *The Ego and the Id*, in: *The Standard Edition* (London: Hogarth, 1956–74), vol. 19, p. 30.

47 Adorno: *Aesthetic Theory* (note 24), p. 13.

to the problem of narcissism. The difficulty left behind by Freud consists in his indecision with respect to the value he places on the concept of sublimation. Though it is distinguished as the cardinal means of coping with suffering, it never fully loses its character as a sad surrogate, the moment in which *das Eigentliche*, the actual object of desire, is renounced. In Freud's theoretical ambiguity there recurs the necessarily ambivalent relationship between the subject and its own sublimations, an ambivalence for which Freud ultimately introduces the concept of an enduring discontent. The question that Freud does not answer – and this may be the principal reason that his doctrine of sublimation remained fragmentary – is whether successful sublimation, a satisfying substitution without the bitter aftertaste of renunciation, can occur at all. This problem arises as early as his lecture on the poet and his relation to daydreaming:

> "As people grow up, then, they cease to play, and they seem to give up the yield of pleasure which they gained from playing. But whoever understands the human mind knows that hardly anything is harder for a man than to give up a pleasure which he has once experienced. Actually, we can never give anything up; we only exchange one thing for another. What appears to be a renunciation is really the formation of a substitute or surrogate. [...] We may lay it down that a happy person never phantasizes, only an unsatisfied one. The motive forces of phantasies are unsatisfied wishes, and every single phantasy is the fulfillment of a wish, a correction of unsatisfying reality."[48]

In Freud's view, the work of the writer is ultimately only a long detour whose goal is not the production of literary works—which are rather only the unloved means to an end—but rather social gratification, in particular anticipated erotic success. What Freud's text on the poet has to say about a special case that permanently marks sublimation as inauthentic, as a surrogate, widens in his later, melancholic study of *Civilization and Its Discontents* into a general explanation of why human beings have never succeeded in feeling content within their culture. In the following passage, Freud verbally differentiates between the sublimation and the renunciation of the drives, yet both processes blur together to the point of being indistinguishable, inasmuch as the sublimation of the drives, as a "forced vicissitude", is effectively no different from a forced renunciation of the drives:

> "Sublimation of instinct is an especially conspicuous feature of cultural development; it is what makes it possible for higher

48 Freud: "Creative Writers and Daydreaming" (note 32), p. 145f.

> psychical activities, scientific, artistic or ideological, to play such an important part in civilized life. If one were to yield to a first impression, one would say that sublimation is a vicissitude which has been forced upon the instincts entirely by civilization. But it would be wiser to reflect upon this a little longer. [...] [F]inally, and this seems the most important of all, it is impossible to overlook the extent to which civilization is built up on a renunciation of instinct, how much it presupposes presicely the non-satisfaction (by suppression, repression or some other means?) of powerful instincts. This 'cultural frustration' dominates the large field of social relationships between human beings. As we already know, it is the cause of the hostility against which all civilizations have to struggle."[49]

If one considers the entire corpus of Freud's writings, the distinction ostensibly established here between the sublimation of the drives and their renunciation—Freud admits, honestly enough, that much more reflection on this point is needed, though he never gets around to this—can ultimately be justified only with recourse to the distinction between the insatiable neurotic and the simple, modest man discussed in the Freud chapter of this book. In a sense, the demands of the drives increase in proportion to one's ability to form ideals. The more refined one's capacity for sublimation, the more keen the awareness that something must be renounced, so that ultimately the relationships are reversed: the more extensive the sublimation, the greater the desire for an unrestricted life. Protest against reality itself, awareness of the negativity of existence thus constitutes for Freud the vanishing point of his double-edged, or rather latently dialectical theory of sublimation. In this way, Freud's distinction produces the recurrence of the archaic: "If it is more than mere indifference, the Kantian 'without interest' must be shadowed by the wildest interest."[50]

The contradictions and non-integrated elements of Freud's doctrine of sublimation are briefly reviewed above so that we may able to discern and acknowledge Adorno's rigor, which is obscured in the text of his *Aesthetic Theory* by a combination of boast and understatement. For Adorno, masterly writing is an essential part of philosophical work; that which is carelessly expressed he considers poorly thought out. And one of the first acts of a stylist is to allow the skeleton of, say, a semantics of sublimation to disappear in the river of language. In the case of

49 Freud: *Civilization and Its Discontents* (note 43), p. 97.
50 Adorno: *Aesthetic Theory* (note 24), p. 11.

Adorno's text, the downside of this process is that readers who love language may not recall his chain of thought as much as his polemical remarks or malicious anecdotes, such as the story of the analyst who is irritated by a neurotic artist who finds the engravings hanging on the walls of his practice hideous and subsequently diagnoses her with aggression.

The differentiation of three kinds of sublimation nonetheless underlies Adorno's reconstruction and critique as much as his knowledge of Freud's description of narcissism as an intermediate step, or the paradox that differentiation may be transformed into an unsuppressible awareness of the drives, which Adorno develops into a dialectic of sublimation. All in all, it is a meticulous study of Freud that exemplifies how Adorno works, reconstructing the scattered elements of a theory, then bringing them together in order ultimately to allow for the recognition of their unresolved contradictions as latently productive ideas.

Reduced to a formula, Adorno's argument reads as follows: only by experiencing a fundamental shock (*Erschütterung*) (Sublimation B: reception) through a work of art (Sublimation A: production) is the subject able to appreciate fully the cost of the process of civilization (Sublimation C) and at the same time recognize that this process is not necessarily synonymous with chronic discontent and the renunciation of happiness. For Adorno, rather the inverse is true. In terms of cultural theory, this is where he departs from Freud, by means of introducing the historically and artistically open. In passing through the shock produced by art, which recalls the lasting pain of the process of civilization, the subject first acquires a valid concept of happiness that maintains a balance between "memory and longing".[51]

As the study of Freud's writings demonstrates, this concept—in which the production and reception of art is assigned a central anthropological role—does not come to its position from outside; rather, all of its elements may be derived from the material at hand through the immanent critique that structures the methodological dimension of Adorno's thinking. The philosophical construction of, in this instance, art arises not *a priori* out of nothing but strictly *a posteriori*, by working through the historically available material above which it is elevated only a hair's breadth.

Adorno's chain of thought begins with the criticism, outlined above, that psychoanalysis mistakes works of art for documents and thus identifies them with the development of neurotic symptoms: "The question is never once broached whether a psychically sound

51 Ibid., p. 14.

Baudelaire would have been able to write *The Flowers of Evil*."[52] At the same time, Adorno asserts the value of Freud's elucidations in comparison to the remnants of a conservative-idealistic theory of art: "The psychoanalytic theory of art is superior to idealist aesthetics in that it brings to light what is internal to art and not itself artistic. It helps free art from the spell of absolute spirit."[53] If, on the one hand, a psychoanalytic approach to art demonstrates its utility by having exposed the libidinal dimension of aesthetic constructs and thus their critical dimension and anthropological relevance, on the other hand, it neglects the objectivity of the work of art as well as the relationship that exists between the artist and his work. Adorno thus condenses into a single sentence the program of his own *Aesthetic Theory*, which takes the ontology of the artwork as its starting point:

> "Psychoanalysis treats artworks as nothing but facts, yet it neglects their own objectivity, their inner consistency, their level of form, their critical impulse, their relation to non-psychical reality and, finally, their idea of truth."[54]

Adorno's outline of his own project may be recognized as an argument against Freud if one considers his examination of the objectivity of the artwork together with the work of the artist. If the work of art is to a certain extent the phantasmatic working through of subjective instinctual impulses that have been frustrated—a purely narcissistic concern—the process of creating art yet reveals that working on oneself is tantamount to working on the world: "[The psychology of art] would need to decipher the artwork not just as being like the artist but as being unlike as well, as labor on a reality resisting the artist."[55]

Adorno's reconstruction of Freud and transgression against him here become subtly intertwined. At first glance, Freud's theory of art appears to be eminently realistic, both as a demystification of artistic work, which is traced back to instinctual impulses, and in its disenchanting view of artworks themselves, which are treated as mere daydreams and then as documents. What had been laid out as a contradiction in Freud's theory of libido displacement is developed to its fullest extent in the case of art. What was originally the purely narcissistic, transitory return of the ego to itself, or to what is allegedly identical to it, is revealed in the confrontation with the artifact to be work on that which is non-identical.

---

52 Ibid., p. 8.
53 Ibid., p. 8f.
54 Ibid., p. 9.
55 Ibid.

In this way, the production of a work of art entails the objectification of the process of a constant differentiation of the ego, which turns towards the world only to turn away from it again and, in working on itself, communicates simultaneously with the world and with itself. Works of art—conceived by Adorno as entities that are non-identical to the artist, that raise their own demands, and, as has been frequently documented, that are experienced by their producers effectively as work on something which resists—turn out to be models of the subject's relationship to the world and to itself.

Adorno can thus argue that the "cult of the reality principle to which psychoanalysis is devoted"[56] is in fact a cult, an abandonment of reflection. Reality is not something that is fixed, that has been defined once and for all, any more than the subject is; rather, each is non-identical to the other and is being constantly redefined by the other. The experience of producing art, which first allows for this insight, is exemplary. What may at first have been conceived as a mere encounter with oneself turns out, once the work has been completed, to be the experience of a discrepancy between the subject and itself, the subject and the world. Reflection on the production of art thus emerges as a complement to the anthropological reformulation of Kantian epistemology begun in the *Dialectic of Enlightenment* as an analysis of projection. If, according to the *Dialectic of Enlightenment*, perception of the world always comprises both objective sensory data *and* projective material, then the subject can comprehend itself only when it comprehends the world. In recognizing the world, it simultaneously recognizes itself, insofar as the constitution of the world always includes projective elements: "The inner depth of the subject consists in nothing other than the delicacy and wealth of the external world of perceptions."[57]

In its working out of the link between Freud's theory of sublimation and the narcissistic intermediate step that facilitates it, Adorno's *Aesthetic Theory* approaches the interconnection of subject and world from the perspective of the productive solitary subject. In the process of sublimation, the subject, encountering resistance in a work of art that it has created, becomes aware of its own relation to the world. The above sentence about perception from the *Dialectic of Enlightenment* may then be reformulated thus: By experiencing, in the course of creating a work of art, the objectivity, coherence, form, impulse and truth of that artwork, the subject grasps both that it is in the world and that it works on this world by working on itself:

---

56 Ibid. Translation slightly altered, JCW.

57 Max Horkheimer/Theodor W. Adorno: *Dialectic of Enlighenment* (trans. John Cumming, New York: Continuum, 1972), p. 189.

> "If art has psychoanalytic roots, then they are the roots of fantasy in the fantasy of omnipotence. This fantasy includes the wish to bring about a better world. This frees the total dialectic, whereas the view of art as a merely subjective language of the unconscious does not even touch it."[58]

Against the backdrop of Freudian theory and the doctrine of projection, the final link in Adorno's chain of thought is thus not an appeal to morality; the moralistic will to a better world does not necessarily belong to artistic work. Things are rather more complicated. Working on a resistive piece of art frustrates the phantasm of the subject's omnipotence even in relation to itself. Working on art, i.e. sublimation, is successful when the working subject surrenders itself to the objectivity of the artwork, following the laws of form that the work's coherence demands and yielding to the direction in which the work wants to go. In this act of surrender, which makes it possible to sublimate the frustration of the archaic fantasy of omnipotence and thus allows for a non-phantasmatic, non-delusional liberation both from fixation and from the strength of the ego, there emerges a relationship to the world that serves as an alternative model to the aggressive domination of nature. By surrending itself, the subject gains not only itself but a differentiated world, independent of any subjective moral intentions.

In order to proceed to the aim of this argument which identifies the experience of happiness in the experience of a work of art, Adorno must follow up his ambitious thesis regarding the artwork's objectivity and his corresponding theory of the production of art with the development of their strict "antithesis",[59] namely the Kantian doctrine of disinterested pleasure.

Adorno must address Kant for two reasons. For one, Kant's doctrine of formal beauty gives historical succor to Adorno's theory of the artwork's objectivity, his argument against Freud's reduction of the work of art to a document. Kant uncovers what Adorno later unfolds in much greater proximity to concrete artworks: the autonomy of the laws of art, the objectivity of its forms and patterns, the tendencies of the materials involved, the objectivity of its coherence. Kant undertakes an "objective attempt to save objectivity through the analysis of subjective elements".[60]

58 Adorno: *Aesthetic Theory* (note 24), p. 9.
59 Ibid., p. 10.
60 Ibid.

The second insight that Adorno takes from Kant, and which was not developed by Freud, consists in the knowledge that through the process of sublimation—insofar as it does not merely replace one drive-object by another, but rather selects instinctual aims that are no longer immediately sexual—the subject itself is changed, becoming more differentiated. In the course of sublimation, the subject to a certain extent loses the ability simply to enjoy what its original primitive desire demanded. Or rather, the subject gains a richer relationship to the world. The idea of happiness thus acquires the Janus face towards which Adorno's argument as a whole is directed: the memory of a lost, ancient fulfillment coupled with the desire for perfection in completing the process of differentiation and thus experiencing fully the world's abundance. By insisting "that aesthetic comportment is free from immediate desire",[61] Kant gains not only a conception of sublimation that substantially changes the subject but also a concept of an "aesthetic sphere"[62] beyond empiricism, which for its part is thus divested of its claim to an alleged totality. The production and reception of art become objectively critical: "Aesthetic disinterestedness has broadened interest beyond particularity."[63]

Inasmuch as the process of producing works of art is conceived as an alternative to the abstract domination of nature, there yet exists the danger that Adorno's *Aesthetic Theory*, in the tradition of the nineteenth century, promotes the artist as the representative of a successful life. In order to confront this tendency, Adorno allows his analysis of the doctrine of sublimation to culminate in a theory of the reception of art—something only rudimentarily developed by Freud—in which the productive dimension (through the moment of surrender) and the philosophical dimension (through the possibility of distant reflection on the entire process) merge. In order to make this synthesis possible, the realist in Kant and the idealist in Freud must first be exposed. Adorno achieves this in a single sentence:

> "If successful sublimation and integration are made the be-all and end-all of the artwork, it loses the force by which it exceeds the given, which it renounces by its mere existence."[64]

Against Kant's disinterested pleasure, Adorno asserts that the work of art, "as the announcement of an immediate praxis", is itself practical:

---

61 Ibid.
62 Ibid.
63 Ibid., p. 11.
64 Ibid., p. 12.

"Only artworks that are to be sensed as a form of comportment have a raison d'être."[65] Against Freud's doctrine of sublimation, he emphasizes its own repressed vanishing point, namely that sublimation itself is the expression of a resistive force that culminates in the protest against an absolute reality and which is not "exhausted in the psychical performance of gaining mastery over instinctual renunciation [nor] in the achievement of conformity".[66] The development of thesis and antithesis ultimately allows for the concept of happiness that will guide Adorno's theory of the reception of art through the phases of surrender and shock (*Erschütterung*):

> "Art's *promesse du bonheur* means not only that hitherto praxis has blocked happiness but that happiness is beyond praxis. The measure of the chasm separating praxis from happiness is taken by the force of negativity in the artwork."[67]

Following this incisive comment, Adorno proceeds quickly. Via his resistance to the concrete enjoyment of art and his description of the genuine response to art as the extinguishing of subjectivity, which may be observed in "reproductive" artists such as musicians, he arrives at an aphoristic condemnation of bourgeois consumer behavior that satirizes the double binds of bourgeois existence as well as the purity fetish of modernity after World War II: "The bourgeois want art voluptuous and life ascetic; the reverse would be better."[68]

The musical dimension of Adorno's writing, his artful stewardship of the text is exemplified by its final pages, inasmuch as the text, following its serious and highly condensed remarks on Freud and Kant, occasionally relaxes its train of thought, on the one hand granting the reader a reprieve from concentrated philosophical work through the proliferation of bon mots and vicious commentary, while at the same time using humor to prepare the issue that it ultimately establishes in a dissonant way, namely the experience of happiness. A philosophical text can hardly convey a feeling of happiness except through humor and the beauty of its prose. The sidelong glance at the aesthetic gourmet, who is convicted as a philistine by expressions like "a feast for the ears", the joke about the cellist who hisses "I just hate music" before playing beautifully under Toscanini, the allusion to the nude Greek statue that had never been a pin-up: all of this prepares the matter at hand, the attempt to establish the

65 Ibid.
66 Ibid.
67 Ibid.
68 Ibid., p. 13.

experience of art as one of happiness by dismantling the concept of enjoying art:

> "The happiness gained from artworks is that of having suddenly escaped, not a morsel of that from which art escaped; it is accidental and less essential to art than the happiness in its knowledge; the concept of aesthetic pleasure as constitutive of art is to be superseded."[69]

The end of the chapter on Freud and Kant presents a surprising and almost scandalous contradiction. On the one hand, there is the repeated doctrine that the appropriate response to a work of art consists in losing oneself in it, in extinguishing oneself through it, in surrendering to it—a doctrine that in its sensuality seems to reproduce directly both the Freudian theory of daydreaming and the narcotic fore-pleasure taken in its peculiarly gentle sensuousness: "Whoever disappears into the artwork thereby gains dispensation from the impoverishment of a life that is always too little."[70] Yet this emphasis on sensual experience is at odds both with Adorno's abolition of artistic enjoyment, which he replaces with the pleasure of *knowledge*, as well as with his final sentence on the feeling of standing firm:

> "Happiness in artworks would be the feeling they instill of standing firm. This holds true for the aesthetic sphere as a whole more than for any particular work."[71]

The contradiction between surrender and knowledge, disappearing and standing firm, is only a seeming one, yet one must study the entire book in order to arrive at its sublation, which in a certain sense could only have been achieved through the *Aesthetic Theory* as a whole. Surrender to the work of art is knowledge; to be shaken by the work of art constitutes standing firm. As in a visual image organized around a central perspective, the chapter's vanishing point, the sublation of the sharp contradiction between surrender and thought, lies beyond these paragraphs, at the end of the *Aesthetic Theory* and in its paralipomena. This vanishing point:

> "is the moment in which recipients forget themselves and disappear into the work; it is the moment of being shaken. The recipients lose their footing; the possibility of truth,

69 Ibid., p. 15.
70 Ibid., p. 14.
71 Ibid., p. 15.

> embodied in the aesthetic image, becomes tangible. [...] Shock [*Erschütterung*], radically opposed to the conventional idea of experience [*Erlebnis*], provides no particular satisfaction for the I; it bears no similarity to desire. Rather, it is a memento of the liquidation of the I, which, shaken, perceives its own limitedness and finitude."[72]

A second articulation of this point again identifies in the concept of aesthetic transcendence

> "the self-negation of the contemplator who is virtually extinguished in the work. [...] Pain in the face of beauty is the longing for what the subjective block closes off to the subject, of which the subject nevertheless knows that it is truer than itself. Experience, which would without violence be free of the block, results from the surrender of the subject to the aesthetic law of form."[73]

Adorno brings together Kant, Freud and the *Dialectic of Enlightenment* under the lofty banner of Plato's *Phaedrus*, which offers a mythological derivation of the experience of pain in the face of beauty through its theory of anamnesis. Great works of art—Beethoven repeatedly serves as Adorno's preferred example—represent a twofold realization. Sublimation is pushed into the realm of the imaginary, which escapes the empirical world, disrupting its claim that it is the only reality. With the appearance of a second world within the first, the constitution of the subject, which anxiously attempts to conform to this first world, is *bodily* shaken: "[A]t other moments creatural sadness has borne witness to metaphysical content"[74]—in the specific sense that the world, blindly interpreted as an object of domination, has demanded its separation from the subject. The shaken subject surrenders itself to the work and recalls the mimetic affinity that it has lost. At the same time, however, the subject surrenders itself not to nature directly but entirely to *a formal aesthetic law* that escapes the empirical world, i.e. both nature and society. The regressive experience of surrender is thus transformed into the desire for a world that would have escaped the archaic grip of nature rather than reconstituted it through its attempts to disrupt it by dominating nature itself. For Adorno, it is the experience of art which as a regressive behavior allows for the knowledge, balanced between memory and desire, that happiness lies beyond raw nature and the practice of its domination.

---

72 Ibid., p. 244f.
73 Ibid., p. 265f.
74 Ibid., p. 14.

The unmediated recurrence of archaic instinctual desires at the apex of sublimation is a consequence of Freud's theory. In thinking this theory through, Adorno moves beyond the antithesis of sublimation and the drives. Only false sublimation, with adaptation and integration (in Freud: narcissistic idealization) as its aim, reproduces the archaic desires of the drives as they once were, because they were never changed. Aesthetic experience as conceived by Adorno differentiates instinctual desire by comprehending sublimation both as differentiation and as a protest against the world under "the rule of brutal self-preservation",[75] which corresponds to the identical, rigid self. In being shaken by a work of art, the callous subject becomes practiced in a certain attitude towards itself and the world that, according to the *Dialectic of Enlightment*, first makes a different world conceivable:

> "Only in that mediation by which the meaningless sensation brings a thought to the full productivity of which it is capable, while on the other hand the thought abandons itself without reservation to the predominant impression, is that pathological loneliness which characterizes the whole of nature overcome."[76]

The whole of nature, subject and world. What is established in the *Dialectic of Enlightenment* is carried out in Adorno's *Aesthetic Theory* through the development of the potentially ambiguous notion of a remembrance of nature within the subject. In becoming aware, through the experience of art, of the nature within itself, the subject begins to change itself *and* nature, thus transcending both. Critical Theory without aesthetic theory would be incomplete. The ambiguity—emancipation from nature and, at the same time, nature's sublation—is itself sublated in the concept of a sublimation of nature: "No sublimation succeeds that does not guard in itself what it sublimates."[77]

---

75 Ibid., p. 12.
76 Horkheimer/Adorno: *Dialectic of Enlightenment* (note 57), p. 189.
77 Adorno: *Aesthetic Theory* (note 24), p. 94.

7. *Das Ding*: Jacques Lacan's Luther

We have lost something. We are missing something that would allow us to be happy. There exists a painful void, a hole that must be filled.[1] Our entire life is oriented towards the recovery of this lost object, this sought-after *Ding*, of whose earlier presence we are supposedly reminded by an "oceanic feeling".[2] Our life is "actually" nothing more than an attempt to reconstitute the delights of primal narcissism, since "[a]s always where the libido is concerned, man has here again shown himself incapable of giving up a satisfaction he had once enjoyed."[3]

We fight off as much as possible anything that frustrates our narcissism; the difference between outside judgment and grandiose self-perception is "repressed". Critical observations that call our magnificence into question are either "rejected with the utmost indignation [...] or even stifled before they enter consciousness".[4] There is a second cardinal rule besides repression: we salvage our ever-threatened self-love by deferring it to an ego ideal that we "project before us"[5] as a beautiful image we have of ourselves. We compensate our present frustrations through happy daydreams and fantasies of a guaranteed brilliant future about which those who currently mistreat

---

1 Cf. Jacques Lacan: *The Ethics of Psychoanalysis 1959–1960* (trans. Dennis Porter, ed. Jacques-Alain Miller, New York: Norton, 1992), p. 88. Citations from *The Ethics of Psychoanalysis* are henceforth indicated by page numbers in parentheses immediately following the quotation.

2 Sigmund Freud: *Civilization and Its Discontents*, in: *The Standard Edition of the Complete Psychological Works of Sigmund Freud* ((eds) James Strachey and Anna Freud, London: Hogarth, 1956–74), vol. 21, p. 65.

3 Freud: *On Narcissism: An Introduction*, in: *The Standard Edition* (London: Hogarth, 1956–74), vol. 14, p. 94.

4 Ibid., p. 93.

5 Cf. ibid., p. 94.

us know nothing. Man's ego ideal is merely "the substitute for the lost narcissism of his childhood in which he was his own ideal".[6]

Potentially, we are capable of striking a compromise, and we admit to ourselves and to others that there is a gaping abyss between our actual ego and our ego ideal. Perhaps we place great demands on ourselves and give our lives meaning by attempting to close the gap between ideal and reality. We are reminded of the discrepancy between the two by our conscience, occasionally through pangs of guilt. If we listen closely to the voice of our conscience, however, we discover that the ego ideal, which is supposed to compensate our frustrations with the glittering promise of an ideal future, is not and never was truly our own. Our private problems of identity are socially mediated, perhaps even constituted by others through a process of primal alienation:

> "For what prompted the subject to form an ego ideal, on whose behalf his conscience acts as watchman, arose from the critical influence of his parents (conveyed to him by the medium of the voice), to whom were added, as time went on, those who trained and taught him and the innumerable and indefinable host of all the other people in his environment—his fellow-men—and public opinion."[7]

The ego ideal turns out to be a double-edged sword. On the one hand, it helps me to overcome the frustrations of narcissism. On the other hand, its demands, programmed by my "milieu," threaten to overwhelm my life, and the question is raised: Is the pain of the discrepancy between ego and ideal a result of the fact that this ideal was largely not mine at all? Who am I beyond an identity constituted through the "advice" of my parents? In technical literature, the process of transformation in which I turn against the "milieu" from which I come in order to find "my true self" is called an "identity crisis"[8] or a "liminal phase".[9] Freud notes at least four possible ways of overcoming this crisis: "the cure by love"[10] according to the "narcissistic type" (I allow myself to

6 Ibid.

7 Ibid., p. 96.

8 Cf. Erik H. Erikson: *Identität und Lebenszyklus* (Frankfurt am Main: Suhrkamp, 1966).

9 Cf. Rolf Parr: "Liminale und andere Übergänge. Theoretische Modellierungen von Grenzzonen, Normalitätsspektren, Schwellen, Übergängen und Zwischenräumen in Literatur- und Kulturwissenschaft", in: *Schriftkultur und Schwellenkunde* (Hg. Achim Geisenhanslüke und Georg Mein, Bielefeld: Transcript, 2008), p. 11–64.

10 Freud: *On Narcissism: An Introduction* (note 3), p. 101.

be admired by a subjected object, or I admire a powerful object to the point of sef-abandonment); "the cure by love" according to the "dependent type" (in caring for an object, I experience a renewal of the devotion I supposedly enjoyed as a small child);[11] commitment to an idealized cause (such as politics or religion), the regressive formations of which Freud analyzes in *Group Psychology and the Analysis of the Ego*; or finally, sublimation (intellectually distancing oneself from all of these possibilities—science, pure thought).

If it is successful, psychoanalysis is capable of elucidating the patterns outlined above, in particular the difference between unconscious narcissistic idealization and sublimation, which if stabilized ultimately makes possible an "ego-syntonic" object-choice. If it is successful, analysis teaches the patient that he "cannot desire the impossible", that he must relinquish the desire to merge with himself, with another person or with the world in the name of the "oceanic feeling". Enlightened desire, embodied in the figure of the analyst, can ultimately put the patient in the position of saying—to quote Lacan, who remained something of a Kantian—"My experience has its limits" (cf. 296, translation slightly altered, JCW):

> "What the analyst has to give, unlike the partner in the act of love, is something that even the most beautiful bride in the world cannot outmatch, that is to say, what he has. And what he has is nothing other than his desire, like that of the analysand, with the difference that it is an experienced desire." (p. 300)

Jacques Lacan's research and thought may be characterized as a comprehensive elaboration of the mechanisms of narcissism described by Freud.[12] His discovery of the so-called "mirror stage" as formative of the function of the I rightly occupies the beginning of Lacan's undertaking; for in asserting it, he places the troublesome divide between self-perception and outside judgment at the start of an individual's life. The "mirror stage"—in which the small child, yet incapable of controlling its own body, catches sight of itself in the mirror, in the eyes of others, and rejoices in the image of an integral whole that does not really exist—"is a drama whose internal pressure

11 Cf. ibid. pp. 88f. and 98f.

12 Cf. regarding Lacan in general: Hermann Lang: *Language and the Unconscious: Jacque Lacan's Hermeneutics of Psychoanalysis* (trans. Thomas Brockelman, Atlantic Highlands, NJ: Humanities, 1997), Peter Widmer: *Subversion des Begehrens. Eine Einführung in Jacques Lacans Werk*, 3. Edition. (Wien: Verlag Turia & Kant, 2004), Christoph Braun: *Die Stellung des Subjekts. Lacans Psychoanalyse* (Berlin: Parodos Verlag, 2007).

pushes precipitously from insufficiency to anticipation".[13] The mirror stage generates the discrepancy between an imaginary self, Lacan's *moi*, and the actual self, silenced and overrun by phantasms, the *je* with which psychoanalysis is concerned. Lacan finds the "discontent" with which Freud had diagnosed civilization at the level of the *constitution* of subjectivity, i.e. prior to any and all later experiences of frustration. That we later feel discontent within civilization is merely an epiphenomenon of a primal, archaic, pre-Oedipal discontent that begins with the mirror stage:

> "In man, [...] this relationship to nature is altered by a certain dehiscence at the very heart of the organism, a primordial Discord betrayed by the signs of malaise and motor uncoordination of the neonatal months."[14]

Terminologically, Lacan condenses the various objects that serve to compensate the subject's frustrated narcissism—ego ideal, love object, political and religious associations, etc.—into a single concept, *das Ding* [the Thing]. The ways in which the ego copes with narcissism and its inevitable frustration within its own, uniquely shaped life-world are startlingly diverse. In order to indicate clearly that, despite this diversity of methods, the ego has only a single concern, namely restituting the delights of primary narcissism, Lacan unites all objects, no matter how categorically different, from phantasms to real persons, under this one concept: *das Ding*. To the extent that the problem of narcissism emerges in Freud's research and in Lacan's as the linchpin of both individual and collective human life, Lacan claims psychoanalysis as a leading science. And here he already announces his engagement with the figure of the "reformer", which he would later study through the example of Martin Luther:[15]

---

13 Jacques Lacan: "The Mirror Stage as Formative of the *I* Function as Revealed in Psychoanalytic Experience", in: *Écrits: The First Complete Edition in English* (trans. Bruce Fink, New York: Norton, 2006), p. 78.

14 Ibid.

15 Erik H. Erikson had already pointed to the importance of Martin Luther to the prehistory of psychoanalysis and devoted a monograph to him (ignored by Lacan) in which he writes: "[O]ne cannot help feeling that Luther often publicly confessed just those matters which Freud, more than three hundred years later (enlightenment having reached the psychological point of no return) faced explicitly, and molded into concepts, when, studying his dreams, he challenged and disciplined the neurotic component of his intellectual search." Erik H. Erikson: *Young Man Luther: A Study in Psychoanalysis and History* (New York: Norton, 1962), p. 50.

> "At this intersection of nature and culture, so obstinately scrutinized by the anthropology of our times, psychoanalysis alone recognizes the knot of imaginary servitude that love must always untie anew or sever.
>
> For such a task we can find no promise in altruistic feeling, we who lay bare the aggressiveness that underlies the activities of the philanthropist, the idealist, the pedagogue and even the reformer.
>
> In the subject to subject recourse we preserve, psychoanalysis can accompany the patient to the ecstatic limit of the '*Thou art that*', where the cipher of his mortal destiny is revealed to him, but it is not in our sole power as practitioners to bring him to the point where the true journey begins."[16]

We have lost something. We are missing something that would allow us to be happy. There exists a painful void, a hole that must be filled. Our entire life is oriented towards the recovery of this lost object, this fervently longed-for Thing, of whose earlier presence we are reminded by an "oceanic feeling". We sometimes believe that returning to Mother Nature would bring this Thing back to us. Yet we must understand that we have fallen from nature, by our own nature. We are an ego because we are no longer one with our mother: "The self is first born in the pain of separation."[17] Every attempt to undo the pain of separation, to heal the wound, is doomed to failure, because we *are* the primal separation, we are the wound:

> "This ego, whose strength our theorists now define by its capacity to bear frustration, is frustration in its very essence. Not frustration of one of the subject's desires, but frustration of an object in which his desire is alienated."[18]

As Robert Spaemann emphasizes, even primitive communities, seemingly closely tied to nature, establish their systems of social order not with recourse to nature directly but rather via cosmogonies and theogonies. The union of the ego with nature is a paradoxical phantasm; natural right, a romantic fiction: "Every nomos suppresses

16 Ibid., p. 80f.

17 Klaus Heinrich: *Versuch über die Schwierigkeit Nein zu sagen*, 3. Edition. (Frankfurt am Main: Stroemfeld Verlag, 1985), p. 69. Translation JCW.

18 Jacques Lacan: "The Function and Field of Speech and Language in Psychoanalysis", in *Écrits* (note 13), p. 208.

that which comes by nature."[19] Inasmuch as separation from nature and the constitution of the ego are one and the same, this union could successfully be restored only by sacrificing the ego, which would destroy any possibility of experiencing the reunion as happiness. This sorrowful insight into the paradox of existence forces us onto the path of civilization, which as such is determined by our respective "milieus" and yet appears to be a clever detour towards *das Ding*. For we will never believe that access to the Thing has been forever forbidden to us. We are willing to make compromises for the sake of this Thing, to inhibit our drives—as natural as they are unnatural—to apply the reality rather than the pleasure principle to our lives. We are even willing to renounce permanently our instinctual aims, so that we might ultimately find happiness in potential co-operation with others. And all of this renunciation and deferral, despite the fact that, given the insatiability of our nature, "we can never give anything up":[20]

> "One might dream of a total, complete, epidermic contact between one's body and a world that was itself open and quivering; dream of a contact and, in the distance, of a way of life that the poet points out to us; hope for a revelation of harmony following the disappearance of the perpetual, insinuating presence of the oppressive feeling of some original curse." (p. 93)

"Cultural frustration", the erection of culture and its institutions upon the all but unbearable renunciation of the drives, "suppression, repression" represent for Freud the cause of the "hostility against which all civilizations have to struggle",[21]the reason for discontent in civilization. On our quest for happiness, everything—from the microcosm to the macrocosm—seems to work against us: "One feels inclined to say that the intention that man should be 'happy' is not included in the plan of 'Creation.'"[22] Our body is frail, inexorably aging and ultimately perishing. Nature remains superior in its power; its contingency can never be overcome. Finally, our "neighbor" is not wholly benevolent but rather potentially dominant, hostile to the point of mortal enmity, the third and most excruciating source of our pain, the most excruciating[23] because we know from our own selves that, unlike our body, or

19 Robert Spaemann: "Natur", in: *Philosophische Essays. Erweiterte Ausgabe* (Stuttgart: Reclam, 1994), p. 20. Translations JCW.

20 Freud: "Creative Writers and Daydreaming", in: *The Standard Edition* (London: Hogarth, 1956–74), vol. 9, p. 145.

21 Freud: *Civilization and Its Discontents* (note 2), p. 97.

22 Ibid., p. 76.

23 Ibid., p. 77.

a thunderstorm, our neighbor has a choice. In Martin Luther's words, "We are our own torturers."[24]

Lacan concisely summarizes Freud's bitter diagnosis: "It is to be found"—this Thing—"at the most as something missed" (p. 52), as suffering. According to psychoanalysis, and not only in its Lacanian orientation, there lies hidden in the innermost heart of desire the "desire of the mother", which Lacan deems "the origin of everything" (p. 283). To the extent that ego formation is connected to the doom of the Oedipus complex, in the working through of which the incestuous object is transformed into an ego ideal, the agent of all sublimation, Lacan is able to achieve this regressive breakthrough only by destroying the structure of the ego. In the light of the paradigmatic trauma of the Oedipus complex, the desirous ego faces a dilemma: all subsequent love objects are insufficient, yet a return to the origin would mean the "psychical death of psychosis".[25]

In overcoming the Oedipus complex, the young child acquires language as a substitute for the forbidden union. It acquires the "gift" of the "symbolic order",[26] according to whose rules it must henceforth articulate its needs, which for their part are thereby substantially altered or which—because they are mediated by the language and "milieu" of others—thus "become other":

> "Drives, insofar as the word is applicable to man in the pressure for a satisfaction, belong to the order of the 'demand' and must fit themselves into it. Still, along with 'demand' and 'need', Lacan also speaks of 'desire'. The transformation of the natural need into a request always leaves something open and thus constitutes the essential *manque à être* of man."[27]

The conflict-based structure of the subject, further intensified by its entry into the symbolic order—"[T]he fashioning of the signifier and the introduction of a gap or a hole in the real are identical" (p. 121)—is rewritten through the two myths of psychoanalysis: the Oedipus myth on the one hand, the myth of the primal father on the other. Whereas the Oedipal conflict condemns the subject to wander through life forever unhappy and dissatisfied and bearing the stigma of an infinite

24 Martin Luther: *Tischreden* (Hg. Kurt Aland, Stuttgart: Reclam, 1981), p. 93. Translation JCW.

25 Peter Zagermann: *Ich-Ideal, Sublimierung, Narzissmus. Die Theorie des Schöpferischen in der Psychoanalyse* (Darmstadt: Wissenschaftliche Buchgesellschaft, 1985), pp. 43 and 23. Translation JCW.

26 Widmer: *Subversion des Begehrens* (note 12), p. 45. Translation JCW.

27 Lang: *Language and the Unconscious* (note 12), p. 124.

lack of Being, the primal father places these wanderings under the banner of *Angst*, of consummate wickedness, at best of transgression—or, after the father has been murdered, under the banner of the dead God and his laws.

Individuals recognize the need for rules, limits and the law if they are to be able to articulate, or even sense in the first place, that need which has been transformed into a desire that cannot be fulfilled. The "black monolith" of Nietzsche, Kubrick and Dotzler returns: "Without the signifier at the beginning, it is impossible for the drive to be articulated as historical. And this is all it takes to introduce the dimension of the *ex nihilo* into the structure of the analytical field" (p. 213). This experience repeatedly generates the bitter frustration that desire must be channeled through the law, that it must exist "in the name of the Father", that it must be articulated at all. Thus desire invariably produces its own frustration and—at best—sublimation, tragically magnifying the hunger that it was supposed to obliterate. Or conversely, order produces the perverse desire to undermine order. The passage from Paul's Letter to the Romans which argues that sin is first created by the law becomes one of the leitmotivs of Lacan's seventh *Seminar*, yet with a slight modification, in that *sin* is here replaced by *the Thing*:

> "Is the Law the Thing? Certainly not. Yet I can only know of the Thing by means of the Law. In effect, I would not have had the idea to covet it if the law hadn't said: 'Thou shalt not covet it.' But the Thing finds a way by producing in me all kinds of covetousness thanks to the commandment, for without the Law the Thing is dead. But even without the Law, I was once alive. But when the commandment appeared, the Thing flared up, returned once again, I met my death. And for me, the commandment that was supposed to lead to life turned out to lead to death, for the Thing found a way and thanks to the commandment seduced me; through it I came to desire death.
>
> I believe that for a little while now some of you at least have begun to suspect that it is no longer I who have been speaking. In fact, with one small change, namely, 'Thing' for 'sin', this is the speech of Saint Paul on the subject of the relations between the law and sins in the Epistle to the Romans, 7–11" (p. 83).

Religion, which promises glory above the law, thus appears as the great consoler; it "in all of its forms consists of avoiding this emptiness" (p. 130). Religion promises compensation: "It is because the soul remains hungry for something more that it needs an afterlife, so that the unrealized harmony may be achieved somewhere or other"

(p. 316). Religion promises that we will regain what we have lost, what we have sacrificed, what we never received.

It might be that religion disappoints us, that God not only remains silent but even appears to act unjustly. It might be that we—like Luther, who repeatedly cites this passage—concur with Job (Job 12:6): "The tabernacles of robbers prosper, and they that provoke God are secure; into whose hand God bringeth abundantly." This bitter insight can lead us into the heart of darkness. With burning impatience, pain, despair and hate we follow the path of intoxication, of suicide or of cruelty and crime, which Lacan defines as behavior "which doesn't respect the natural order" (p. 260), i.e. as the dark side of civilization that emerges along with it. Crime does not even come to an end with the death of the other, who being dead is only an object and no longer a bearer of *das Ding*. This is why Sartre (repressed by Lacan) describes hate as essentially powerless and hence a "*black* feeling".[28] Thus in the potential unleashing of hate we desire the death of the other even after his death; we desire it again and again, this "second death" (p. 260). Because the other seems to deny us access to happiness, we make his life a hell on earth or, if we fail in doing so, we wish upon the hated eternal agony in hell, a second death; we succumb to the "fantasm of eternal suffering" (p. 261). Against this backdrop, psychoanalysis must approach religion in two ways. It may shed light upon the psychological genesis of religion, yet must always keep in mind that human beings, structured by conflict, will always remain "creationist" (p. 309). In this twofold sense, theology, the reflection of religion, illuminates what man is, as in the theology of Martin Luther:

> "'*Who* (you say) *will endeavor to amend his life?*' I answer, No man! No man can! [...] '*Who will believe* (you say) *that he is loved of God?*' I answer, no man will believe it! No man can!"[29]

We have lost something. We are missing something that would allow us to be happy. What has been lost might also be a citation, here an important quote from Martin Luther. I have read the translation of *De servo arbitrio* over and over and yet have not found the quote. I begin to doubt my abilities as a reader; ultimately, I doubt my memory and my reason. Everyone has recourse to this quote about the Father, yet I cannot find it. For "[t]o understand Freud's position relative to the

---

28 Jean-Paul Sartre: *Being and Nothingness* (trans. Hazel E. Barnes, New York: Washington Square Press, 1993), p. 533.

29 Martin Luther: *The Bondage of the Will* (trans. Henry Cole, Peabody, MA: Hendrickson, 2008), p. 53.

Father, you have to go and look up the form it is given in Luther's thought" (p. 97). Luther's 1525 treatise on the bondage of the will, *De servo arbitrio*, paints the image of a Father who deeply hates his children, hates them even before the creation of the world. Nothing these children do—not even their best works—helps to put the Father in a merciful mood. The most impeccable conduct cannot guarantee the attainment of grace. All works are worthless. We have free will only with respect to trivialities; when it comes to matters of grace, our will is enslaved, no longer free, irrelevant. Psychological research on Luther, brilliantly refined by Dieter Groh among others, has emphasized his conception in *De servo arbitrio* of a schizophrenic God who puts his human children in "a classic double-bind situation": Behave in a way that is pleasing to God, which you cannot do. Human beings stand in relation to a strict, demanding God from whom they cannot escape (the parallel to the helpless child) whom they must satisfy and yet cannot satisfy. The universal promise of salvation confronts the absolute, unimpressionable arbitrariness of whether or not this promise will be honored.[30]

The passage to which Lacan, Erikson, Groh and others all refer, however, was not to be found in the German version of *De servo arbitrio*. The solution to the riddle: The stern mother, the *Evangelische Verlagsanstalt*, had censored that paragraph in which the son Martin Luther despairingly laments God's cruelty. There are translations of the Latin passage, in English as well as in German, that exist outside the realm of theology. In order to be able to glean from Luther what Freud understood as the conception of a father who hates his children simply because they exist, one must master Latin, the language of Catholicism inasmuch as Luther's pathos lay in making the doctrines of the Church accessible to the laity through translation. Or one must free oneself from paternalism via the Protestant Church, which practices fidelity to scripture by emending any objectionable passages. As this philological anecdote teaches, we can only find what we have lost—in this case a quotation—through enlightenment and through the dissolution of theology's censoring authority. In Groh's translation (re-translated into English here), the text that Lacan endeavors to interpret, that had been shrouded in the mystery of Latin, reads as follows:

> "Admittedly, what most offends natural reason and that spirit of community is the fact that God arbitrarily leaves humanity in the lurch, indurated and condemned, as if he took delight

30 Dieter Groh: *Schöpfung im Widerspruch. Deutungen der Natur und des Menschen von der Genesis bis zur Reformation* (Frankfurt am Main: Suhrkamp, 2003), p. 563f. Translation JCW.

> in the sins and the intense, eternal agonies of the wretched, he who is so praised for his great mercy and benevolence, etc. It is this unjust, this cruel, this unbearable image of God at which so many important men of so many generations have taken offense. And who would not take offense at this? I myself have more than once taken offense to the point of despair, that hellish abyss, and wished that I had never become a human creature, until I understood how redemptive was that despair and how near it was to grace."[31]

That grace is near does not mean that grace is assured. It is not only the hideous portrait of a sadistic God that disappears from the German edition of *De servo arbitrio* when the mother stifles the son's cry of despair "in the name of the Father". A fundamentally different image emerges of Martin Luther, who appears to be sovereign and free of those temptations that haunt mankind. Through the excision of this human confession, Luther himself becomes a superhuman, inhuman father figure, before whom the faithful writhe in despair and shame. Yet knowledge of Luther's all-but-uncontrollable despair is necessary in order to understand why, for example, he argues—as he does in his *Table Talks*, in an affront to the ethics of the Catholic Church—that suicide should not be condemned as a sin but understood as analogous to a robbery-homicide. A person who kills himself out of desperation does not sin but rather is stolen away by satanic despair.[32]

The year 2006 saw the publication of the first volume of a new German edition of Luther's Latin writings, a bilingual edition of which was necessary because, as the introduction laments, young theologians today are no longer proficient in the necessary languages.[33] In this introduction there comes a turning point that documents theology's historical maneuverability. The section that had been discreetly emended in the old edition of *De servo arbitrio* is not only translated in its entirety; it is singled out as a key passage for contemporary readings of Luther.[34]

What do Jacques Lacan, the French psychoanalyst, and Martin Luther, the German reformer, have to do with each other? At first glance, nothing. Yet a closer look reveals ever more striking parallels. Luther

31 Ibid., p. 564. Translation JCW.

32 Cf. Luther: *Tischreden* (note 24), p. 261.

33 Luther: *Der Mensch vor Gott. Lateinisch-Deutsche Studienausgabe*, vol. 1. (Hg. Wilfried Härle, Leipzig: Evangelische Verlagsanstalt, 2006), p. vi.

34 Ibid., p.v.

laid claim to being the first person in a long time actually to read closely and interpret the Bible, the holy scripture of the Father. Lacan laid claim to being the first person in a long time actually to read closely and interpret the writings of Sigmund Freud, the father of psychoanalysis. Both Luther and Lacan uncompromisingly follow the principle of *sola scriptura*, reading signifiers as precisely as possible. Both Luther and Lacan were first reformers, then renegades and ultimately founders of an alternative community that turned its back on orthodoxy. Both were accused by their enemies of having the ambition to become new popes. For Luther, the sale of indulgences was reason enough to go his way as a Protestant after nailing his *95 Theses* to the church doors in 1517. Indulgences were the promise of being able to reduce the duration of one's sojourn in purgatory by acquiring a letter from the pope—at bottom, a promise that happiness and salvation are not tied to faith, penance and grace, but rather can be purchased. The Reformation that Lacan initiated in the psychoanalytic world derived its pathos from its attack on the promise made by second-generation psychoanalysis, that undergoing treatment will not only make the patient happy, but ultimately will also enable him to grasp precisely that Thing which psychoanalysis knows must always remain inaccessible: "[A] demand for happiness is doubtless involved here" (p. 292). For Lacan, analysts who promise happiness through treatment are the "pardoners" of the twentieth century; they commit "a form of fraud" (p. 303). He harkens back to Freud's harsh statement that the goal of analysis is to transform hysterical misery into common unhappiness.

Luther and Lacan both reject Aristotelian ethics. Lacan demonstrates that the doctrine of the mean conceals a power structure that, as "the morality of the master" (p. 315), does not allow itself to be questioned. Luther recognizes that it is primarily the privileged who are able to walk on the Aristotelian "middle path" extolled by Erasmus. In a stunning theological aphorism, he articulates a social critique of Erasmus' noble skepticism—which was protected by worldly power—that suddenly mutates into religious fundamentalism: "The Holy Spirit is not a Skeptic."[35] Luther's rejection of Aristotle is theologically necessary, as the latter's ethics derive moral character from works. That is a social measuring stick, not a theological one. It is not only his battle against the sale of indulgences that compels Luther to destroy the status of works. He must inevitably insist on the nullity of works and bet on faith alone, in accordance with Romans 3:28, if he hopes to avoid the problems of theodicy. In this world, living as a good person is not at all synonymous with being favored or given special treatment by God the Father. As illustrated by its implicit reception in Kant's

35 Luther: *The Bondage of the Will* (note 29), p. 22.

Anthropology, Luther's treatise *On Good Works* describes an alternative to Aristotelian ethics.

Lastly, Luther's insistence on a faith that is to be regarded more highly than knowledge—which leads to laziness, insanity and death by excessive happiness[36]—corresponds with Lacan's doctrine of the perpetual deferral of desire, inasmuch as restituted *jouissance* amounts to a radical regression of psychosis. What faith is for Luther, the deferral of happiness is for Lacan. Again, both Luther and Lacan adhere strictly to the level of the signifier, which according to Lacan is also a promise of meaning that necessarily points to a "beyond". In the light of these parallels, one could say that Lacan is the Martin Luther of psychoanalysis, and with a view to the pope suggest a merging of the two prodigal sons of Catholicism: the Holy Father is not holy, because he is not a father. Or stated differently: celibacy is desire, but marriage is sublimation, because it raises an object to the level of *das Ding*.

Yet these remarkable correspondences cannot hide the fact that there appears to exist a yawning abyss between Luther and Lacan. Leaving aside the banal fact that Lacan repeats Nietzsche's claim that God is dead, the chasm really seems to open up with respect to the question of desire. "I propose then," Lacan says at the end of his seminar on ethics, "that, from an analytical point of view, the only thing of which one can be guilty is of having given ground relative to one's desire" (p. 319). One could scarcely conceive of a greater contrast to this statement than the commandment formulated by Luther in accordance with Paul's Letter to the Romans: "Thou shalt not covet."[37] Whereas the Mosaic commandments lay out in detail what it is that one should not covet (your neighbor's wife, slave, maid, ox and ass—in short, everything that belongs to your neighbor), in Paul as in Luther desire itself is forbidden altogether. Yet because man can do nothing other than desire, he is always and everywhere sinful.[38]

The contradiction between Luther and Lacan is only a seeming one; having a father means being always and everywhere guilty, being subject to a prohibition that applies to everything, whether it involves food, goods or men and women. Everything is always either allowed or forbidden by the father. The neurotic who suffers the consequences of a Christianity founded by Paul and reformed by Luther thus wishes for something beyond the symbolic order, longs to be able to grasp the

---

36 Cf. Luther: *Tischreden* (note 24), p. 238.

37 Luther: "Concerning Christian Liberty", in: *Basic Luther* (Springfield, IL: Templegate 1984), p. 111.

38 Friedrich Nietzsche offers a powerful account of the consequences of this rewriting of the Ten Commandments for the history of civilization. Cf. the chapter on Nietzsche above.

Thing, the will "to make a fresh start" (p. 212). According to Lacan, the destructive drive, inherent in the pleasure principle and capable of being made productive through the process of analysis, announces itself in this longing. Lacan offers therapeutic practice a particularly insightful piece of advice. The outbreak of aggression, in effect an auto-aggressive reaction against the neurotic constitution of the subject, is regularly expressed on the couch in the form of references to the metaphysics of the saving word, which allegedly catapults forth out of the stranglehold of the symbolic order and always "belongs to the register of a destructive drive":

> "It is at the very moment when a thought is clearly about to appear in a subject, as in the narration of a dream, for example, a thought that one recognizes as aggressive relative to one of the fundamental terms of his subjective constellation, that, depending on his nationality, he will make some reference to a passage from the Bible, to an author, whether a classic or not, or to some piece of music." (p. 239)

Lacan expands on Freud's studies of monotheistic religion through his analysis of Luther's Protestantism, identifying the most prominent elements of Lutheran theology as confirming the theory of the dead God's origin in the murder of the primal father: the capriciousness of God, the nullity of works, the utter sinfulness of man, and finally the notorious severity of Luther's language. Luther invents what three centuries later Freud must analyze. Given Luther's obsession with the scatological, Lacan is able to claim that Luther in effect—i.e. through "the power of images"—allows us to return from the world of theology to ourselves, "that is to say, [to] our body, and nowhere else" (p. 92). Luther's table talks and sermons are "in the end far more analytic than all that modern phenomenology has been able to articulate in the relatively gentle terms of the abandonment of the mother's breast; what kind of negligence is that which causes her milk to dry up? Luther says literally, 'You are that waste matter which falls into the world from the devil's anus'" (p. 93). If on the one hand Lacan is able to read in Luther's language the analytical dimension of religion, infantile sexology projected onto heaven and the anal theory of birth, Luther's image of the hateful father for whom not even the best children can do anything right appears to him on the other hand as a theological variant of the myth of the primal father, who severed the dyad of mother and child and thus bestowed the gift of the symbolic order which the child keeps at a distance from both its parents and itself. Given this despair over the father, hard to rethink as a religious virtue, all that remains for Luther is resignation, hope in the beyond.

Thus we come to the final element of the analytical theory of religion, consolation for a hopeless world:

> "There is a life after this life, in which all will be punished and repaid, everything that is not punished and repaid here, for this life is nothing more than an entrance to, and a beginning of, the life which is to come!"[39]

What do these parallels between Luther and Lacan have to do with the question of sublimation discussed in this book—with the question of nature's spirit, idealistically expressed, or to use Nietzsche's words, with the question of the "transfigured *physis*?" Freud develops a theory of sublimation that implies a theory of dominating nature—i.e. dominating not only the nature of our drives, but also nature as the object of modern science—through his discussion of the question of the need for religion. This fragmentary and contradictory theory is pursued further by Lacan, for whom it becomes apparent that taking recourse to elements of religious tradition is unavoidable. The elaboration of a psychoanalytic theory of civilization widens into an ontopsychology. Lacan allows Luther to teach him what human beings are, who struggle to breathe spirit into their nature, to sublimate. Large sections of his seventh *Seminar*, dedicated to the ethics of psychoanalysis, examine the concept of sublimation. Expressed schematically, it is the drives, according to Freud, that represent our most intimate bond with nature. The human concept of happiness rests on the notion of following the pleasure principle without restraint. Given that frustration is guaranteed, Freud mentions various modes of fending off suffering: distraction, substitution, intoxication. These are measures without which the individual could not endure life on a planet of frustrations. There is ultimately one other possibility: that human beings join forces and launch an "attack against nature".[40] Freud's concept of nature is that of modern science since the seventeenth century, which has abandoned notions of animism, teleology and theology and instead understood nature as the entirety of the observable world, which on the one hand is overpowering and the substance of us all, yet which is also mathematically and physically predictable and therefore reliable.[41]

For Freud, as for many theorists since the 1600s, man is by nature a being that steps outside of nature. Nature is where we originate, our *terminus a quo*. Minimization of frustration is made possible through

---

39 Luther: *The Bondage of the Will* (note 29), p. 276.

40 Freud: Civilization and Its Discontents (note 2), p. 77.

41 Cf. Spaemann: "Natur" (note 19).

the three elements of civilization: science; the regulation of social interactions in order to facilitate both science and survival; and finally all individual techniques for avoiding suffering, from intoxication and distraction to meditation and the creation of products of the imagination (art), which have a compensatory effect. Lacan offers a pithy summary of this cultural process: "To set out to find the instinct again is the result of a certain loss, a cultural loss, of the object" (p. 99).

Structurally, the institution of the reality principle is made possible by the existence of sublimation, a change in the object of the drive.[42] Yet as I attempted to demonstrate in the corresponding chapter of this book, Freud develops his apparently critical theory of sublimation only in fragments that, moreover, contradict themselves. Freud's theory of civilization rests on a concept that remained obscure. This obscurity pertains both to sublimation's structure in the context of metapsychology and drive theory as well as to its valuation. At the heart of Freud's soberly formulated theory of civilization lurks an unresolved "Thing". As was described again in the previous chapter on Adorno, Freud recognizes at least three forms of sublimation, which are not categorically linked with each other: a sublimation A, the production of art, and a sublimation B, the reception of art, which are supposed to be exemplary instances of the human talent for a sublimation C, that broad renunciation of the drives that makes civilization possible.

Why did Freud never formulate a theory of sublimation or write anything that specifically elaborates this concept? The problem lies primarily in the fact that, except in his portraits of great individuals like Leonardo or Goethe, Freud never succeeded in establishing a concept of sublimation that would be free of the aftertaste of the surrogate, the bitter renunciation of *das Eigentliche*. Freud later discovered that sublimation is always linked to a transitory, narcissistic intermediate step. A narcissistic turn which establishes the ego ideal is necessary to allow for the transition from one object to a new one. Meanwhile, what happens with the ego, which assumes characteristics of the lost object in order to offer itself to the id as a transitional object and subsequently to project again the lost object into the world as an ideal? It is in mourning, or at worst melancholic. Mourning and melancholia are already inscribed as a black trace in the process of civilization at the level of sublimation's *constitution*. Thus sublimation, civilization is necessarily mournful. Civilization is the work of mourning. Freud moreover recognizes that the drives' demands increase along with the capacity for ideal formation. The more keenly the capacity for ideal formation is developed, the more acutely and painfully does

42 Freud: *Instincts and Their Vicissitudes*, in: *The Standard Edition* (London: Hogarth, 1956–74), vol. 14, p. 126.

the subject become aware that it must renounce those ideals. Freud finds himself confronted with the fact that it is the differentiated and not the primitive man who has a problem with sublimation if he does not succeed in ultimately giving up his ideal. At the pinnacle of civilization, the archaic may return, undaunted and neurotically intensified. By introducing narcissism, Freud discovered the dialectic of enlightenment. The enormous task at hand, then, is to discover ways of confronting mourning and discontent.

Successful sublimation could occur if the emphasis in subjective experience were shifted from the egoistic desire to satisfy the drives onto the object itself, i.e. if the transition from *amour propre* to *amour pur*—or, at the very least, an amalgamation of drive and object—were possible. Love as love of an object in its freedom and not love of one's own drive: that would be successful sublimation. Or, more romantically, sublimation *is* love. Freud never fully developed this project; rather, he left behind the open question of whether or not successful sublimation can even be said to exist.

In his text on the mirror stage, Lacan defined the task of "love" as the perpetual untying or severing of the knot of imaginary servitude. As this love is supposed to make our *earthly* journey possible, it is vital to remember that Freud, from his 1898 essay on *Sexuality in the Etiology of Neuroses* through 1930's *Civilization and Its Discontents* to 1938's *Outline of Psychoanalysis*, distinguished perverse experience as an access point for understanding normality. Neurosis cannot be cured nor civilization understood without first appropriating perverse experience. Jacques Lacan gives an edge to this perspective on culture seen from its margins by asserting that the major achievements of civilization emerged from psychical crises. In connection with Freud, he offers a poignant thesis "which [brings] together the respective mechanisms of hysteria, obsessional neurosis and paranoia with three forms of sublimation, art, religion and science" (p. 129). Accordingly, art is a hysterical dance around the tormenting void in our heart; science, to the extent that it blasphemously structures itself as radical "*Unglauben*" [lack of belief] (p. 130), represents the paranoid attempt to expose the nature of an evil God's conspiracy against our happiness; and religion "in all its forms consists of avoiding this emptiness" (p. 130).[43]

With respect to the function of art, Lacan's seventh *Seminar* consistently aims towards a reading of Sophocles' *Antigone*, in order "to illustrate a function that we have shown is inherent in the structure

43 Cf. Sigmund Freud: *Totem and Taboo*, in: *The Standard Edition* (London: Hogarth, 1956–74), vol. 13, p. 73: "It might be maintained that a case of hysteria is a caricature of a work of art, that an obsessional neurosis is a caricature of religion and that a paranoic delusion is a caricature of a philosophical system."

of the ethic of tragedy, which is also that of psychoanalysis' (p. 258). Lacan defines beauty, which he sees embodied in the form of the young Antigone, a figure for whom "the race is run" (p. 272), as a "stopping place" that halts us but at the same time "points in the direction of the field of destruction" (p. 217). In an elegant turn, he asserts that beauty is not a polish on ugly truth but rather its "glaze", the shimmering amber that envelops the prehistoric mosquito, as it were. Lacan's reading of *Antigone* culminates in a new and shocking definition of catharsis, that moment of horror that makes the severity of sublimation tangible:

> "[T]he function of desire must remain in a fundamental relationship to death. The question I ask is this: shouldn't the true termination of an analysis—and by that I mean the kind that prepares you to become an analyst—in the end confront the one who undergoes it with the reality of the human condition? It is precisely this, that in connection with anguish, Freud designated as the level at which its signal is produced, namely, *Hilflosigkeit* or distress, the state in which man is in that relationship to himself which is his own death [...] and can expect help from no one." (p. 303f.)

A work of art that reveals its dual character as both promise and warning sign—Lacan repeatedly speaks of beauty's "blindness effect" (p. 281)—and that *unambiguously* seeks to annul this distance pushes the limit, tears down sublimation. Beyond this limit lies the sadistic need not only to establish violently the *Hilflosigkeit* of the hated other in this world, but also to prolong it phantasmatically beyond this world, to usher in the Second Death, eternal agony in hell.[44] The work of the Marquis de Sade, according to Lacan, transgresses this limit:

> "It has been called an unsurpassable body of work, in the sense that it achieves an absolute of the unbearable in what can be expressed in words relative to the transgression of all human limits. One can acknowledge that in no other literature, at no other time, has there been such a scandalous body of work. No one else has done such deep injury to the feelings and thoughts of mankind. [...] [Sade's work represents] the approach to a center of incandescence or an absolute zero that is physically unbearable. [...] The work of art in this case is an experiment that through its action cuts the subject loose from his psychological moorings—or

44 Cf. Augustine: Confession, Book 5 regarding the concept of the second death: Adam's biological death, for example, is the first death; the hellish existence in limbo of the unbaptized and the damned, the second.

> to be more precise, from all psychosocial appreciation of the sublimation involved." (p. 200f.)

One can see clearly here why for Lacan a work of art that pursues the ideal of breaking free of the symbolic order is a work of art at the limit. Art according to Lacan has a dual ethic function, maintaining distance between us and *das Ding* on the one hand, on the other hand showing us the direction in which we are not allowed to go. Art emerges from the liminal phase and as a "glaze" defines the limit between us and psychosis. Embedded in the shimmering amber of representation, the mosquito—in reality painfully uncomfortable—bestows gentle forepleasure, or in Lacan's words: "[I]t's always fine from the side of the work" (p. 122).

Art can point to the tragic dimension of the human condition but cannot provide a solution that would quench the thirst for fulfillment or obliterate the harrowing experience of utter helplessness. Lacan takes up the challenge raised by the phenomenon of *Angst* by clearly emphasizing the severity of the problem. Freud demonstrates that the concept of the world's sovereign good, so important to pre-analytical ethics, stems from the pleasure principle, "that the Sovereign Good, which is *das Ding*, which is the mother, is also the object of incest, is a forbidden good, and that there is no other good" (p. 70). The search for "a natural ethics", the optimistic aim of civilization "that the maturation of the instincts would naturally lead to" (p. 88), the hope for "an improved nature or a natural amelioration" (p. 89) is always already a failed venture if this quest is oriented toward the phantasm of the sovereign. That the sovereign good is in fact a great evil becomes evident in a phenomenon discovered by Freud that seems paradoxical only beyond the Oedipal situation, namely that "the moral conscience [...] shows itself to be the more demanding the more refined it becomes, crueler and crueler even as we offend it less and less" (p. 89). The more the subject strives for the sovereign good, the stronger the "parasite" of the guilt-producing moral conscience, which "is fed by the satisfactions accorded it" (p. 89) becomes. Accordingly, sublimation means recognizing that the idea of the sovereign good is a product of narcissism and thus renouncing it. On the other hand, sublimation then means nevertheless becoming and remaining conscious of the fact that we will never be rid of our longing for the good.

In contrast to Freud's depiction of the unshakable calmness of stoic individuals, Lacan insists on the ineluctable "creationist" dimension of our lives (p. 309), on the fact that we begin to quarrel with our imagined father precisely at the moment we discover that our real father is not the "Great Fucker" (p. 307) but "an idiot or quite simply an old fogey" (p. 308). The "function of the superego in the end, from its final point of view, is hatred for God" (p. 308). Lacan suggests no future for illusion but also offers a clearer illumination of the religious scenario than Freud does. The conflict with the great other emerges from the shadow of the conflict with our real father. Prayer is nothing but the attempt to move beyond language through the use of language. It is for this reason that Lacan finds the portrait of God painted by Luther to be so revealing:

> "[I]n my opinion Luther is much more interesting. That hatred which existed even before the world was created is the correlative of the relationship that exists between a certain influence of the law as such and a certain conception of *das Ding* as the fundamental problem and, in a word, as the problem of evil. I assume that it hasn't escaped your attention that it is exactly what Freud deals with when the question he asks concerning the Father leads him to point out that the latter is the tyrant of the primitive horde, the one against whom the original crime was committed, and who for that very reason introduced the order, essence and foundation of the domain of law." (p. 97)

To the extent that striving for the sovereign good entangles us ever more deeply in the barbed wire of guilt, the situation becomes even more problematic when two inevitably narcissistic subjects suddenly encounter each other in love. Strict limits are placed on the path to one's neighbor, as one discovers

> "that my neighbor possesses all the evil Freud speaks about, but it is no different from the evil I retreat from in myself. To love him, to love him as myself, is necessarily to move toward some cruelty." (p. 198)

Lacan ignores here wide swaths of the extremely pessimistic anthropology of Luther (for whom even the world of nature was rotten and corrupt: "the older the bleaker, the longer the worse [*je elter je kerger, jhe lenger je erger*]"),[45] alluding only to Luther's advice for those who wish to marry: pray, pray, pray.[46] This is meant less facetiously than it sounds. Luther knows that two people, directly confronted with each other, will soon discover cruelty: "Like fleas and lice, desire arrives without any particular occasion."[47] As Julia Kristeva notes, what is

45 Cf. Groh: *Schöpfung im Widerspruch* (note 30), p. 581. Translation JCW.

46 Cf. Luther: *Tischreden* (note 24), p. 285.

47 Ibid., p. 286. Translation JCW.

needed is a mediating third, a higher authority, an ideal, a God, if two people are to be able to live together successfully.[48]

Inflated by a narcissistic ideal, the quest for the sovereign good stumbles ever deeper into the trap of guilt. Love is the discovery of cruelty; it is not natural. Even beyond these focal points, the quest for good reveals itself as a quest for power. That which is good is that which I can command: "The domain of the good is the birth of power" (p. 229). In the heart of the good lurks not only psychotic self-destruction but also the will to empowerment:

> "The true nature of the good, its profound duplicity, has to do with the fact that it isn't purely and simply a natural good, the response to a need, but possible power, the power to satisfy. As a result, the whole relation of man to the real of goods is organized relative to the power of the other, the imaginary other, to deprive him of it." (p. 234)

The picture of human life painted by Lacan in accordance with Luther is one of life enmeshed in self-hatred, the mutual infliction of cruelty, and an endless competition for power: "In the first place, the neighbor [...] is bad" (p. 186). Its dominating force is an insatiable desire for what the other has; this is life in the shadow of *Lebensneid*, that is to say, envy for the life that someone else supposedly enjoys. *Lebensneid*, however, is itself tragic, inasmuch as it constitutes desire for the other in a double sense: the desire to become like the other by stealing what the other has. Here, too, the perpetrator of this theft acquires only objects, never the longed-for Thing. His hunger remains unsated.

Given this ruthless phenomenology, an ethics of psychoanalysis must be an ethics of limits, as well as an apologia of institutions. It must first call attention to the limits that are individually set for human beings structured by conflict:

> "[C]omplete sublimation is not possible for the individual. With the individual [...] we find ourselves faced with limits. There is something that cannot be sublimated; libidinal demand exists, the demand for a certain dose, for a certain level of direct satisfaction, without which harm results, serious disturbances occur." (p. 91f.)

---

48 Julia Kristeva: *Geschichten von der Liebe* (Frankfurt am Main: Suhrkamp, 1989), p. 11.

Civilization must thus be ready to provide asylums of regression, distractions. Moreover, it must be able to cope with the misconception that is love. As Lacan writes,

> "[T]he most general formula that I can give you of sublimation is the following: it raises an object—and I don't mind the suggestion of a play on words in the term I use—to the dignity of the Thing." (p. 112)

It must be possible in the subject's intimate relationships to process the structurally generated frustration which ensues the moment that the object which has been sublimated to the level of *das Ding* reveals itself to be what it really is: another human being. Here Lacan articulates a highly sophisticated solution to the problem of sublimation. He proposes not working on the drive or on the object but rather favoring the exchange of objects. Permanent exchange makes it possible to follow the pull of the insatiable drive without falling into the deadly trap of desire for the *Ding*. Promiscuity, avoiding a hopeless fixation, establishes a healthy distance to one's parents and their revenants in transference:

> "In the definition of sublimation as satisfaction without repression, whether implicitly or explicitly, there is a passage from not-knowing to knowing, a recognition of the fact that desire is nothing more than the metonymy of the discourse of demand. It is change as such. I emphasize the following: the properly metonymic relation between one signifier and another that we call desire is not a new object or a previous object, but the change of object in itself." (p. 293)

The work of sublimation then requires compensation beyond romantic relationships:

> "Sublimate as much as you like; you have to pay for it with something. [...] That good which is sacrificed for desire—and you will note that that means the same thing as that desire which is lost for the good—that pound of flesh is precisely the thing that religion undertakes to recuperate." (p. 322)

On the whole, the ethics of psychoanalysis consists in a double move. It recognizes and exposes human desire, inflamed by the fear of death, as unavoidable, while at the same time setting strict limits on it: "The flowers of desire are contained in this vase whose contours we attempt to define" (p. 298). From an analytic perspective—which in recognition of our "creationist" disposition assumes an eschatological perspective on the Thing that in this world is forever lost—fear of the superego and the feeling of guilt that corresponds to it merely serve to mask the only guilt that exists in the context of analytic drive theory. The perhaps central passage of Lacan's *Seminar VII* thus reads:

> "In the last analysis, what a subject really feels guilty about when he manifests guilt at bottom always has to do with—whether or not it is admissible for a director of conscience—the extent to which he has given ground relative to his desire." (p. 319).

For Lacan, as for Goethe before him, it is not civilization that bears responsibility for our discontent but we ourselves, our unnatural constitution, which makes of us starvelings hungering for the unobtainable. We are uncomfortable with ourselves. Civilization sets limits to our self-hatred, and this is what constitutes Lacan's inversion of Freud as a reflection on religion.

In enumerating Lacan's responses to the problem of sublimation, I have chosen an additive-administrative style in order to illustrate that according to Lacan there evidently must exist a higher authority that sets the rules for both social and private life, an authority that both strictly and flexibly organizes our perpetual fluctuation between desire and frustration and that ultimately prevents the explosion of the whole. If we wish to stop the bombs from going off (Lacan always writes with one eye on the Cold War), then there must exist subjects who successfully create the most sublime work of sublimation by reformulating our longing for *das Ding* as responsibility for the social community (cf. p. 43ff.):

> "The question of the Sovereign Good is one that man has asked himself since time immemorial, but the analyst knows that it is a question that is closed. Not only doesn't he have that Sovereign Good that is asked of him, but he also knows there isn't any. To have carried an analysis through to its end is no more nor less than to have encountered that limit in which the problematic of desire is raised" (p. 300).

This clear answer stands in marked contrast to another passage in which Lacan just as decisively emphasizes that "as analysts we believe that there is no knowledge which doesn't emerge against a background of ignorance" (p. 171). Lacan solves the paradox—knowing that it is necessary to set limits on the one hand, and on the other hand having to admit being ignorant as to why limits ought to exist at all—with an eminently challenging turn that integrates both spiritual and social factors. To wit, the son must become a father.

In accordance with Freud, Lacan underscores "the exquisiteness of that virile identification which flows from the love for the father" and which among other things is assigned the task of announcing "the normalization of desire" qua castration, which averts our gaze from origin and nirvana (p. 181). Successful sublimation means acting in the name of the sublime father: "[R]ecognition of the function of the Father is a sublimation that is essential to the opening up of a spirituality that represents something new, a step forward in the apprehension of reality as such" (p. 181).

Lacan's interest in Luther is explained by this horrifying demand to love the monster that is the father, and to such an extent that one no longer fears becoming a father oneself. We find hidden in the father the flip side of our longing for *das Ding*:

> "the elementary horror of such a renewed, consciousness-obliterating mergence with the mother, with the primary matrix, which finds its personification in the imago of the father and his function of prohibiting incest."[49]

Lacan is less interested in Luther as a religious author who promises an afterlife that will compensate for the happiness human beings have been denied; rather, Luther interests Lacan primarily as the suffering son whose theology takes as its starting point the insight that, as sons, we are hated because we were born.[50] Luther's theology documents the sorrowful stations that mark the path of a son who struggles to attain the position of the father. In comparison with this conflict, Luther describes "popery, purgatory, indulgences, and other like things" as "more trifles than real problems".[51] The pope is not a father but only a surrogate figure mired in narcissistic desire. Along the path to assuming the position of the father, the son Martin Luther encounters three different kinds of light: the faint light of nature, the flickering light of grace and the glowing light of glory:

> "By the light of nature, it is insolvable how it can be just, that the good man should be afflicted and the wicked should prosper; but this is solved by the light of grace. By the light of grace it is insolvable, how God can damn him, who, by his own powers, can do nothing but sin and become guilty. Both the light of nature and

49 Zagermann: *Ich-Ideal, Sublimierung, Narzissmus* (note 25), p. 9. Translation JCW.

50 Cf. Luther: *The Bondage of the Will* (note 29), p. 257.

51 Ibid., p. 279. Translation slightly altered, JCW.

> the light of grace here say, that the fault is not in the miserable man, but in the unjust God; nor can they judge otherwise of that God, who crowns the wicked man freely without any merit, and yet crowns not, but damns another, who is perhaps less, or at least not more wicked. But the light of glory speaks otherwise. That will show, that God, to whom alone belongs the judgment of incomprehensible righteousness, is of righteousness most perfect and most manifest."[52]

The spirituality and radical worldliness emphasized by Lacan converge in Luther's description of this gleaming light. There is an admirable depth to Lacan's observation that spirituality marks a step toward grasping reality as such. The childish laments raised in the light of nature and of grace are incinerated in the glowing light of glory, an allegory for the process of maturity. To gaze into the indifferent light of glory is to somersault out of the world of laments for a single ecstatic yet fatal moment, in order to discover reality in its fullness after this brief second of total blindness. The light of glory reveals the abundance of a world in which there is no reason to lament because the father no longer exists. Theology is sublated in its culmination. There is no authority to which to turn except those entities and institutions which humans themselves have erected over an abyss of ignorance. At the moment of insight, the son assumes the position of the father and loses his faith. Under the law of the father, life was the compulsion "to labor under a continual uncertainty, and to beat the air only".[53] In the light of glory, the specter of the dead father to whom such desperate laments were raised disappears. What remain are the sons and daughters and their real conflicts with each other. Lacan thinks through Freud's theory of sublimation in the light of glory. Sublimation is not renunciation of the world but rather the *via regia* to its discovery. The glowing light of glory returns in Lacan's essay on the mirror stage as the ecstatic limit to which psychoanalysis leads those who have *abandoned* their ideals of happiness:

> "At this intersection of nature and culture, so obstinately scrutinized by the anthropology of our times, psychoanalysis alone recognizes the knot of imaginary servitude that love must always untie anew or sever.
>
> For such a task we can find no promise in altruistic feeling, we who lay bare the aggressiveness that underlies the activities of the philanthropist, the idealist, the pedagogue and even the reformer.

52 Ibid., p. 277.
53 Ibid., p. 273.

> In the subject to subject recourse we preserve, psychoanalysis can accompany the patient to the ecstatic limit of the '*Thou art that*', where the cipher of his mortal destiny is revealed to him, but it is not in our sole power as practitioners to bring him to the point where the true journey begins."[54]

---

54 Lacan: "The Mirror Stage as Formative of the *I* Function as Revealed in Psychoanalytic Experience' (note 13), p. 78.

Bibliography

Adorno, Theodor W. *Aesthetic Theory*. Trans. Robert Hullot-Kentor. Eds Gretel Adorno and Rolf Tiedemann. Minneapolis: University of Minnesota Press, 1997. Vol. 88 of *Theory and History of Literature*. 88 vols. 1981–97.

—*Against Epistemology. A Metacritique*. Trans. Willis Domingo. Cambridge, MA: The MIT Press, 1983.

—"Aus Sils Maria". *Gesammelte Schriften*. Band 10.1. Hg. Rolf Tiedemann. Frankfurt am Main: Suhrkamp, 1997.

—*The Jargon of Authenticity*. Trans. Knut Tarnowski and Frederic Will. Evanston, IL: Northwestern University, 1973.

Andreas-Salomé, Lou. *Looking Back: Memoirs*. Trans. Breon Mitchell. Ed. Ernst Pfeiffer. New York: Paragon House, 1991.

Becker, Aloys. "Arthur Schopenhauer – Sigmund Freud. Historische und charakterologische Grundlagen ihrer gemeinsamen Denkstrukturen". *Schopenhauer-Jahrbuch 1971*. pp. 114–56.

Benjamin, Walter. *Selected Writings, Volume 1: 1913–1926*. Eds Marcus Bullock and Michael W. Jennings. Cambridge, MA: Belknap Press of Harvard University Press, 2004.

Benn, Gottfried. *Sämtliche Werke*, Band 3. Hg. Gerhard Schuster in Verbindung mit Ilse Benn. Stuttgart: Klett-Cotta-Verlag, 1987.

Bernfeld, Siegfried. "Zur Sublimierungslehre". *Antiautoritäre Erziehung und Psychoanalyse*. Band 2. Hg. Lutz von Werder and Reinhart Wolff. Frankfurt am Main: März Verlag, 1974.

Bieri, Peter. *Das Handwerk der Freiheit. Über die Entdeckung des eigenen Willens*. 8. Aufl. Frankfurt am Main: S. Fischer Verlag, 2007.

Böhm, Karl Werner. *Zwischen Selbstzucht und Verlangen. Thomas Mann und das Stigma Homosexualität*. Würzburg: Verlag Königshausen & Neumann, 1991.

Böschenstein, Renate. *Idylle*. Stuttgart: Metzler Verlag, 1967.

Brown, Norman O. *Life Against Death: The Psychoanalytical Meaning of History*. Middletown, CT: Wesleyan University Press, 1985.

Bürger, Peter. *Theory of the Avant-Garde*. Trans. Michael Shaw. Minneapolis: University of Minnesota, 1984. Vol. 4 of *Theory and History of Literature*. 88 vols. 1981–97.

Buschendorf, Bernhard. *Goethes mythische Denkform. Zur Ikonographie der "Wahlverwandtschaften"*. Frankfurt am Main: Suhrkamp, 1986.

Butler, Judith. *Gender Trouble: Feminism and the Subversion of Identity*. New York: Routledge, 1990.

Castoriadis, Cornelius. *The Imaginary Institution of Society*. Trans. Kathleen Blamey. Cambridge, MA: The MIT Press, 1998.

Erikson, Erik H. *Young Man Luther: A Study in Psychoanalysis and History*. New York: Norton, 1962.

Foucault, Michel. "Nietzsche, Genealogy, History". *Language, Counter-Memory, Practice: Selected Essays and Interviews*. Ithaca, NY: Cornell University Press, 1977.

Freud, Anna. *The Ego and the Mechanisms of Defense*. New York: International Universities, 1966. Vol. 2 of *The Writings of Anna Freud*. 8 vols. 1966–81.

Freud, Sigmund. *The Standard Edition of the Complete Psychological Works of Sigmund Freud*. Trans. James Strachey et al. Eds James Strachey and Anna Freud. 24 vols. London: Hogarth Press, 1956–74.

Gadamer, Hans-Georg. *Truth and Method*. 2nd revised edition. Trans. Joel Weinsheimer and Donald G. Marshall. New York: Continuum, 1989.

Gasser, Reinhard. *Nietzsche und Freud. Monographien und Texte zur Nietzsche-Forschung*. Band 38. Hg. Ernst Behler et al. Berlin/New York: De Gruyter, 1997.

Gay, Peter. *Freud: A Life For Our Time*. New York: Norton, 1988.

Gebhard, Walter. *"Der Zusammenhang der Dinge:" Weltgleichnis und Naturverklärung im Totalitätsbewusstsein des 19. Jahrhunderts*. Tübingen: De Gruyter Verlag, 1984.

Gehlen, Arnold. *Man: His Nature and Place in the World*. Trans. Clare McMillan and Karl Pillemer. New York: Columbia University Press, 1988.

—"Die Resultate Schopenhauers". *Gesamtausgabe*, Band 4. Frankfurt am Main: Vittorio Klostermann Verlag, 1989.

Goethe, Johann Wolfgang. *Conversations of Goethe with Johann Peter Eckermann*. Trans. John Oxenford. Ed. J. K. Moorhead. New York: Da Capo, 1998.

—*Elegie von Marienbad: Urschrift September 1823*. Jürgen Behrens and Christoph Michel. Frankfurt am Main: Insel Verlag, 1991.

—*Faust I & II*. Vol. 2 of *The Collected Works*. Trans. and ed. Stuart Atkins. New York: Suhrkamp, 1984.

—*From My Life: Poetry and Truth (Parts One to Three)*. Trans. Robert R. Heitner. Eds Thomas P. Saine and Jeffrey L. Sammons. New York: Suhrkamp, 1987.

—*Selected Poems*. Trans. John Whaley. Evanston, IL: Northwestern University, 1998.

—*The Sorrows of Young Werther--Elective Affinities--Novella*. Vol. 11 of *The Collected Works*. Trans. Victor Lange and Judith Ryan. Ed. David Wellbery. New York: Suhrkamp, 1988.

—*Verse Plays and Epic*. Vol. 8 of *The Collected Works*. Trans. Michael Hamburger, Hunter Hannum and David Luke. Eds Cyrus Hamlin and Frank Ryder. New York: Suhrkamp, 1987.

—*Werke*. Hamburger Ausgabe. Erich Trunz. 14 Bänden. München: C. H. Beck Verlag, 1982-2008.

Groh, Dieter. *Schöpfung im Widerspruch. Deutungen der Natur und des Menschen von der Genesis bis zur Reformation*. Frankfurt am Main: Suhrkamp, 2003.

Heidegger, Martin. *Being and Time*. Trans. John Macquarrie and Edward Robinson. Oxford, UK: Blackwell, 1962.

Heinrich, Klaus. *Versuch über die Schwierigkeit Nein zu sagen*. 3. Auflage. Frankfurt am Main: Stroemfeld Verlag, 1985.

Herrmann, Hans-Christian von. "'Induction psycho-motrice.' Zur technischen Wiederkehr der Kunst in Hysterie und Hypnose". *Electric Laokoon. Zeichen und Medien, von der Lochkarte zur Grammatologie*. Michael Franz et al. Berlin: Oldenbourg Akademieverlag, 2007.

Hirsch, Rudolf and Werner Vortreide. *Dichter über ihre Dichtungen*, Vol. 14/ II. *Thomas Mann Teil II: 1918–1943*. München/Frankfurt am Main: Heimeran Verlag, 1979.
Hobbes, Thomas. *Leviathan*. Ed. J. C. A. Gaskin. Oxford, UK: Oxford University, 1998.
Horkheimer, Max and Theodor W. Adorno. *Dialectic of Enlightenment*. Trans. John Cumming. New York: Continuum, 1972.
Kaufmann, Walter. *Nietzsche: Philosopher, Psychologist, Antichrist*. 4th ed. Princeton: Princeton University, 1974.
Kernberg, Otto. *Borderline Conditions and Pathological Narcissism*. Northvale, NJ: Jason Aronson, 1985.
Klein, Melanie. "Mourning and its Relation to Manic-Depressive States". *Love, Guilt and Reparation and Other Works 1921–1945*. New York: Free Press, 1984.
Kommerell, Max. *Gedanken über Gedichte*. Frankfurt am Main: Vittorio Klostermann Verlag, 1985.
Lacan, Jacques. *Écrits: The First Complete Edition in English*. Trans. Bruce Fink. New York: Norton, 2006.
—*The Ethics of Psychoanalysis 1959–1960*. Trans. Dennis Porter. Ed. Jacques-Alain Miller. New York: Norton, 1992. Vol. 7 of *The Seminar of Jacques Lacan*. 20 vols. 1988-.
Lang, Hermann. *Language and the Unconscious: Jacque Lacan's Hermeneutics of Psychoanalysis*. Trans. Thomas Brockelman. Atlantic Highlands, NJ: Humanities, 1997.
Laplanche, Jean and Jean-Bertrand Pontalis. *The Language of Psychoanalysis*. Trans. Donald Nicholson-Smith. London: Karnac, 2006.
Lethen, Helmut. *Cool Conduct: The Culture of Distance in Weimar Germany*. Trans. Don Reneau. Berkeley: University of California Press, 2002.
Loewald, Hans W. *Sublimation: Inquiries into Theoretical Psychoanalysis*. New Haven: Yale University Press, 1988.
Lukács, Georg. *The Theory of the Novel*. Trans. Anna Bostock. Cambridge, MA: The MIT Press, 1971.
Luther, Martin. *Basic Luther*. Springfield, IL: Templegate, 1984.
—*The Bondage of the Will*. Trans. Henry Cole. Peabody, MA: Hendrickson, 2008.
—*Tischreden*. Kurt Aland. Stuttgart: Reclam, 1981.
Lütkehaus, Ludger. *"O Wollust, o Hölle". Die Onanie. Stationen einer Inquisition*. Frankfurt am Main: Imago Psychosozial-Verlag, 1992.
Mann, Thomas. *The Beloved Returns: Lotte in Weimar*. Trans. H. T. Lowe-Porter. New York: Knopf, 1940.
—*The Black Swan*. Trans. Willard R. Trask. Berkeley: University of California, 1990.
—*Death in Venice*. Trans. Michael Henry Heim. New York: Ecco, 2004.
—*Death in Venice and Seven Other Stories*. Trans. H. T. Lowe-Porter. New York: Vintage, 1936.
—*Doctor Faustus*. Trans. John E. Woods. New York: Knopf, 1997.
—*Essays of Three Decades*. Trans. H. T. Lowe-Porter. New York: Knopf, 1965.
—*Gesammelte Werke*. 13 Bände. Frankfurt am Main: S. Fischer Verlag, 1990.
—*Große kommentierte Frankfurter Ausgabe*. 38 Bände. Frankfurt am Main: S. Fischer Verlag, 2003.
—*Last Essays*. Trans. Richard Winston. New York: Knopf, 1966.
—*The Magic Mountain*. Trans. John E. Woods. New York: Vintage, 1995.

Marcuse, Herbert. *Eros and Civilization: A Philosophical Inquiry into Freud*. New York: Vintage, 1962.

Marquard, Odo. *Skeptische Methode mit Blick auf Kant*. 3. Aufl. Freiburg/München: Verlag Karl Alber, 1982.

Menninghaus, Winfried. *Das Versprechen der Schönheit*. Frankfurt am Main: Suhrkamp, 2003.

Mitscherlich, Alexander. *Die Idee des Friedens und die menschliche Aggression. Vier Versuche*. Frankfurt am Main: Suhrkamp, 1970.

—"Wesensbestimmung der Aggression". *Die Motivation menschlichen Handelns*. Hans Thomae. 3. Aufl. Köln/Berlin: Kiepenheuer & Witsch, 1966.

Münkler, Herfried. *Thomas Hobbes*. 2. Revised edition. Frankfurt am Main: Campus Verlag, 2001.

Nietzsche, Friedrich. *The Anti-Christ, Ecce Homo, Twilight of the Idols, and Other Writings*. Trans. Judith Norman. Eds Aaron Ridley and Judith Norman. Cambridge, UK: Cambridge University Press, 2005.

—*Basic Writings of Nietzsche*. Trans. and ed. Walter Kaufman. New York: Modern Library, 2000.

—*Daybreak: Thoughts on the Prejudices of Morality*. Trans. R. J. Hollingdale. Eds Maudemarie Clark and Brian Leiter. Cambridge, UK: Cambridge University Press, 1997.

—*The Gay Science*. Trans. Josefine Nauckhoff. Ed. Bernard Williams. Cambridge, UK: Cambridge University Press, 2001.

—*Human, All Too Human: A Book for Free Spirits*. Trans. R. J. Hollingdale. Cambridge, UK: Cambridge University Press, 1996.

—*On the Genealogy of Morality and Other Writings*. Trans. Carol Diethe. Ed. Keith Ansell-Pearson. Cambridge, UK: Cambridge University Press, 2006.

—*Thus Spoke Zarathustra: A Book for None and All*. Trans. Walter Kaufmann. New York: Penguin, 1966.

—*Untimely Meditations*. Trans. R. J. Hollingdale. Ed. Daniel Breazeale. Cambridge, UK: Cambridge University Press, 1997.

Panofsky, Erwin. *Meaning in the Visual Arts*. Chicago: University of Chicago Press, 1982.

Plato. *The Symposium*. Trans. Christopher Gill. London: Penguin, 1999.

Rapaport, David. *The Structure of Psychoanalytic Theory: A Systematizing Attempt*. New York: International Universities, 1960. *Psychological Issues*. Vol. 2, No. 2.

Reich, Wilhelm. *Character Analysis*. Trans. Vincent R. Carfagno. Eds Mary Higgins and Chester M. Raphael. 3rd ed. New York: Farrar, Straus and Giroux, 1972.

Ritter, Joachim. *Subjektivität*. Frankfurt am Main: Suhrkamp, 1989.

Safranski, Rüdiger. *Nietzsche: A Philosophical Biography*. Trans. Shelley Frisch. New York: W. W. Norton, 2003.

Sartre, Jean-Paul. *Being and Nothingness*. Trans. Hazel E. Barnes. New York: Washington Square Press, 1993.

Schelling, Friedrich Wilhelm Joseph. *Philosophical Investigations into the Essence of Human Freedom*. Trans. Jeff Love and Johannes Schmidt. New York: State University of New York, 2006.

Schiller, Friedrich. *Essays*. Eds Walter Hinderer and Daniel O. Dahlstrom. New York: Continuum, 1993. Vol. 17 of *The German Library*. 100 vols. 1982–2007.

—"On Grace and Dignity". Trans. Jane V. Curran. *Schiller's "On Grace and Dignity" in Its Cultural Context*. Eds Jane V. Curran and Christophe Fricker. Rochester, NY: Camden House, 2005.

Schmidt, Jochen. *Die Geschichte des Geniegedankens in der deutschen Literatur, Philosophie und Politik 1750–1945*, Band 1., 2. Aufl. Darmstadt: Wissenschaftliche Buchgesellschaft, 1988.

—"Letters on the Aesthetic Education of Man". Trans. Elizabeth M. Wilkinson and L.A. Willoughby. *Essays*. Eds Walter Hinderer and Daniel O. Dahlstrom. New York: Continuum, 1993. Vol. 17 of *The German Library*. 100 vols. 1982–2007.

Schopenhauer, Arthur. *On the Basis of Morality*. Trans. E. F. J. Payne. Indianapolis: Hackett, 1998.

—*The World as Will and Representation*. Trans. E. F. J. Payne. 2 vols. New York: Dover, 1969.

Spaemann, Robert. *Philosophische Essays. Erweiterte Ausgabe*. Stuttgart: Reclam, 1994.

Sterba, Richard. *The Collected Papers*. Trans. Richard Sterba. Ed. Herman Daldin. Croton-on-Hudson, NY: North River, 1987.

Tillich, Paul. *The Socialist Decision*. Trans. Franklin Sherman. New York: Harper & Row, 1977.

Tugendhat, Ernst. *Vorlesungen über Ethik*. Frankfurt am Main: Suhrkamp Verlag, 1993.

Wiegmann, Hermann. *Die Erzählungen Thomas Manns. Interpretation und Materialien*. Bielefeld: Aisthesis Verlag, 1992.

Wünsch, Marianne. "Zeichen – Bedeutung – Sinn. Zu den Problemen der späten Lyrik Goethes am Beispiel der 'Trilogie der Leidenschaft.'" *Goethe Jahrbuch*. Band 108. Werner Keller. pp. 179–90. 1991.

Zagermann, Peter. *Ich-Ideal, Sublimierung, Narzissmus. Die Theorie des Schöpferischen in der Psychoanalyse*. Darmstadt: Wissenschaftliche Buchgesellschaft, 1985.

Index